CLASSIC LEGENDS FOR KIDS:

Heroes, Gods, and Myths From Rome, Egypt & Greece

ROMAN LEGENDS FOR KIDS:

Emperors, Gladiators, History, Myths & More from Ancient Rome

History Brought Alive

CONTENTS

INTRODUCTION

Imagine stepping back thousands of years in time to the grand and bustling empire of Rome. An era of mighty emperors and powerful women, heroic gladiators, and lofty gods, each playing a part in crafting a civilization that shaped our world today. It's a journey that might seem overwhelming, as the history is packed with events and characters that may feel as distant as the stars. But don't worry! This is the perfect guide to make this ancient world come to life right before your eyes.

We'll march with Julius Caesar as he expands Rome's borders, stand in awe of Cleopatra, cheer for the brave gladiators fighting in the Colosseum, and ascend Mount Olympus to meet with the gods and goddesses of Rome.

Here's a sneak peek of what you'll explore inside:

- **Chapter 1: Mighty Emperors of Rome** — From Julius Caesar's nearly successful grab for ultimate power to Constantine's establishment of a new capital, witness the rise and fall of Rome's greatest leaders.

- **Chapter 2: Powerful Women of Rome** — Discover the stories of the empire's strongest women, who influenced the male-dominated realms of politics and power.

- **Chapter 3: Brave Gladiators of the Colosseum** — Enter the arena to experience the gladiatorial games that captivated Roman citizens, from the lowest commoners to the most noble senators.

- **Chapter 4: Mighty Gods & Goddesses of Rome** — Climb the steps to Mount Olympus, where gods and goddesses like Jupiter, Minerva, and Venus shaped the fates of humans below.
- **Chapter 5: Heroes, Legends & Myths That Shaped Rome** — Discover myths and legends like the founding of the city by Romulus and Remus or the noble sacrifices of heroes like Mucius Scaevola.

We don't just want to tell you these stories but to transport you back in time. You'll feel the excitement, the curiosity, and the drama as if you were a Roman yourself. These are more than simple stories; they are windows into how the ancient Romans lived, thought, and influenced the world around them. These stories teach us lessons that are still relevant today.

So, are you ready for an adventure like no other? Then it's time to turn the page and dive into "Roman Legends for Kids." Let's start our journey through history right now!

(Pay attention to the tales and facts—see if you can become an expert on ancient Rome when you reach the end!)

CHAPTER 1: MIGHTY EMPERORS OF ROME

Welcome! In this opening chapter, we will step back in time to meet some of the most influential leaders of the ancient Roman Empire. From the wise Augustus, who founded the Empire, to the bold Constantine, who reshaped it entirely, these emperors crafted the history of Rome with their decisions, battles, and laws.

Get ready to explore the lives, accomplishments, and, sometimes, scandals of Rome's greatest emperors. Discover how they came to power, ruled, and the impact of their legacies today.

Julius Caesar | The Almost-Emperor (49 BC - 44 BC)

In the grand, busy world of ancient Rome, full of soldiers in shiny armor and senators in flowing robes, there lived a man who would change everything. His name was Julius Caesar. While he never wore the golden crown of an emperor, his daring actions and clever mind paved the way for those mighty rulers who came after him.

Early Life of a Future Legend

Julius Caesar was born into a time when Rome was a republic, meaning people voted for leaders to make decisions together. But Caesar's family was noble; they were related to heroes of Roman myths! From the time he was just a boy, Caesar knew he was meant for greatness. He was clever and always the first to raise his hand in class. He loved learning about the history of his powerful city.

As a young man, Caesar left Rome to explore the world. He joined the army and traveled far from home, from the sun-baked hills of Spain to the mysterious forests of Germany. Everywhere he went, Caesar fought bravely and thought quickly, earning medals and the respect of his men. But Caesar wanted more than just adventures; he wanted to lead. So, when he returned home, he set his eyes on the biggest prize of all—becoming the leader of Rome.

The Conquest of Gaul

One of Caesar's most famous adventures was in Gaul. Gaul was a region of Western Europe. This was not just a quick battle— it was long and exhausting and lasted several years. Caesar was not only fighting fierce warriors but also the harsh weather and tough terrain. However, with his skills in strategy and bravery, Caesar won many battles. He added vast lands to Rome's territories. Back home, people celebrated his victories with parades and parties, and cheered his name in the streets.

But, not everyone was happy with Caesar's success. Some powerful people in Rome thought he was becoming too influential. They ordered him to come back to Rome without his army and give up his power. Caesar faced a difficult choice at the river Rubicon, which was the border of Italy. Roman law said no general could cross it with an army, or it would mean declaring war on Rome itself.

On a chilly morning, standing by the Rubicon, Caesar made a decision that would change history. He whispered, "The die is cast," and led his army across the river, into Italy. This started a civil war. Caesar knew there was no turning back.

After many battles, Caesar won the civil war. He entered Rome not as a criminal, but as its ruler. He became a dictator, but not the kind we think of today with absolute power. Caesar made many changes during his rule. He gave land to the poor, made laws that were fairer to everyone, and introduced a new calendar, which is the basis for the calendar we use today!

The Ides of March and Caesar's Legacy

Caesar's story doesn't have a happy ending. In 44 BC, on the 15th of March—a day now known as the Ides of March—some of the senators who feared losing their power betrayed him. This day marked the end of Caesar's life, but not his influence. His actions and ideas laid the foundation for the emperors who would follow, starting with his adopted son, Augustus, the first official emperor of Rome.

Julius Caesar's life was like a grand play filled with adventure, danger, and big decisions. Though he never became emperor, his spirit and rules shaped the future of Rome and created a path for emperors to come. His story teaches us about courage, wisdom, and the impact one person can have on the world.

So, remember Julius Caesar, the almost-emperor who dreamed big and dared even bigger.

Augustus | Founder of the Roman Empire (27 BC - AD 14)

In the ancient city of Rome, filled with grand marble buildings, bustling markets, and chariots zipping down the cobblestone streets, there lived an emperor who would forever change history. His name was Augustus, and he was the first emperor of the Roman Empire. From his bold changes to government to grand building projects, Augustus's story is filled with adventure and great achievements.

Augustus was born in 63 BC, during a time of many changes in Rome. His name was originally Gaius Octavius. After

Julius Caesar was betrayed and murdered, young Octavius discovered that Caesar had adopted him as his son. This was a huge surprise to everyone, including Octavius, who was just a teenager at the time. So, he changed his name to Gaius Julius Caesar Octavianus, often called Octavian, stepping into big shoes at a very young age.

Octavian was smart and understood that he needed to act carefully to claim his inheritance. He formed an alliance with Mark Antony, one of Caesar's closest allies, and Marcus Lepidus, a powerful politician. Together, they defeated Caesar's assassins, but it wasn't long before the alliance broke apart. Octavian and Mark Antony became rivals. Their friendship turned into a fierce competition for control of Rome.

The rivalry between Octavian and Mark Antony came to a head in a naval battle at Actium in 31 BC. Octavian's forces defeated Antony's, because Octavian had allied himself with the enchanting Queen Cleopatra of Egypt. This victory was a turning point for Rome. It marked the end of the Roman Republic and the beginning of the Roman Empire.

Augustus, Emperor of Rome

In 27 BC, the Roman Senate changed Octavian's name to Augustus, which means "the respected one." He was now the emperor of Rome. As emperor, Augustus wanted to make Rome into a powerful, organized, and splendid city.

Augustus used to say that he found Rome built of bricks and left it covered in marble. He rebuilt much of the city, adorning it with splendid buildings, statues, and temples that glistened in the sun. Augustus's Rome became a place where art and culture flourished alongside politics and power.

Augustus knew that to build a strong empire, he needed more than just beautiful buildings. He dramatically enlarged the empire, bringing peace and stability to regions that had seen chaos for generations. He reformed the Roman system of taxation to make it fairer and more efficient. Augustus also helped fund grand projects.

He also developed a network of roads that crisscrossed the empire. With the roads, Augustus created a sort of ancient post office system, making communication across long distances faster than ever. This network helped manage the empire and spread Roman culture and influence.

The Founder of the Praetorian Guard

To protect himself and the city, Augustus established the "Praetorian Guard." The members were elite soldiers who served as the personal bodyguards of the emperor, official police and fire fighters.The city became safer and more organized than it had been in years.

Under Augustus's rule, Rome now had a permanent army. The soldiers were ready to defend Rome's borders or expand its territories at a moment's notice.

A Legacy of Peace and Prosperity

Augustus ruled for over 40 years, and his time as emperor was marked by peace and prosperity. This was a period known as the *Pax Romana* or "Roman Peace." He created a strong government that would guide Rome through many more centuries of history.

When Augustus died in AD 14, he left behind an empire that was vastly different from the troubled republic he had inherited. His legacy is not just in the buildings and statues that dotted Rome but the idea of how to run an empire.Through Augustus's story, we see how courage, intelligence, dreams, and a great heart can bring about change and create a legacy that lasts forever.

Tiberius | The Steady Hand of Rome (AD 14 - 37)

Tiberius's story is full of battles, big decisions, and the heavy weight of a crown. As the second emperor of Rome, following his famous stepfather Augustus, Tiberius had big sandals to fill. He was a quiet man, but don't let that fool you—he was also one of Rome's greatest generals and a smart leader.

From Young Soldier to Emperor

Tiberius was born into a noble family in 42 BC, a time when Rome was still figuring out whether it wanted to be a republic or an empire. As a boy, Tiberius learned how to fight and lead soldiers, which was a good thing to know in those days of constant battles.

When he grew up, Tiberius became a famous general. He marched his armies across large parts of Europe, conquering lands and peoples for Rome. He fought in places like Pannonia, Dalmatia, and Raetia, and even ventured into the wild forests of Germania. These conquests helped Rome secure its borders and made Tiberius a hero back home.

Chosen as Successor

Although Tiberius was a great warrior, he didn't jump straight into being an emperor. At first, Augustus wasn't sure who should become the next emperor. But after other possible successors passed away, Augustus picked Tiberius. To prepare Tiberius, Augustus let Tiberius co-lead the empire for a while..

When Tiberius finally became emperor in AD 14, it wasn't easy. The Senate wasn't too happy about having an emperor. They missed the old days when they had more power. Tiberius found it hard to get along with them, and he was always worried that they wanted his crown.

Despite these troubles, Tiberius was really good at his job. He made sure that Rome was well-run, its money well-spent, and its borders secure. He wasn't the kind to spend all day throwing parties or parades; instead, he spent his free time working hard at his job.

Tiberius ruled Rome until AD 37. During this time, he showed that an emperor could be a great general and a careful leader, even if it wasn't always exciting or dramatic.

Tiberius's story is a reminder that being in charge isn't always about glory and fame. Sometimes, it's about doing the hard work behind the scenes, making tough decisions, and looking after a great empire. Thanks to Tiberius's efforts, Rome stayed strong and secure, ready for the many emperors who would come after him.

Caligula | The Wild Emperor (AD 37 - 41)

Caligula is one of Rome's most legendary rulers for all the wrong reasons.His real name was Gaius Julius Caesar Augustus Germanicus. He was called Caligula, which means "little boot," because as a little boy he wore a tiny soldier's outfit, including boots, that the army loved. He became emperor in AD 37, after the death of his grand-uncle and adoptive grandfather, Tiberius.

When Caligula first became emperor, the people of Rome were hopeful. He was young, energetic, and ready to lead. He promised to be a fair ruler, different from Tiberius, who was unpopular by the end of his time.

Caligula started his rule with good deeds. He freed people who had been unjustly imprisoned and got rid of some unfair taxes. He held magnificent games for the entertainment of the citizens, which made him popular. Everyone in Rome was talking about the wonderful new emperor who seemed like a breath of fresh air.

However, things began to change about six months into his rule. Caligula got very sick and was not the same when he recovered. He started doing strange and mean things. He began spending money wildly to build himself huge palaces and stage more extravagant games that emptied the empire's treasury.

Caligula's behavior became more and more unpredictable. He forced Romans to pay heavy taxes to fund his lifestyle.

When he needed more money, he accused rich citizens of crimes, took their properties, and sometimes even ordered their execution. Caligula even said that he was a god! He wanted to put statues of himself in temples across Rome.

Caligula also had a bad relationship with the Roman Senate. He thought that many senators were untrustworthy and wanted his crown. To protect himself, he had several senators executed.

Caligula's strange behavior didn't stop at being mean; he also had some very weird ideas. He once decided to build a bridge made of boats across the Bay of Baiae so he could ride his horse across it wearing the armor of Alexander the Great (who was a famous Greek king and general). He also talked about giving his favorite horse, Incitatus, one of the highest positions in the Roman government as a consul.

The End of His Rule

Caligula didn't last long as emperor because he made too many enemies. In AD 41, after only four years as emperor, one of his bodyguards killed him. The people of Rome, who had once been so hopeful, were happy to get rid of such a wild and unpredictable ruler.

Caligula's time as emperor serves as a reminder that power can be tricky. It shows that it is important for leaders to be kind and fair to everyone. Caligula started with the promise of greatness but will always be remembered for how he became crazy and heartless.

Claudius | The Unexpected Emperor (AD 41 - 54)

One of Rome's most surprising emperors was Tiberius Claudius Caesar Augustus Germanicus, who we will just call Claudius. His effective leadership style was surprising to everyone, and his reign from AD 41 to AD 54 was full of unexpected successes and strange twists of fate.

Though Claudius was born into a royal family, no one expected he would become emperor. He had a tough childhood due to several physical ailments, like tremors in his head and hands, a limp, and other issues that made his own family doubt him. They thought he was too weak to rule such a vast empire, and often made fun of him. However, Claudius would prove them all wrong.

Unlike many of his predecessors, Claudius didn't rush into the chaotic world of Roman politics. He entered the scene relatively late in life, spending much of his younger years out of the public eye, often lost in his books and studies. He was an accomplished historian and a scholar who loved learning about the past.

Claudius became emperor quite unexpectedly after the assassination of the notorious Caligula, his nephew. The Praetorian Guard, aka Rome's elite military force, found

Claudius hiding behind a curtain in the palace during the chaos that followed Caligula's death. Seeing an opportunity, they declared him emperor, thinking they could control him easily. This decision would lead to significant changes in the empire.

Expanding the Empire

One of Claudius's greatest achievements was the expansion of Rome's territories. He completed the Roman annexation of Britain, something other emperors failed to achieve. His military campaigns in Britain were so successful that they added a vast new province to the Roman Empire. This secured Claudius's fame as a conqueror.

He also pushed Rome's borders into parts of Africa and the Middle East, making the empire larger and more diverse than ever before. Under his rule, Rome's influence and power grew significantly.

Reforms and Rights

Claudius was not just a conqueror; he was also a wise leader who made many improvements to the empire. He updated the judicial system to make it more fair, passed laws to protect workers, and extended Roman citizenship to more people. He gave citizens new rights that helped improve their lives, showing that he

cared about his people and their well-being.

Love of Games and Personal Struggles

Claudius loved the Roman games, which were grand events featuring gladiators and wild beasts. These games were not just entertainment; they were a way for the emperor to connect with his people and show off Rome's prosperity.

However, Claudius's personal life was not as successful as his public life. He was notoriously unlucky in love, with several troubled marriages that ended in scandal and tragedy.

The way Claudius died is still a mystery. Some say he was poisoned by his own wife, who wanted her son to become the next emperor. Others think it might have been a sudden illness.

His death marked the end of a surprisingly effective reign that had seen Rome grow stronger and more organized. Despite being underestimated by almost everyone in his early life, Claudius showed that being a good emperor involves more than just looking strong. It's about making smart decisions, caring for your people, and sometimes, surprising everyone by turning weakness into strength.

Claudius expanded an empire, reformed laws, and left a legacy that historians still praise today. He's a reminder that sometimes, the most unlikely person can become a truly mighty leader.

Nero | The Emperor and the Great Fire (AD 54 - 68)

Nero ruled from AD 54 to AD 68. His famous reign was filled with tales of mystery, music, and a very big fire.

Nero became emperor when he was a teenager, stepping into power after the death of his stepfather, Claudius. He was the last emperor of the family line that had started with Augustus. Nero started out well enough with guidance from his advisors, but as he grew older, his rule took a turn for the worse.

In the beginning, Nero was popular. He reduced taxes and gave more power to the Senate, which gave people hope. He loved arts and sports, especially music and chariot racing. Nero wasn't just a fan; he was also a performer who often played the lyre and sang, though it's not clear if he was any good.

Trouble Begins

As Nero got more comfortable in his role, his decisions became more and more controversial. He spent a huge amount of money on arts and building projects, including a massive palace for himself called the Golden House. Manypeople who thought this spending was too extravagant. Nero also did some bad things, like the assassinations of people he didn't trust, including his own mother and his wife. These actions made many people in Rome start to fear and distrust him.

The Great Fire of Rome

One of the most famous events during Nero's time as emperor was the Great Fire of Rome in AD 64. This huge fire lasted for several days and destroyed a large part of the city. Rumors flew around that Nero had played his lyre and sang while Rome burned, although this is probably just a myth. What is true is that after the fire, Nero built his new palace where some of the city had been, which made people even more suspicious that he had let the fire burn on purpose.

Despite the rumors, Nero tried to help the city recover. He opened his palaces to give shelter to those who lost their homes and arranged for food supplies to be distributed. He also made new fire safety laws to try to prevent a similar disaster.

Nero is also known for his harsh treatment of Christians. He blamed them for the Great Fire, among other things. Under his orders, many Christians were persecuted. This was one of many reasons he became unpopular in the empire.

As the years went by, Nero's rule faced increasing problems. Rebellions started in the provinces, and eventually, the Roman Senate turned against him. In AD 68, the Senate declared him to be an enemy of the state. Nerois discovered that even his guards had turned on him, so he took his own life and ended his controversial reign.

Nero's legacy is a mix of good and bad. He was a patron of the arts and a performer, which showed his love for culture. However, his name is often remembered for the negative aspects of his rule—his extravagance, his ruthless actions, and the great fire. His life serves as a reminder of how power can be both a gift and a curse, depending on how it is used.

Vespasian | The Builder of Rome (AD 69 - 79)

Nero's death did not slow down the busy world of ancient Rome. Instead, a new emperor, Vespasian, replaced Nero. He brought peace and grand buildings to the empire. His story is a great adventure filled with challenges and victories, showing us how a strong leader can make a big difference.

Vespasian was born into a family that wasn't particularly famous or powerful, which was unusual for an emperor. He climbed the ranks of the Roman army and became known for his skill as a general. In AD 69, after a year of chaos known as the "Year of the Four Emperors," where four different leaders tried to claim the throne, Vespasian took over. This was a big job, especially after such a turbulent time.

One of the first things Vespasian did as emperor was to stabilize Rome's shaky finances. He was practical and made smart changes to how taxes were collected, which helped fill Rome's empty treasury. He also cut back on unnecessary spending, making sure that the money was used for important things that would help everyone in the empire.

But Vespasian didn't just save money; he also knew when to spend it wisely. He launched a huge building program across Rome, which included some spectacular projects that we can still see ruins of today. The most famous of these is the Colosseum, a giant amphitheater where people watched gladiator fights and other events. It was Vespasian's idea to build a place where Romans could gather for entertainment, bringing joy and pride to his people.

He also built the Temple of Peace and restored the Capitol, which had been damaged by fires during the chaos before he became emperor. These buildings weren't just beautiful; they were symbols of Rome's strength and stability.

With Vespasian in charge, the empire also enjoyed a period of peace and consolidation. This means he worked hard to strengthen the areas Rome already controlled, rather than trying to conquer new lands. This strategy helped make the empire more secure and allowed the people to prosper.

Vespasian was known for being down-to-earth and having a good sense of humor, which helped him connect with people from all walks of life. He often joked about his own policies and even made fun of himself! That was quite unusual for an emperor, but it made him quite popular.

Vespasian ruled for ten years. When he passed away in AD 79, he left behind a stronger, more stable Rome than the one he had inherited. He was succeeded by his sons, who continued his good work, especially in building projects like the Colosseum, which was completed after his death.

Vespasian is remembered as a wise and practical leader who valued peace and stability. He showed that being a good leader isn't just about winning battles or having a famous family; it's also about making smart decisions and caring for your people, and making the world a better place.

Vespasian's story is a great chapter in the tale of Rome's mighty emperors. So, next time you see a picture of the Colosseum, remember Vespasian—the emperor who gifted it to his people as a sign of peace and fun for everyone.

Titus | The Emperor of Good Deeds (AD 79 - 81)

After Vespasian's reign, which focused on stability and the prosperity of the people, a new emperor took the stage. His name was Titus. Although he ruled for just two years, from AD 79 to AD 81, his reign was as brief as it was bright.. Let's dive into the story of this fascinating leader.

Titus was the son of the Colosseum's creator. As a young prince, Titus learned how to lead by watching his father and helping him with important duties. He was a skilled soldier and a smart thinker, which made him a good choice to become emperor after his father.

When Vespasian passed away, Titus took over. At first, people weren't sure if they liked him. They remembered some of the not-so-nice things he had done when he was younger, like destroying a great temple in Jerusalem during a war. But Titus was about to prove everyone wrong.

A Time of Tragedy

Just as Titus was getting started as emperor, a huge disaster struck. Mount Vesuvius, a big volcano near the city of Pompeii, erupted in AD 79. This was the same year Titus became emperor. It was one of the biggest eruptions in history, and it buried the cities of Pompeii and Herculaneum under ash and lava. The eruption trapped thousands of people.

Instead of sitting back in the palace, Titus acted quickly. He sent help to the survivors and spent a lot of money to support the rescue and rebuilding efforts. He showed that he cared deeply about his people's suffering, and this made him very popular.

The Emperor of Good Deeds

During his short time as emperor, Titus did many kind things. He finished building the Colosseum and opened it with grand games that lasted for 100 days. These first games were free for everyone to enjoy!

Elephants, tigers, and gladiators entertained the crowds. Titus often joined the people to watch the games, cheering and laughing along with them. Titus also made laws that were fair and tried to make life better for the ordinary people of Rome. He used the empire's money wisely, to help those in need rather than just making the rich richer.

Mysterious End

Sadly, Titus's time as emperor was very short. He died suddenly after only two years in power, probably from a fever. Some people wondered if his brother, Domitian, who was next in line for the throne, might have had something to do with his death.But, no one knows for sure what happened.

Even though he was emperor for just a little while, Titus is remembered as one of the "good emperors." He showed that being a leader isn't just about power and glory; it's also about taking care of your people when they need help the most.

Titus's story teaches us that you can make a big difference even in a short time. He used his days as emperor to spread joy and help those in need, leaving behind memories of a ruler who truly cared. His legacy is like a shooting star—bright, beautiful, and remembered long after it's gone. This makes him a special chapter in the book of Rome's mighty emperors, teaching us about the power of good deeds and a kind heart.

Domitian | The Builder of Rome's Glory (AD 81 - 96)

In the colorful tapestry of Rome's history, woven with stories of heroes and emperors, one figure stands out for his long reign and big projects. His name was Domitian, who took over after his older brother died suddenly. He was emperor from AD 81 to AD 96. During his 15 years as leader, Domitian worked hard to make Rome a strong and shining capital, even though he was often misunderstood by his people.

When Domitian became emperor after Titus's sudden death, he had big shoes to fill. Unlike his brother, Domitian was serious and private. Because of this, some Romans didn't trust him. But Domitian had great plans for the empire, and he was determined to see them through.

Domitian took over at a time when Rome needed a strong hand. The city had suffered from fires and other disasters, and the empire's borders were always threatened by enemies. Domitian rolled up his sleeves and got to work, making sure Rome was safe and strong.

One of the first things Domitian did was to fix the economy. The money in Rome had been losing its value, which made everything more expensive for the people. Domitian introduced new coins that were worth more and made sure that everyone knew they could trust this new money. This helped everyone from bakers to soldiers buy what they needed without worrying about their coins being worthless.

Domitian loved architecture and believed that a beautiful city was a strong city. He started a massive building program all over Rome. He repaired temples, built new statues, and improved the roads. One of his biggest projects was rebuilding the Capitol, which was an important temple that had been damaged by fire. Under Domitian's orders, Rome began to sparkle again, filled with marvelous buildings that awed everyone who saw them.

But Domitian didn't just focus on the inside of the empire; he also looked outwards to its borders. He knew that safe borders meant a safe Rome. Domitian strengthened the defenses along the empire's edges, building forts and training soldiers to make sure that no enemies could sneak in. These efforts kept the people inside the empire safe and made Domitian popular with the soldiers.

A Controversial Figure

Even though he did many good things for Rome, Domitian wasn't very popular with the Senate. They thought Domitian wanted too much power for himself. This tension made it difficult for him to rule, and many senators did not trust him.

Unfortunately, the distrust of the Senate and others that surrounded him led to a sad end for Domitian. In AD 96, after 15 years of ruling, Domitian was betrayed and assassinated in a palace conspiracy. His death marked the end of the Flavian dynasty, which included his father, Vespasian, and his brother, Titus.

Domitian shows us that being a leader isn't always about being popular; it's about making tough decisions that can help people in the long run. His story teaches us about the importance of having goals as a leader. Domitian reminds us that even the most misunderstood rulers can have a positive impact on history.

Trajan | The Great Builder and Conqueror (AD 98 - 117)

Domitian's successor, the emperor Trajan, stands out as one of the greatest. Ruling from AD 98 to AD 117, Trajan was known for his kindness, his love for building, and his adventurous spirit through the expansion of Rome's borders.

Trajan was born in a place called Hispania, which is now part of Spain, which made him the first Roman emperor born outside of Italy. This gave him a unique perspective and helped him connect with many different people across the vast empire. Before he became emperor, Trajan was a famous general who won many battles and earned the respect of his soldiers and the people.

When Trajan took the throne in AD 98, he decided to make Rome even greater. He was a fair and wise ruler. The people loved him due to his fairness. He also made Rome a stable and prosperous place. Unlike some emperors who only wanted power for themselves, Trajan truly cared about the well-being of his citizens.

A Vast Building Program

Trajan loved architecture. He believed that building impressive structures could make Rome even more glorious. He started a vast building program that saw the creation of new roads, bridges, and buildings all over the empire. One of his most famous projects was "Trajan's Market," which was like a big shopping mall where people could buy all sorts of goods. It was a bustling place where traders from all over the empire came together.

One of the most amazing things Trajan built was "Trajan's Column." This tall column is covered in detailed carvings that tell the story of Trajan's wars in Dacia, which is now the country of Romania. It's similar to a giant comic strip, but made of stone. It shows battles, soldiers, and the people of Dacia. "Trajan's Column" not only celebrated his victories but also served as a reminder of how he expanded the empire and his legacy.

Expanding the Empire

Trajan was not only a builder, but also a great conqueror. He believed that Rome needed to expand to become stronger. Under his rule, the empire was the biggest in history. It stretched from the sands of the Sahara to the rainy lands of Britain, and east to the rich cities of the Middle East. He led his armies with courage and skill, winning territories and securing Rome's borders against its enemies.

What made Trajan truly special was his care for all people throughout the empire. He set up programs to help poor children, giving them food and educating them. This showed that he was both powerful and kind-hearted. Trajan wanted to make sure even the least fortunate could have a good life.

The Legacy of Trajan

Trajan ruled Rome for nearly twenty years. When he died in AD 117, he was deeply mourned by the people. He was called *Optimus Princeps*, which means "the best leader," because he was seen as the ideal emperor. He left behind a stronger, more beautiful Rome.

Trajan's ability to combine the might of a warrior with the heart of a caretaker shows us that being a great leader is about much more than just winning battles; it's about making life better for your people.

Hadrian | The Traveling Emperor (AD 117 - 138)

Emperor Hadrian shines as a unique character. He took over immediately after his adopted father, Trajan, died. He ruled from AD 117 to AD 138. Unlike many emperors who focused on war, Hadrian loved peace, culture, and especially everything Greek! Let's travel back in time and see what made Emperor Hadrian such a memorable leader.

From the start, Hadrian decided to do things a bit differently. He believed that the Roman Empire was big enough. It was time to make sure the people were secure and happy, rather than trying to conquer more lands. This idea made him very popular in some places but not so much in others.

A Lover of Greek Culture

One of Hadrian's biggest passions was his love for Greek culture, which he thought was the best way to learn and live. Greeks had great ideas about art, science, philosophy, and government. Hadrian wanted to spread these ideas throughout his empire. To show his dedication, he even spent a whole year living in Greece. He spent a lot of time in Athens, which was like the New York City of ancient culture!

While living in Athens, Hadrian wasn't just sitting around enjoying the views. He helped make the city even more beautiful and functional. He built new public buildings, such as a fabulous library where people could read and learn, and an aqueduct. Aqueducts served as a kind of water bridge and brought fresh water to the city's people.

Hadrian's most impressive project was finishing the vast Temple of Olympian Zeus, a huge temple that had been under construction for over 500 years! When Hadrian completed it, the temple was one of the largest and most stunning in all of Greece, showing how much he adored and respected Greek culture.

Hadrian didn't just want to build things; he wanted to be a part of Greek life. He joined in religious festivals and rituals, celebrating the gods and goddesses of Greek mythology with the people. This wasn't just for fun; it was a way for Hadrian to show that he was one of them, not just their ruler from afar in Rome.

Hadrian's Wall

Back in the Roman Empire, Hadrian knew that to keep peace he needed strong borders. One of his most famous projects was building Hadrian's Wall across what is now Northern England. This massive wall was meant to keep out invaders and mark the northern limit of his empire. It was so well built that parts of it still stand today!

Under Hadrian's rule, the Roman Empire enjoyed a period of peace and prosperity. He made laws that were fairer. He tried to make sure that governors in different parts of the empire were doing their jobs right and improved the lives of many people. His focus on building and culture brought a lot of beauty and joy to the empire.

Hadrian passed away in AD 138 after a long and eventful reign. He was remembered as a wise and cultured emperor who made the Roman Empire a better place through his understanding and respect for different cultures.

Emperor Hadrian shows us that leadership is also about learning, sharing culture, and making the world more beautiful and safe for everyone. Hadrian's journey as emperor teaches us the importance of celebrating the things that make us all unique.

Antoninus Pius | The Peaceful Emperor (AD 138 - 161)

Antoninus Pius took over after Hadrian, ruling from AD 138 to AD 161. Unlike many emperors before him who spent their days on battlefields, Antoninus Pius preferred to bring peace and happiness to the empire.

Antoninus Pius was born into a noble family and grew up learning about the ways of government and leadership. When Emperor Hadrian chose him as his successor, he knew Antoninus was wise and kind enough to lead Rome well. Upon becoming emperor, Antoninus was given the name Pius because he showed great respect and piety towards Hadrian. Pius honored all Hadrian's wishes, including adopting two young men, Marcus Aurelius and Lucius Verus, who were to become the next emperors after him.

A Time of Peace

What made Antoninus Pius's reign remarkable was how peaceful it was. For 23 years, the Roman Empire saw no major revolts or invasions. It was a golden time when people could focus on their crops, their crafts, and their families without the constant worry of war. This peaceful period allowed Antoninus to improve the lives of his people. He repaired roads and cities, made laws that were fair, and worked hard to ensure that justice was served throughout the empire. He believed that a good emperor must be like a good father, looking after all his citizens with care and fairness.

The Antonine Wall

Even though his reign was peaceful, Antoninus Pius knew the importance of a strong defense. Early in his rule, he ordered the construction of a new wall in southern Scotland, called the Antonine Wall. This wall was built north of Hadrian's Wall. It was meant to protect the Roman Empire from the tribes in the north. It stretched from coast to coast and was fortified with ditches, ramparts, and forts. The Antonine Wall was a massive project and showed the might of Rome even in peaceful times. It was a symbol of how Antoninus Pius extended Roman influence without extensive warfare, preferring strong defenses and clear boundaries.

Life in the Empire under Antoninus Pius

During the time of Antoninus Pius, the Roman Empire flourished. Cities grew larger and markets bustled with traders from all over the world. Artists and philosophers could create and think without the interruptions of war.

Antoninus was also known for his generosity. He used the empire's money to help cities struck by disasters like earthquakes and fires. He believed that the empire's strength didn't just come from its army but from the happiness and health of its people.

Antoninus Pius died in AD 161, leaving behind an empire that was stable and strong. His peaceful approach to ruling was a breath of fresh air in the turbulent history of Rome. He proved that with wise management and a focus on the welfare of the people, an emperor could be just as mighty in peace as in war.

His adopted sons, Marcus Aurelius and Lucius Verus, took over after him, and they continued his policies of careful, thoughtful leadership. Antoninus's reign is often seen as the height of the Roman Empire's peace and prosperity.

Antoninus Pius teaches us that peace, strong borders, and care for the people can lead to a golden age just as much as victory in battle. His wise and gentle rule left a lasting impression on Rome.

Marcus Aurelius | The Philosopher Emperor (AD 161 - 180)

When Marcus Aurelius took over for his adopted father, he ruled with wisdom and power. His reign lasted from AD 161 to AD 180. Marcus wasn't just an emperor; he was also a philosopher who wrote down his thoughts on how to live a good life, which are still read by people around the world today.

Marcus Aurelius was born into a wealthy and important family. From a young age, he was trained in the art of leadership and the studies of philosophy, particularly Stoicism—a type of philosophy that teaches the importance of reason and self-control in facing life's challenges. Stoics believe that a good life comes from doing your duty and accepting your fate with courage. When Marcus became emperor, he continued to live by these lessons. He tried to rule wisely and fairly, and always worked to improve himself and his empire.

Becoming Emperor

Marcus Aurelius and Lucius Verus started by sharing the duties of emperor in AD 161. Together, they ruled over an empire that was peaceful thanks to the efforts of their predecessor, Antoninus Pius. However, Marcus's reign soon faced challenges, including wars on the empire's frontiers and a devastating plague that swept through the land. Despite these troubles, Marcus tried to maintain peace and stability within the Roman Empire. He believed that it was his duty to look after his people and protect them as best he could.

The Philosopher on the Throne

What made Marcus truly unique was his commitment to Stoic philosophy even while being an emperor. He often wrote about his ideas and reflections in a book called *The Meditations*. At first, this wasn't a book meant for others to read—it was his personal diary, filled with notes to himself on how to be a better person and a better leader.

In *The Meditations*, Marcus wrote about the importance of accepting what you can't change and dealing calmly with other people. He wrote that you should always try to do the right thing, no matter how hard it might be. These writings offer a rare glimpse into the mind of an emperor who deeply cared about being moral and fair.

As a leader, Marcus Aurelius was known for his efforts to bring peace whenever possible. He worked hard to protect the empire's borders, but preferred to solve conflicts without fighting. When wars were necessary, he led his soldiers with courage and care, always mindful of the hardships of battle.

Marcus was also fair in his dealings with people from all walks of life. He passed laws to help the poor and made sure that slaves could have a chance to gain their freedom. He believed that all people, no matter their status, deserved respect and justice.

Legacy of a Wise Emperor

When Marcus Aurelius died in AD 180, his death marked the end of the Pax Romana, the long period of relative peace and stability within the Roman Empire. He was succeeded by his son, Commodus, who unfortunately did not share his father's wisdom or commitment to philosophy.

Today, Marcus Aurelius is remembered not just as a powerful emperor, but as a wise and thoughtful philosopher. His life reminds us that being a good leader is about much more than giving orders—it's also about setting an example of how to live a good and meaningful life.

We can learn a lot from Marcus Aurelius, like how to stay calm in tough situations, how to be fair to others, and why it's important to always keep learning and growing...no matter who you are or what challenges you face.

Septimius Severus | The Warrior Emperor (AD 193 - 211)

After the Pax Romana ended, Rome started to face many changes and challenges. During this time, Septimius Severus became emperor. He ruled from AD 193 to AD 211. His story is full of battles, adventures, and big building projects. Let's take a closer look at this fascinating emperor who left a lasting mark on Rome.

Septimius Severus came from the city of Leptis Magna, which is in modern-day Libya. He was the first Roman Emperor from Africa, which made his rise to power quite unique. Severus was known for being a strong and determined leader. He became emperor after winning a civil war against other rivals who also wanted to become emperor.

When Severus became emperor, Rome was going through a turbulent time. He knew he needed to make it clear to everyone in the empire that he was in charge. To do this, he showed both his might as a warrior and his skill as a leader.

The Triumphal Arch

One of the most famous things Severus did was to build a grand arch in the Roman Forum. This wasn't just any arch— it was a triumphal arch, which is a big, decorative structure that celebrates victories in battle. The Arch of Septimius Severus is still standing today, and it tells his story of success as a leader.

This arch was beautifully decorated with carvings that, like a comic book, showed scenes of his victories over the Parthian Empire (modern-day Iran). By building this arch, Severus told everyone that he was a strong emperor who could protect and lead Rome.

Severus also wanted to make sure that his family, the Severan dynasty, would keep ruling Rome after he was gone. So, the arch also served as a way to show that his family was rightful and legitimate, and deserved to be in charge because of their strength and leadership.

Severus made many changes during his reign. He strengthened the army by increasing pay for the soldiers. He made sure they were loyal first to him and then to Rome. He also traveled a lot around the empire, from Britain to Syria, making laws and improving cities wherever he went. In Britain, he fought against the tribes in the north and even tried to strengthen Hadrian's Wall. He wanted to make sure that all parts of the empire were well-protected and governed.

A Family Man

Severus was also a family man. He had two sons, Caracalla and Geta, whom he tried to prepare to rule after him. He wanted them to learn how to be good leaders, just like he was. Unfortunately, his sons didn't get along, and this caused problems later on.

Severus died in AD 211 in the city of York during a battle in Britain. His rule had seen the Roman Empire stabilize and grow stronger after a period of uncertainty. He left behind a legacy of strong military power and impressive architecture, like his famous arch, which people from all over the world still go to see today.

Septimius Severus shows us that a great leader can come from anywhere, and that a ruler looks out not only for his own time but for the future as well. His triumphal arch, still standing in the heart of Rome, reminds us of his power and his legacy, which have lasted through the ages.

Diocletian | The Emperor Who Divided Rome (AD 284 - 305)

Let's jump forward to Emperor Diocletian, who stands out as a mastermind of change. His rule from AD 284 to 305 brought significant reforms that helped stabilize the struggling Roman Empire during tough times. Let's explore how this clever leader made a big difference.

Diocletian was born around AD 245 in the region of Dalmatia (now part of modern Croatia). He rose from humble beginnings, climbing the ranks of the Roman military through determination and skill. His real name was Diocles, but he took the name Diocletian when he became emperor. His leadership came at a time when Rome desperately needed strong hands to guide it.

A Time of Trouble

Before Diocletian became emperor, Rome was going through the "Crisis of the Third Century." This was a difficult period marked by economic problems, invasions, and the empire nearly breaking apart. Multiple emperors came and went, each unable to fix the deep issues facing Rome.

Diocletian had a revolutionary idea: the empire was too big for one person to manage, especially in such chaotic times. So, he decided to split the empire in half. In AD 285, he divided Rome into the Eastern and Western Empires. But Diocletian didn't stop there. He introduced the Tetrarchy, a system where four rulers would share power—two senior emperors called Augusti and two junior emperors called Caesars.

Diocletian ruled the Eastern part of the empire, which included the wealthier provinces that were less troubled by invasions. This decision helped each part of the empire get the attention it needed to manage its specific problems, making governing more efficient and effective.

Reforms and Recovery

Under Diocletian's rule, the empire saw major improvements. He reorganized the government to make it more structured. This way, the emperors could better serve the people and handle crises. He also reformed the economy by introducing new coins to replace the old, less valuable ones.

To strengthen the military, Diocletian increased the number of soldiers and built stronger defenses along the empire's borders. These actions helped protect the empire from outside attacks and brought more stability.

For ordinary people, Diocletian's reign brought mixed feelings. On one hand, his economic reforms eventually led to higher taxes, which some people found difficult. On the other hand, the empire was becoming more stable, and there were fewer invasions disrupting their lives.

Diocletian's Retirement: A Historic First

Diocletian did something no Roman emperor had done before; he retired, which shocked everyone. In AD 305, after 21 years as emperor, he decided to step away from power. He believed that fresh leadership could bring new ideas and keep the empire strong. Diocletian spent his last years in a palace he built in his homeland, enjoying a quiet life away from the stress of ruling.

Diocletian's reforms set the stage for a more organized and stable empire, even though the peace didn't last forever. The Tetrarchy eventually broke down, leading to new conflicts, but his ideas about dividing the empire influenced future leaders, including Constantine the Great.

Emperor Diocletian teaches us that sometimes solving big problems requires bold, new ideas. His decision to split the empire and share power showed that teamwork and smart planning can help solve even the toughest issues. Diocletian's story is a chapter in Roman history that highlights the importance of adaptability and innovation in leadership.

Constantine | The Great (AD 306 - 337)

In the grand story of the Roman Empire, Emperor Constantine the Great shines as one of the most transformative figures. He ruled from AD 306 to AD 337, making decisions that reshaped the empire's spiritual landscape and founded a city that would stand as a beacon of power for centuries. Let's step back in time and discover the life of this remarkable leader.

Constantine was born in the year AD 272, in a region that is now part of Serbia. His father was a powerful Roman officer who would become emperor. So, Constantine grew up in the emperor's courts, learning the arts of leadership and war. When his father died in AD 306, Constantine was declared emperor by his father's troops.

The Path to Power

Becoming emperor was just the beginning for Constantine. When his reign began, the Roman Empire was not united under one leader but was divided among several, leading to a period of chaos and conflict. Constantine had to fight a series of battles against these other rulers to secure his position as the sole emperor. The most famous of these battles was the Battle of the Milvian Bridge in AD 312.

Before the Battle of the Milvian Bridge, Constantine experienced a profound moment that would define his rule. According to stories, on the night before the battle he saw a sign in the sky. It was a cross made of light. He also saw the words, "In this sign, you will conquer." Believing this to be a divine message, Constantine had his soldiers paint the Christian symbol on their shields. After winning, Constantine attributed his success to the Christian God.

A New Religious Path for Rome

After his victory, Constantine made a big decision: he would support Christianity, a religion whose followers had been persecuted under previous Roman emperors. In AD 313, he issued the Edict of Milan, which granted religious freedom to Christians and allowed them to worship openly. This paved the way for Christianity to become the empire's dominant faith.

Constantine's vision extended beyond religion. He saw the need for a new capital city that could reflect his riches and the empire's renewed strength. Thus, he founded Constantinople in AD 330 on the site of the ancient city of Byzantium.

Constantinople was strategically located on the crossroads between Europe and Asia. It was a vibrant hub for trade and culture. Massive walls helped to protect the city that was filled with grand palaces and decorated with splendid churches. Constantinople would later become known as one of the most powerful cities in the world. It became the capital of the Byzantine Empire long after the fall of the Western Roman Empire.

Legacy of a Visionary

Constantine ruled until his death in AD 337. His reign marked a significant turning point in the history of the West, as he transformed the Roman Empire in ways that still resonate today. Constantine was significant in both establishing Christianity as a major world religion as well as laying the foundation for what would become the Byzantine Empire.

Constantine the Great was more than just a conqueror; he was a visionary who redefined the ancient world. His story teaches us about the power of faith and the importance of bold leadership.

Theodosius I | The Great Peacemaker (AD 379 - 395)

The next significant ruler after Constantine was Theodosius I, who holds a special place in the history of Roman emperors as a peacemaker. Known as Theodosius the Great, he ruled the Roman Empire from AD 379 to AD 395. He was the last emperor to rule over both the eastern and western parts of the empire (before it split into two separate empires). Let's explore the life of this important leader.

Theodosius was born in Spain around AD 347. He grew up in a time when the Roman Empire was facing many challenges, including attacks from outside groups called "barbarians." Theodosius learned about military strategy and leadership from his father, who was a high-ranking officer in the army. This training prepared him well for the big role he would later take on as emperor.

Becoming Emperor

In AD 379, Theodosius was chosen to be the new emperor of the Eastern Roman Empire after the death of the previous leader. His first big challenge was to deal with a group called the Goths, who were causing trouble in the eastern parts of the empire. The Goths were a powerful group that had moved into Roman territory looking for a new place to live. Previous emperors had tried to push them out with military force, but these attempts had often led to more conflict and problems. Theodosius had a different idea. He decided to make peace with the Goths. So, he allowed them to live within the empire's borders in the territory between the lower Danube and the Balkan mountains. This was a bold move.

Theodosius treated the Goths fairly. He allowed them to have their own leaders and live by their own laws as long as they remained loyal to Rome. This agreement brought peace to the region and showed that different groups could live together under one empire.

As emperor, Theodosius worked hard to keep the empire united. He believed that a strong and united Rome was better for everyone. He made laws that were fair and worked to make sure that people in both the eastern and western parts of the empire felt connected and supported by the government.

Promoting Christianity

Another important part of Theodosius's reign was his support for Christianity. He was a devout Christian and made decisions that helped strengthen the Christian church within the empire. In AD 380, he issued a law that made Christianity the official religion of the Roman Empire. This was a significant change because it meant that Christianity was now the main religion supported by the emperor himself.

Theodosius ruled for 16 years. When he died in AD 395, his two sons inherited different parts of the empire. One son took over the east and the other took the west. This division marked the official split of the Roman Empire into the Eastern Roman Empire and the Western Roman Empire, which would have very different futures.

Theodosius I is remembered as a wise and thoughtful leader who tried to bring peace and stability to a vast and diverse empire. His ability to make peace with the Goths and his efforts to unite the empire under Christianity had long-lasting impacts on the history of Europe. Theodosius shows us that sometimes, making peace can be more powerful than winning a battle.

Chapter conclusion

We've traveled through the reigns of Rome's most formidable emperors, exploring their monumental achievements, their struggles, and the unforgettable marks they left on history. From Augustus's establishment of peace through the Pax Romana to the transformative rule of Constantine, these leaders not only shaped the political landscape of their time but also laid the foundations for modern governance and civilization.

As we conclude this chapter, we reflect on the complex legacy of these rulers—their vision, their power, and their human flaws. Their stories remind us of the profound impact leadership can have on the fate of nations and the course of history.

Now, as we turn the page, we look forward to diving deeper into the rich tapestry of Roman life. We will explore their daily experiences, cultural achievements, and enduring mysteries of one of history's most fascinating civilizations. Let's continue our journey through ancient Rome!

CHAPTER 2:
POWERFUL WOMEN OF ROME

In this chapter, we'll meet some of ancient Rome's most amazing women.. Though men of this time made most of the big decisions, these women found ways to leave their mark on history. From Livia Drusilla, who was smart and a good planner, to Cornelia, a brave mom who raised famous sons, their stories are full of adventure and inspiration. Let's discover how these incredible ladies showed that anyone can make history. Get ready for some exciting tales about Rome's most powerful women!

Livia Drusilla: The Emperor's Confidante (30 January 59 BC – AD 29)

In the ancient city of Rome, there once lived a remarkable woman named Livia Drusilla. In this busy city, Livia stood out. Not just as a queenly figure beside her husband, Emperor Augustus, but as a powerful woman whose whispers could move mountains within the palace walls.

Livia Drusilla was more than just the wife of Augustus; she was his closest advisor, friend, and confidante. When Augustus became the first emperor of Rome, it wasn't just his wisdom that led the empire—it was also Livia's clever counsel. Though women in Rome didn't typically rule openly, Livia found her way to influence. She was like a skilled puppeteer, subtly pulling the strings behind the majestic red curtains of the empire.

Livia used her intelligence and charm to help Augustus make big decisions. From deciding which roads to build, to solving squabbles in the Senate, Livia was always ready with smart ideas. She knew how to play the game of politics just as well as any of the men in government, and sometimes even better!

A Mother Shapes an Emperor

Livia wasn't just important to Rome; she was also a super mom! She had two sons, Tiberius and Drusus. From a young age, Livia had big dreams for Tiberius. She imagined him becoming a great leader, just like his stepfather, Augustus. While Drusus grew up to be a brave general, Livia focused her attention on preparing Tiberius for the ultimate role: Emperor of Rome.

Livia taught Tiberius how to understand what people needed or feared. This wasn't always easy, as Tiberius was shy and serious (unlike the charming Augustus). But under his mother's guidance, Tiberius learned the art of leadership and diplomacy. Livia also arranged for Tiberius to marry someone who would help him boost his popularity and power. These actions made Livia seem like a chess player, as she carefully moved her pieces to ensure Tiberius's path to the throne was clear.

Her plans worked well because eventually, after many years and the sad passing of his younger brother Drusus, Tiberius became emperor. Thanks to Livia's early influence, Tiberius knew how to keep the empire together, even during tough times.

Legacy of a Powerful Matron

Livia Drusilla's story is not just about power and politics; it's about the strength of a woman in a man's world. She showed that being a queen isn't only about wearing a crown; it's about using your mind and heart to make a difference. Livia's influence reminds us that behind every great leader, there might just be a wisewoman with a brave heart.

Agrippina the Younger: Mother of an Emperor (6 November AD 15 – 23 March AD 59)

Next we will step into Emperor Nero's time, where a woman named Agrippina the Younger lived. Agrippina was a fierce and ambitious mother who would stop at nothing to see her son, Nero, rise as emperor. Let's embark on a journey through her thrilling and dramatic life!

Agrippina was born into a family that was very close to the throne. So, her family was no stranger to power, as her brother was the Emperor Caligula, and her uncle was Claudius. From a young age, Agrippina knew she was meant for greatness.

Agrippina dreamed not just of standing beside powerful men, but of holding power herself. As she grew up, Agrippina became known for her sharp mind and fearless spirit. Like Livia, Agrippina could be compared to a chess player. She made very calculated moves, thinking many steps ahead of everyone else. But her ultimate goal was to see her son Nero wear the emperor's purple robe—a symbol of supreme power in Rome.

The Master Plan

When Agrippina married her uncle Claudius, who was emperor at that time, many people in Rome whispered behind closed doors. They were shocked because it was unusual and a bit scandalous. But for Agrippina, this was a strategic move. As the wife of the emperor, she had a direct path to guide her young son Nero toward the throne.

Agrippina worked hard to position Nero as the next emperor. She persuaded Claudius to adopt Nero and make him heir. This meant that Claudius pushed aside his own son, Britannicus. Agrippina made sure that when this chess game ended, her son, Nero, would shout "checkmate!" as he took the throne.

As expected, Agrippina's clever planning paid off. When Claudius died under mysterious circumstances (some say Agrippina might have plotted against him), Nero became emperor, meaning that Agrippina's dream came true! She was the mother of the emperor and the most powerful woman in Rome. But, as in many tales of power and ambition, reaching the top was not the end of Agrippina's story.

Getting to the top can be tricky, but staying there can be even trickier. Nero, once a puppet in his mother's hands, started to grow up and wanted to rule on his own. He didn't like his mother controlling every move he made. Like a bird that wants to fly after learning how to use its wings, Nero wanted to be free from his mother's tight grip.

As Nero asserted his independence, Agrippina lost her influence. The once unbreakable bond between mother and son began to crack. In a dramatic turn of events, their relationship ended tragically. Nero, feeling threatened by his mother's power, decided there was only one way to keep his throne secure—to have Agrippina removed. In a dark twist of fate, Nero ordered his own mother to be taken away, never to be seen again.

Remembering Agrippina

Agrippina the Younger's story is a powerful reminder of the heights to which ambition can soar and the depths to which it can fall. She was a woman who played the political game as cunningly as any great leader of her time. She showed the world that a woman, too, could orchestrate the rise of emperors and shape the course of history.

Julia Domna: Philosopher and Empress (170 AD-217 AD)

After discussing Agrippina, who got as close to ruling Rome as possible through her son, we will move onto someone who became an empress. Her name is Julia Domna. Julia was not only a queen but also a philosopher, a mother, and a political strategist. Her story is one of intellect and influence, showing that the power of the mind can be just as mighty as the power of an army.

The Empress Who Loved to Think

Julia Domna was born in Syria, far from the bustling streets of Rome. She was known for her brilliant mind and love for philosophy. Philosophy is all about thinking deeply about life's big questions—such as what is right and wrong and how we should treat others. Julia believed that understanding these big ideas was just as important as any treasure.

When she married Septimius Severus, who would become one of Rome's greatest emperors, she moved to Rome, bringing her love of learning with her. As empress, Julia was not content to sit quietly in her palace; instead, she created a gathering place for some of the smartest thinkers of the day. Imagine a place where every room buzzes with ideas, and poets, philosophers, and scholars debate under glittering chandeliers. That was Julia's palace!

A Queen in the World of Politics

Julia's influence didn't stop at philosophical discussions. She was deeply involved in the politics of Rome, advising her husband on important decisions. When Septimius Severus went on military campaigns to expand the empire, Julia was right there with him. She didn't just act as his supportive wife, but also a crucial advisor. She showed that a queen could be just as savvy and strategic as her king, steering the empire through times of war and peace.

Her role as a political advisor didn't just make her popular—it made her essential. Julia Domna was like the coach of a team. Her husband was the captain, and the empire was their field. She helped plan their moves and was a key player in the game of empire-building.

Even after her death, the ideas and values that Julia left with her sons and court continued to shape Roman politics and culture. Her intellectual gatherings were remembered as golden moments in Rome's history, where the mind was celebrated alongside the might of the sword.

Julia Domna's life reminds us of the importance of thinking deeply about the world and our place in it. In museums today, we can still see statues of Julia with thoughtful, wise eyes. These statues show us that, long ago, this empress of Rome knew the value of a good question and thoughtful conversation.

So, as you turn the pages of this book and explore more tales of ancient Rome, remember Julia Domna as a philosopher and empress who believed in the power of ideas. Her story shows that even during times of emperors and battles, the pen—or the philosopher's stone—could be just as mighty as the sword!

Boudica: Warrior Queen against Rome

Now, let's travel to the misty, green lands of Britain, where a fierce queen named Boudica lived. Her story is one of courage and defiance, as she stood tall against the mighty Roman Empire. Boudica was not just a queen; she was a warrior, a leader, and a hero to her people. Let's ride with her on her incredible journey against one of the most powerful forces in the ancient world.

The Spark of Revolt

Boudica was the queen of the Iceni tribe in what is now eastern England. The Iceni were proud and strong, living peacefully under their own laws and leaders. However, their peace was shattered when the Romans came. The Romans were like a storm that swept across the land, taking control of everything in their path. They took lands, demanded heavy taxes, and treated the local tribes unfairly.

The trouble truly began when Boudica's husband, the king, died. His wish was that his kingdom would be shared between his daughters and the Roman emperor, hoping to protect his family and people. But the Romans had other ideas. They ignored his wishes, took everything, and treated Boudica and her daughters cruelly. This injustice lit a fire in Boudica's heart, and she promised to fight back.

Leading the Charge

Boudica's spirit and call to arms ignited a fierce desire for freedom among her people and neighboring tribes. She became the leader of a massive rebellion, rallying thousands of warriors to her cause. Boudica was not just fighting for revenge; she was fighting for the freedom of her land and people.

Imagine seeing Boudica in her chariot, red hair blazing, her voice thundering over the crowds, stirring her warriors to battle. She led her army with such courage that even the mighty Romans trembled. Her army marched through cities, reclaiming them from Roman rule. Their message was clear: this land belonged to the Britons, not distant emperors.

The Romans were shocked and scared by the strength of Boudica's uprising. They had thought it would be easy to rule over the Britons, but Boudica proved them wrong. She showed that even the most powerful empire could be challenged by the heart and spirit of those oppressed.

Although Boudica's rebellion was eventually crushed by the well-trained Roman legions, her story did not end there. Her courage made her a legend, a symbol of resistance against tyranny. The tale of Boudica teaches us that standing up for what is right, even in the face of overwhelming odds, is a true hero's path.

Fulvia: A Woman in the Civil War (83 - 40 BC)

After Boudica fought her rebellion, while senators debated in the Forum, there lived a woman of remarkable strength and influence. Her name was Fulvia. She was not like the quiet, reserved women of her time. Instead, Fulvia was a powerful figure in Roman politics, and her life was intertwined with the republic's most turbulent years.

Fulvia and the Game of Politics

Fulvia was not just any Roman matron; rather, she was a political powerhouse. She married three of the most influential men in Rome, each of whom played a pivotal role in the Republic's final years. Her husbands included Publius Clodius Pulcher, a radical politician; Gaius Scribonius Curio, a passionate supporter of Julius Caesar; and finally, Mark Antony, a daring and ambitious leader known for his alliances with Julius Caesar and later, Cleopatra.

During her relationship with Mark Antony, Fulvia became heavily involved in Roman politics. She was not content to stay behind the scenes. Instead, she actively participated in the complex and often messy political arena like a coach whose team was always in the middle of the most important play of the game. She managed estates, rallied troops, and even issued orders, much like a queen in a game of chess, moving her pieces across a board filled with danger and intrigue.

The Perusine War: A Stand Against Octavian

One of Fulvia's most famous—and dramatic—political moves was during the Perusine War. This was not just any conflict; instead, it was a fierce struggle for power between Fulvia (and her brother-in-law, Lucius Antonius) and Octavian, who was Mark Antony's rival and the future emperor Augustus.

So, why did this war start? After Julius Caesar's death, Rome was full of power struggles. And, Fulvia was right in the middle of it all. She felt that Octavian was taking too much power and sidelining Mark Antony, her husband. So, what did Fulvia do? She didn't just stand by; she took action!

Fulvia and Lucius Antonius gathered an army and took control of the city of Perusia (modern-day Perugia in Italy). Imagine her, a woman in a world of soldiers and senators, commanding forces and making strategic decisions. They held the city against Octavian's forces through a harsh winter, showing incredible resilience and determination.

However, the Perusine War did not end well for Fulvia. Octavian's troops eventually broke through, and Fulvia was forced to flee. The war showed Octavian's ruthless side and led to further struggles between him and Mark Antony. Still, the war highlighted Fulvia's incredible courage and her willingness to fight for her family's position in the swirling chaos of Roman politics.

Fulvia's life was a series of battles, not just with swords and shields, but with words, alliances, and wills. She showed that a woman, even in ancient Rome, could wield power in ways that echoed through the halls of history. As you explore more tales of ancient Rome, remember Fulvia not as a figure in the shadows, but rather a blazing force in the spotlight. She was a woman who might have used a stylus more often than a sword but who fought just as fiercely for her place and her principles.

Cornelia Scipionis Africana: Mother of Reformers (c. 190 – 115 BC)

Where Fulvia shone most brightly in her political strategies, another woman proved herself to be extraordinary due to her wisdom and dignity—Cornelia Scipionis Africana. Known not just for her noble birth but for her remarkable role as a mother and mentor, Cornelia's story is one of inspiration and influence. She was the mother of the Gracchi brothers, Tiberius and Gaius, who were famous for their bold reforms in Roman politics.

A Mother's Guidance

Cornelia was born into one of Rome's most important families. Her father was Scipio Africanus, a celebrated general who defeated Hannibal in the Punic Wars. With such a heritage, Cornelia grew up steeped in the values of courage, duty, and public service—values she would, in turn, deeply instill in her own children.

As a mother, Cornelia's most enduring legacy was the education and upbringing she provided to her sons, Tiberius and Gaius Gracchus. She didn't just teach them to read and write; however, she also filled their minds with ideas of justice, equality, and the importance of serving the common people. Imagine a classroom where lessons are about how to improve the world—a place where young Tiberius and Gaius learned not only about the past heroes of Rome but also about how they could become heroes themselves.

Cornelia knew that Rome was filled with inequality; the rich were getting richer, and the poor were struggling. Her lessons often highlighted the need for change and reforms that would help everyone in Rome, not just the wealthy. These discussions around their dinner table ignited a fire in the hearts of the young brothers.

The Gracchi Brothers' Reforms

Inspired by their mother's teachings, Tiberius and Gaius grew up to propose revolutionary reforms. Tiberius, the elder, became a tribune and introduced laws to redistribute land to the poor. Gaius, following in his brother's footsteps, also became a tribune and pushed for laws that provided grain at reduced prices for the poor. He even suggested citizenship for all Italians, not just Romans.

Their efforts, though initially popular, faced fierce opposition from the elite classes. Yet, the courage and conviction that Cornelia had instilled in them drove the brothers to fight for their beliefs, reshaping Roman policies and stirring significant changes in the republic.

Revered for Her Virtues

Cornelia's influence was not limited to her immediate family. In Rome, she was revered as a model of Roman virtue. She was known for her intelligence, her eloquence, and her stoic grace, especially in the face of personal tragedy. Even after the tragic deaths of both her sons—who were assassinated because of their political reforms—Cornelia remained a pillar of strength.

Because of this reputation, people from all over both Rome and Italy would come to see her. She often spoke about the pride she felt in her sons' efforts to make Rome a better place for all its citizens rather than bitterness at their unexpected deaths.

Cornelia's Enduring Legacy

Today, Cornelia Scipionis Africana is remembered not just as the mother of the Gracchi brothers but as a symbol of maternal influence and civic duty. Her story teaches us that behind great leaders are often great teachers. In Cornelia's case, she taught her sons that true nobility comes not from one's heritage but from one's service to the community.

As you walk through the historical tales of Rome, remember Cornelia as an example of how one person's teachings can ignite the flame of change and inspire generations to come. Just like the stars that shine above the ruins of ancient Rome, Cornelia's virtues and wisdom continue to shine..

Cleopatra VII: The Queen Who Swayed Rome (51 - 30 BC)

Now we will jump to the ancient and mysterious land of Egypt, where a queen who had a mind as sharp as the point of a pyramid and a will as strong as the stones that built them lived. Her name was Cleopatra VII, and she was the last pharaoh of Egypt. Cleopatra was not just any queen; she also played a pivotal role in the history of both Egypt and Rome.

Cleopatra's Royal Alliances

Cleopatra came to power in a time of turmoil. She was both queen and diplomat. She knew that forming alliances was key to maintaining power and protecting her kingdom. Her most famous alliances were with two of the most powerful men in Rome: Julius Caesar and Mark Antony.

It was in Egypt, where the Nile River flowed and pyramids touched the sky, that Cleopatra first allied with the mighty Roman general, Julius Caesar. Caesar had come to Egypt chasing his rival, Pompey. In this coincidence, Cleopatra saw an opportunity. In a famous event, she was wrapped in a rug and delivered to Caesar. At her arrival, she unveiled herself as a queen who sought his support. With Caesar's help, she solidified her grip on the Egyptian throne.

After Caesar's tragic assassination, Cleopatra found another Roman ally in Mark Antony, a dashing and ambitious leader. Together, they dreamed of creating a new empire that would combine the strengths of Egypt and Rome. Their partnership was not only political but also romantic, and they had three children together.

Impact on History

Cleopatra's alliances with these powerful Roman figures were not just love stories; they were strategic moves that shaped the fates of Egypt and Rome. With Julius Caesar, Cleopatra hoped to stabilize her country and assert her power against her rivals. With Mark Antony, she aimed to further expand her influence, envisioning a world where her son could rule Rome and Egypt.

Unfortunately, Cleopatra's dreams would lead to dramatic and deadly results. Her involvement with Roman leaders plunged Egypt into the complex political struggles of Rome. When Mark Antony declared his loyalty to Cleopatra over Rome, it sparked a conflict with Octavian (the future Emperor Augustus), who saw Antony as a traitor influenced by a foreign queen. The rivalry turned into a great sea battle at Actium, where Octavian's forces defeated Antony and Cleopatra. This defeat marked the end of the Ptolemaic dynasty in Egypt and the beginning of Roman rule.

Cleopatra's Legacy

Cleopatra's life was a tapestry woven with ambition, romance, and tragedy. Her death—by a supposed snake bite—marked the end of an era in Egypt. However, her impact on history remains as enduring as the sands of her Egyptian desert.

Cleopatra is remembered not only as a beautiful and charismatic queen but also as a shrewd and capable ruler who navigated her kingdom through the treacherous waters of Roman politics. Her story teaches us about the power of intelligence and determination, showing that a queen can influence the rise and fall of empires.

As you reflect on the stories of powerful women in Roman history, remember Cleopatra as the queen who swayed Rome. Her tale reminds us that history is not just about battles and conquests, but also about the alliances and decisions that can shape the world.

Chapter Conclusion

We've explored the lives of some incredible women who played key roles in ancient Rome. Through their stories, we learned how women were able to navigate a world dominated by men, using their intelligence, courage, and determination to influence the course of history. From Livia's strategic thinking to Cornelia's nurturing yet firm guidance of her sons, these women showed that strength comes in many forms.

As we close this chapter, we carry with us the inspiring tales of these powerful women. Their contributions remind us that everyone has the potential to make a difference. Now, let's turn the page and continue our journey through ancient Rome, ready to uncover more fascinating aspects of this historic empire. Onto the next adventure!

CHAPTER 3:
BRAVE GLADIATORS OF THE COLOSSEUM

Now, it's time to step into the world of ancient Rome's most thrilling entertainers. In this chapter, we'll meet the fearless gladiators who battled in the grand Colosseum. These were not just fighters; they were real-life heroes to the people who watched them. From the swift and strategic Retiarii with their nets and tridents to the heavily-armored Murmillo, each gladiator had a unique style and a brave heart.

Get ready to discover what made these fighters tick, how they lived, and how they became the stars of the most spectacular shows in all of ancient Rome. Let's dive into the exciting and daring world of the gladiators!

TYPES OF GLADIATORS

In ancient Rome, the Colosseum roared with the cheers of spectators as gladiators clashed in epic battles. These warriors were not only skilled fighters but also masters of different combat styles, each with their unique weapons and tactics. Among them, the Retiarii, Secutores, Bestiarii, Murmillo, and Thraex stood out for their distinctive roles and thrilling performances. Let's dive into the fascinating world of these ancient superstars and explore what made each type of gladiator a favorite in the sands of the arena.

Retiarii: The Net Fighters of the Arena

Imagine going fishing, but instead of catching fish, you're trying to catch other gladiators in a big, sandy arena! That's what it was like to be a *Retiarius* (that's the singular form of *Retiarii*). These gladiators carried a trident, which is a long three-pronged spear. Many Tridents would have been similar to what you see the sea god Neptune. These gladiators also had a *rete*, or a net, which they used to entangle their opponents from a distance.

In addition to their net and trident, *Retiarii* wore minimal armor. They usually had a shoulder guard on their left side, called a *galerus*, which protected their head and neck from incoming blows. This light armor allowed them to move quickly and freely, which was crucial for their fighting technique.

Fighting Style and Strategy

The *Retiarii* were like the sneaky tricksters of the gladiator world. Their strategy was to keep their distance and use their net to snare their opponents. Once the enemy was tangled, the *Retiarius* would use his trident to strike. If the net missed or the opponent got free, the *Retiarius* had to rely on his speed and agility to dodge attacks and prepare for another chance to throw his net.

Retiarii typically fought against heavily armored gladiators like the *Secutores* or the *Murmillos*. These opponents carried big shields and swords but moved slower due to their heavy gear. The battles between the lightly equipped *Retiarii* and the heavily armored secutores were dramatic and full of suspense, showcasing a classic matchup of speed versus strength.

The Challenge of Being a *Retiarius*

Being a *Retiarius* was not easy. Their lighter armor meant they had less protection, making them vulnerable to strikes from their opponent's sword. This required the *Retiarius* to be very skillful and clever. They had to use their nets not just to entrap but also to protect themselves and to create opportunities for attack.

The crowd loved watching *Retiarii* because their fights were unpredictable and filled with clever tactics. A successful net throw could change the outcome of a match in an instant. Crowds would cheer wildly whenever a *Retiarius* managed to ensnare his heavily armored opponent.

Today, when we think about gladiators, we can imagine the *Retiarii* as the clever artists of the arena. They could turn what could have been a straightforward fight into a display of strategy and skill. Their legacy teaches us the value of quick thinking and adaptability, andshowing that that sometimes, being smart and swift is just as important as being strong.

Secutores: The Chasing Gladiators

Secutores, were known as the "chasers." These powerful gladiators were famous for their battles against the tricky *Retiarii*, who fought with nets and tridents. The games between *Secutores* and *Retiarii* were like a dramatic dance of cat and mouse, where strength and strategy clashed in exciting displays.

The Armor of the *Secutores*

Imagine dressing up in a suit of armor that's not just for show, but for protection in fierce battles! That was the life of a *Secutor*. Each piece of their gear was designed to help them succeed in their main job: catching and overcoming the swift *Retiarii*.

The Secutor's helmet was heavy and unique, and looked almost like a big metal bucket with only two small eye-holes. Though this design protected him from being hooked by a Retiarius's trident, it also made it hard to see. Their helmets were smooth with no sharp edges that a Retiarius's net could snag on. It was like wearing a big, metal bucket on your head, but much more carefully designed! They also carried a large rectangular shield, called a "scutum," which covered most of their body. This shield was their main defense against the Retiarius's trident and net. Along with the shield, they wore armor on their arms and legs, and a padded linen guard over their torso, making them look like knights ready for a battle.

The Life of a *Secutor*

Secutores had to be very strong and also quite clever. They carried heavy weapons and armor, which meant they needed to be powerful enough to move quickly and withstand long fights. Their main weapon was a short sword, called a "*gladius*," perfect for close combat once they managed to get past the swirling net of a *Retiarius*.

In the arena, the Secutores job was to chase down Retiarius, who would try to keep his distance and entangle Secutore from afar. This made fights between a Secutores and a Retiarius extremely suspenseful. The audience never knew if the Secutore would manage to shield himself from the net and close in on the Retiarius, or if he'd get caught and face the sharp point of the trident.

The Challenges and Strategies

Being a Secutore wasn't just about strength; it was also about smarts and strategy. They had to judge the right moment to advance and the right moment to hold back, all while carrying heavy gear and looking through tiny holes in a massive helmet. They also had to be patient, waiting for the Retiarius to make a mistake. When their opponent faltered, they had to act quickly. Not only did their bodies have to handle the weight, and the heat of the battle but also their minds to react to the cunning tactics of their opponents.

So, when you think of the *Secutores*, remember them as the brave gladiators who were "chasers' ' of the arena, always ready to face challenges head-on. They show us how determination and protection can lead to victory in the face of adversity. They were not just fighters; they were heroes of the Roman world, whose stories of bravery continue to inspire us today.

Bestiarii: The Wild Animal Fighters of Rome

The *Bestiarii* were also gladiators, but their role was unique. Instead of clashing swords with other warriors, they took on wild beasts like lions, bears, and even elephants. These fights were part of the broader spectacle of Roman games, which included chariot races, theatrical plays, and much more. The *Bestiarii*'s battles were a big draw for the public, offering a mix of danger and excitement.

Training and Gear

Becoming a *Bestiarius* was a serious choice as they only fought. These fighters trained specifically to handle wild animals. They had to move quickly, stay alert, and use their weapons effectively against unpredictable opponents. Their main tools were usually a spear or a short sword, designed to keep the animals at bay while delivering a decisive blow.

Unlike their fellow gladiators, *Bestiarii* often wore lighter armor. This allowed them more speed and agility, which were crucial in outmaneuvering large and dangerous animals. However, this also meant they were less protected, making their role both spectacular and incredibly risky.

The Day of the Battle

On the day of the games, the atmosphere in the Colosseum would be electric. Spectators from all walks of life, from the wealthiest senators to the common folk, filled the stands. They were all eager to watch the *Bestiarii* in action. The arena floor would be transformed for these fights, sometimes filled with elaborate scenery to mimic the natural habitats of the animals being fought.

When the *Bestiarius* entered the arena, the crowd would erupt in cheers. Then, the gates would open, and the wild animals would be released. Imagine the tension in the air as a Bestiarius stood alone, spear in hand, facing down a roaring lion. Each movement had to be calculated and precise—; a single mistake could be fatal.

The Challenges They Faced

The life of a *Bestiarius* was filled with constant danger. Like the *Secutores* and *Retiarii,* These gladiators had to be both physically strong and mentally sharp. But, they also needed to understand the behaviors of different animals and use this knowledge to survive. Their fights were not just brute force; they were moments of intense strategy and daring.

Despite the risks, being a *Bestiarius* brought fame and admiration. Successful *Bestiarii* were celebrated as the heroes who were able to conquer nature itself. Their victories were a testament to human bravery and skill, themes loved by the Roman public.

Murmillo: The Heavily- Armored Gladiator

The *Murmillo* gladiators were imposing figures in the arena, equipped with a large shield and a *gladius* (the same short sword used by *Secutores)* known as a gladius. Their helmet was distinctively large and often featured a fish-like crest on top. – Unsurprisingly, "*murmillo*" comes from the Greek word for a type of fish, hinting at the shape of their helmets. This unique gear not only provided excellent protection but also added to their intimidating presence.

The Armor and Weapons

Imagine wearing the armor of a *Murmillo*—going into a battle wearing a heavy helmet that covers your whole head, a large rectangular shield that protects most of your body, and carrying a sharp sword to defend you. This was the daily uniform of a Murmillo. Their armor was designed to offer maximum protection during fights, making them look like walking fortresses.

The *Murmillo*'s shield was called a *scutum*. It was their primary defense tool., It was used to block attacks from opponents and counterattack when an opportunity presented itself. Like other gladiators, the *gladius*, a deadly short sword, was their main offensive weapon, ideal for close combat and powerful, precise strikes.

Training and Life in the *Ludus*

Becoming a *Murmillo* required rigorous training. These gladiators spent countless hours practicing with their weapons, strengthening their bodies to carry heavy armor, and learning tactics to best opponents with different fighting styles. Life in the *ludus* (which was what they called gladiator school) was strict and disciplined, with every day centered around enhancing physical strength and combat skills.

Young readers might find it interesting to know that despite their fearsome appearances in the arena, many *Murmillo* gladiators formed friendships with their fellow fighters and even with their trainers. The bond formed in the *ludus* was strong, as they relied on each other for survival and success.

The Legacy of the *Murmillo*

The *Murmillo* were not just fighters; they were a symbol of strength and endurance. Their battles in the arenas of ancient Rome left a lasting impression on the public, both for the ferocity of their fighting style and the resilience they displayed against different types of gladiators.

As you think about the Murmillo, imagine them as the ancient superheroes of the arena., Theirtheir battles are a testament to the human spirit's capability to strive for victory in the face of overwhelming odds. Their story is not just one of combat but of the enduring human desire to excel and triumph.

Thraex: The Swift Warriors of the Arena

The *Thraex* gladiators were dressed to resemble the warriors of Thrace, famous for their courage and fighting prowess. In the grand arenas of Rome, these gladiators captivated crowds with their exotic weapons and swift movements, offering a glimpse into the warrior culture of Thrace.

Gear and Weapons of the *Thraex*

Imagine stepping into an arena with a small, square shield and a curved sword. This was the typical gear of a *Thraex* including a small, square shield and a curved sword. Their shield, called a *parma*, was much smaller than the large rectangular *scutum* used by many other gladiators. *Parmas* allowed for quicker, more agile movements so the *Thraex* could. The shield was designed to protect themselves while also enabling swift offensive maneuvers, reactive combat maneuvers.

Fighting Style and Strategy

The *Thraex* gladiators had to use their speed and agility to compensate for their smaller shields and lack of heavy armor. They were trained to be quick on their feet, using their agility to dodge blows and to position themselves advantageously against slower, more heavily armored opponents.

Training and Life as a *Thraex*

Becoming a *Thraex* required intense training. These gladiators spent hours each day honing their skills with the *sica*, learning how to make the most of their weapon's unique shape. They practiced maneuvers to dart in and strike quickly before slipping away from an enemy's counterattack, much like modern fencing athletes.

The Legacy of the *Thraex*

The *Thraex* gladiators brought a distinct flavor to the Roman games, showcasing the art of Thracian warfare. Their battles demonstrated that in the arena, as in life, being adaptable and quick-thinking often leads to success. The sight of a Thraex, darting with his curved sword, became a symbol of agility and cunning in combat. Imagine them as the agile dancers of the arena, their battles a thrilling spectacle dance of swords and shields. They show us that even in the toughest situations, using one's unique strengths creatively can pave the way to victory.

LEGENDARY GLADIATORS

Spartacus: The Gladiator Who Fought for Freedom

Let's begin in the Roman Republic with Spartacus—one of the most legendary heroes of ancient times. Spartacus was not just any gladiator; rather, he was a leader who dared to challenge the vast and powerful city of Rome in a fight for freedom. His story is one of courage, strength, and the unyielding desire for liberty.

Spartacus was originally from Thrace, a place near modern-day Bulgaria. Thrace was not part of Rome, but it did have its own wild and fierce history. Spartacus was a strong man who was skilled with weapons that was ultimately captured by Roman soldiers. Instead of working quietly as a slave, Spartacus was trained to be a gladiator—a fighter who entertained crowds by battling other gladiators or wild animals in large arenas (like the Colosseum).

Imagine being taken to a strange land and forced to fight for your life for the amusement of others. That was the harsh world Spartacus lived in. But he had a heart filled with hope and a mind sharp as a sword. Spartacus was more than a fighter; he was a thinker and a dreamer. His dream was to achieve freedom for himself and his fellow slaves.

The Great Escape

Spartacus's desire for freedom eventually turned into action. Along with about 70 fellow gladiators, he orchestrated a daring escape from a gladiator school in Capua. Using nothing more than kitchen utensils to start the rebellion, the gladiators fought their way out, capturing real weapons from their defeated guards along the way.

Once free, Spartacus and his band of gladiators found refuge on the slopes of Mount Vesuvius. There, they set up camp and planned their next moves. Spartacus's bravery and wisdom quickly made him the leader of the group. He knew that staying free would be even harder than breaking free.

But Spartacus was ready to face whatever challenges came his way.

The Third Servile War

What started as a small group of escaped gladiators soon became a massive army. As word spread of Spartacus and his fight against Rome, thousands of slaves joined him, growing his army to over 70,000 members. These were not just men who wanted to fight; they were people who craved freedom, who wanted to return to their homes, and who no longer wished to live under the harsh rule of their masters.

Spartacus's army of freed slaves won several battles against Roman forces, which was a big embarrassment for Rome. Imagine the most powerful empire in the world being challenged by a group led by a former gladiator! Spartacus and his followers were soon seen as heroes to some and dangerous rebels to others.

The Legacy of Spartacus

The story of Spartacus does not have a happy ending. After two years of fighting, the Roman army finally defeated Spartacus's forces. Historians believe that Spartacus himself fell in battle and his body was never found. However, the spirit of Spartacus could not be defeated. He became a symbol of hope and resistance for all those oppressed. His story has been told and retold in many ways—through books, movies, and songs—each celebrating his strength and his struggle for freedom.

Remember Spartacus not just as a gladiator who fought wild beasts for entertainment but as a hero who fought for a much greater cause of freedom. His courage reminds us that even in the face of overwhelming odds, fighting for what is right is the bravest battle of all.

Crixus: The Gladiator Who Dreamed of Freedom

Among the mighty gladiators that clashed in the grand arenas of ancient Rome, Spartacus was not the only warrior whose heart beat with the fierce rhythm of freedom. There was another gladiator named Crixus, which meant "one with curly hair" in his native language, Gaulish. Crixus was not just any gladiator—he was a leader in one of the biggest slave revolts in Roman history, the Third Servile War.

From Gaul to Gladiator

Crixus was born in Gaul, a vast area covering modern France and parts of its neighboring countries. As a young man, he was captured by Roman forces, taken from his homeland, and sold into slavery. Though the details of his capture are a mystery, his destiny was to become one of the most famous gladiators in Rome.

Imagine being taken from your home and forced to fight for the entertainment of those who captured you. That was the life Crixus was thrown into. He trained in the gladiator school of Capua, where he learned to fight. His education taught him not just to survive, but to excel. Crixus became a powerful warrior, skilled with various weapons and the art of combat.

The Spark of Revolt

Despite his fame in the arena, Crixus's heart longed for freedom. He found a kindred spirit in Spartacus, as both were determined to break the chains of slavery. Together with Spartacus and a small group of other gladiators, Crixus made a bold escape from the gladiator school.

Once free, Crixus and Spartacus gathered other slaves and disenchanted souls, forming an army that would challenge the very foundation of Rome. Crixus was not only a fierce warrior, but also a charismatic leader. He inspired his followers with dreams of returning to their homes and escaping the tyranny of their masters.

As their numbers grew, the rebels, led by Spartacus and Crixus, won several battles against Roman forces. Crixus's bravery and fighting skills were crucial to these victories. He fought with a passion that ignited courage in the hearts of his comrades. However, as the war progressed, differences in strategy began to emerge between Spartacus and Crixus. Spartacus wanted to escape over the Alps, believing that dispersing their forces would keep them safe from Roman retaliation. Crixus, however, wanted to strike directly at Rome until every slave in Italy was free.

The Legend of Crixus

Eventually, Spartacus and Crixus differences caused them to split, each with part of the army. Crixius continued to harass Roman forces, achieving great feats on the battlefield. But, the divided army would eventually lead to Crixus's downfall. In a fierce battle near Mount Gargano, Crixus and his followers faced a large Roman army. Despite their bravery, Crixus and many of his warriors were killed, marking a tragic end to his quest for freedom.

Crixus's life was a testament to the spirit of resistance. He may not have successfully freed all of the slaves in the empire, but his actions left a mark on history. His courage and determination in the face of overwhelming odds inspired not only his contemporaries but generations to come.

Today, when we think of gladiators, we often picture them fighting in the arena. But Crixus reminds us that some gladiators fought for something greater: their freedom. His story teaches us about the power of hope and the unbreakable human spirit that can thrive even in the darkest of times.

Flamma: The Gladiator Who Chose the Arena

While the once-gladiators Crixus and Spartacus stood out due to their fight for freedom, another gladiator was notable for his dedication to stay in the arena even when the gates of freedom were opened to him. His name was Flamma, which means "flame" in Latin. And, true to his name, Flamma was a fiery and fierce warrior who captured the hearts of many.

Flamma came from Syria, a land rich with history and culture, and far from the bustling streets of Rome. As a young man, he was captured and brought to Rome, where he was trained to be a gladiator. This was a tough life, filled with danger at every turn, but Flamma excelled in the art of combat.

Gladiators like Flamma fought in grand arenas like the famous Colosseum. Here, battling against other gladiators, wild animals, and sometimes staged reenactments of famous battles, gladiators gained honor and recognition, even though they were slaves.

A Champion in the Arena

Flamma was a powerhouse in the arena. He fought 34 battles, winning 21 of them. With each victory, his fame grew. He soon became a favorite among the Roman spectators. Gladiators who performed well in the arena were sometimes rewarded with a *rudis*—or, a wooden sword that symbolized their freedom. It was the ultimate prize for a gladiator, a ticket to a new life away from the deadly sands of the arena.

However, Flamma was no ordinary gladiator. He was offered the *rudis* not just once, but four times throughout his career. Each time, he rejected this offer of freedom. Flamma's decision to stay a gladiator baffled many, but to him, the arena was where he felt most alive. The thrill of the fight, the cheers of the crowd, and the glory of victory were what he cherished most.

Why Stay a Gladiator?

You might wonder, why would someone choose the dangerous life of a gladiator over freedom? For Flamma, the reasons could be many. Perhaps he felt a sense of belonging in the arena, a place where he was respected and admired rather than just another slave. Or maybe he loved the thrill of competition and the camaraderie with other gladiators, sharing a bond forged in the heat of battle.

Being a star in the arena also gave Flamma a sense of purpose and achievement. He knew the risks, but he also knew the glory. Every time he stepped into the Colosseum, he wasn't just fighting for survival; he was fighting to be remembered, to leave a legacy that would outlive him.

Flamma's choice to remain a gladiator made him a legend. He showed that sometimes, we find our true calling in the most unexpected places. For Flamma, the arena was his home, and ultimately the gladiator's life was his chosen path. Today, Flamma is remembered not just for his victories in the arena, but for his courage to follow his heart. His story teaches us about the values of determination, bravery, and the pursuit of what makes us truly happy, even if that choice is unexpected.

Tetraites: The Hero of the Arena

Flamma was not the only gladiator who was extremely skilled in the Colosseum. Another famous gladiator, Tetraites, became a legendary fighter as well. He was a *murmillo*, or a type of gladiator known for wearing a large helmet with a fish-like crest on top and also carrying a big shield and sword. But Tetraites wasn't just a fighter; rather, he was also a symbol of bravery and skill who captured the imagination of all who saw him battle.

A Star in Roman Culture

Tetraites's popularity went beyond the arena. His exploits were talked about in the streets, written about in poems, and even painted as graffiti on the walls of Rome. People admired his strength and prowess, and he soon became a part of Roman pop culture, much like movie stars today.

Artifacts from that time, like small figurines and mosaics, are proof of just how admired he was. These items often depicted Tetraites in his *murmillo* armor after a victory. People in Rome might have kept these as souvenirs, much like we might keep posters or action figures of our favorite heroes today.

Being a star gladiator like Tetraites was a strange mix of fame and danger. On the one hand, Tetraites enjoyed fame and the adoration of fans. On the other hand, every time he stepped into the arena, he faced real danger. Gladiators often fought to the death, and even though many battles ended with mercy—when the defeated gladiator was spared—every fight could have been his last.

This mix of danger and fame made Tetraites's life exciting but also very challenging. He had to maintain his strength and skills, always preparing for the next battle, knowing that his survival depended not just on his ability to fight but also on his ability to win over the crowd.

Tetraites's Legacy

Tetraites's impact on Roman culture shows us how sports and entertainment have always been important. Just like modern sports stars, gladiators brought excitement and drama into people's lives, giving them heroes to cheer for and stories to tell.

Tetraites's legacy teaches us about how the love for stories of struggle and triumph is a part of the human experience. He remains a symbol of the timeless appeal of heroes and the games that showcase their courage still today.

Priscus and Verus: The Gladiator Brothers

Though gladiators like Tetraites often became legendary due to their skill in the arena alone, two warriors defied this stereotype. They were Priscus and Verus, two gladiators who were not brothers by birth, but became brothers in battle. They shared one of the most famous fights in the history of the gladiators.

Priscus and Verus were both originally slaves, captured in wars and brought to Rome to train as gladiators. Gladiators like Priscus and Verus trained for months, learning how to fight with various weapons, how to protect themselves, and how to entertain a crowd. Their lives were tough, but they knew that if they could win the favor of the public, they might earn their freedom with the *rudis*.

The Battle of Equals

The day that Priscus and Verus stepped into the Colosseum to face each other was a day of celebration in Rome. It was the 100th day of games commissioned by the Emperor Titus to inaugurate the opening of the Colosseum, and the city was alive with excitement. People from all over the empire came to watch, eager to see the grand battles.

During these special games, Priscus and Verus faced off. They were well-matched in skill and courage. So, as they fought, it became clear that this was no ordinary match. They exchanged blow for blow, their swords clashing, shields banging, and the crowd roaring with each move. The battle was long and fierce, and neither warrior could gain the upper hand.

As the fight wore on, both gladiators grew tired, but neither would yield. Their respect for each other grew with every pass of their swords, and so did the crowd's respect for them. The fight seemed to last forever, and the spectators were held spellbound by the spectacle of these two incredible warriors. Priscus and Verus fought not just for their lives but for honor and freedom.

Finally, both gladiators were too exhausted to continue, and the battle was declared a draw. This was a rare occurrence in the gladiatorial games, where usually only one gladiator could be victorious. The crowd, moved by the bravery and endurance of both men, erupted in cheers, calling for their freedom. The emperor, impressed by their skill and spirit, granted both Priscus and Verus their freedom. They were awarded the *rudis*, (the same symbolic wooden sword that Flamma denied many times) which freed them both from their service as gladiators. The poet Martial, who witnessed the fight, wrote about it to celebrate their courage and the historic nature of their battle.

Heroes of the Arena

The story of Priscus and Verus is more than just a tale of a fight; it's a story about determination, skill, and mutual respect. These two men proved that they were not just entertainers—rather, they were warriors of the highest order. Their battle showed that even in the harsh world of the gladiators, there was room for honor and brotherhood.

Today, Priscus and Verus are remembered not only for their epic battle, but also as proof that even in the face of great challenges, friendship and respect can prevail.

Chapter Conclusion

Now we've journeyed alongside many Roman heroes, including the brave gladiators of ancient Rome. We explored their fierce battles and learned about the lives they led both in and out of the Colosseum. These gladiators were more than just fighters; they were symbols of bravery and skill, capturing the imaginations of thousands of spectators who watched them perform in the arena.

As we close this chapter, we reflect on the incredible courage these individuals displayed, facing formidable foes and dangerous beasts for the entertainment of others. Their legacy teaches us about the Roman values of strength and honor, and their stories continue to fascinate us today.

CHAPTER 4:
MIGHTY GODS & GODDESSES OF ROME

In this chapter, we're going to meet the amazing gods and goddesses that the ancient Romans believed in and worshiped. From Jupiter, the powerful king of the gods, to Juno, the queen who watched over all marriages, each deity had their own special powers and exciting stories. Get ready to explore the magical myths and fascinating roles these celestial characters played in the daily lives of the Romans. Welcome to a new adventure full of mighty deeds and divine wonders!

Saturn: The God of Time and Renewal

In the ancient Roman pantheon, where gods held dominion over everything from the depths of the sea to the expanse of the sky, Saturn reigned over some of the most fundamental aspects of life and the universe. Known as the god of time, agriculture, wealth, and renewal, Saturn was a complex deity whose influence touched the lives of all Romans, from farmers tilling the fields to citizens celebrating the new year.

Saturn was often depicted as a wise old man holding a sickle, which he used to harvest crops but also symbolized his connection to the cycles of creation and dissolution. This tool highlighted his dual role as a god of both agriculture and time.

The Role of Saturn in Roman Mythology

Saturn's mythology is rich with stories of power, loss, and revival. According to legend, Saturn was once the king of the gods., He ruleding during a golden age of prosperity and peace. During his reign, there was abundance and joy, and the earth provided without the need for extra worktoil. However, Saturn was overthrown by his son Jupiter.

Though he was conqueredDespite his overthrow, Saturn's spirit of abundance and liberation lived on. He was celebrated as a liberator, freeing those bound by time and fate. His return at the end of each year during the festival of *Saturnalia* brought a temporary return to the golden age he once ruled over.

Saturnalia: The Festival of Saturn

The festival of *Saturnalia* was one of the most important and joyous events in the Roman calendar. It was hHeld in December, during the winter solstice, it celebrated the return of the golden age. For a week, social norms were turned upside down;: slaves were served by their masters, all work and business were suspended, and the streets filled with merry celebrations.

Families exchanged gifts such as, especially wax candles. These candles signified the light returning after the solstice, symbolizing the hope and the rebirth of life that comes with the new agricultural year. *Saturnalia* showcased Saturn's roles as the god of time, renewal, and liberation from the usual social and physical constraints.

Saturn's Legacy

Today, Saturn's name lives on in the planet Saturn, known for its beautiful rings that circle endlessly, much like the cycles of time he governed. His legacy also continues in the celebration of *Saturnalia.*, which This festival has influenced modern holiday traditions, such as Christmas and the New Year.

As you think about Saturn, remember him as a god who reminds us of the importance of time, the joy of renewal, and the value of freedom.

Jupiter: The King of Roman Gods

Imagine a grand figure, towering with strength, wearing a robe that sparkles like the stars, and holding a lightning bolt as fierce as his gaze. This is Jupiter, the supreme deity of the Roman pantheon. His role was to oversee all aspects of life and rule over the other gods, making sure that peace and order prevailed.

Maybe you know Jupiter by his Greek name, Zeus. Since the Romans gave him his own distinct personality and stories, the name Jupiter is just as important. He was the god of the sky, which meant he controlled the weather (especially thunderstorms and lightning). These served as his weapons to show his displeasure or to fight against those who crossed him.

Jupiter's Family and Friends

Jupiter was part of a divine family that ruled the skies and the Earth. He was the son of Saturn, the god of time, and Ops, the goddess of wealth. Jupiter's brothers and sisters included Neptune, the god of the sea, and Pluto, the god of the underworld.

Jupiter was married to Juno, the goddess of marriage and childbirth, who was also his sister. Together, they lived on Mount Olympus, the mythical home of the gods, which was said to be perched high above the clouds, unreachable by mere mortals.

Jupiter, the Protector of Rome

Jupiter was not only a powerful god but also a champion of the Roman people. The Romans believed that Jupiter watched over their city and protected its people from harm, whether from natural disasters or enemy attacks. This made him an extremely important figure in Roman religion.

The worship of Jupiter was at the heart of Roman religious life. The largest temple in Rome, the magnificent Temple of Jupiter Optimus Maximus, was dedicated to him. It stood on Capitoline Hill, one of the seven hills of Rome. The temple served as a place where Romans offered prayers and sacrifices, hoping to gain Jupiter's favor.

Stories and Myths Involving Jupiter

Jupiter was central to many Roman myths and stories, which often involved his adventures, his battles to maintain order, and his relationships with other gods and mortals. One famous myth is how he became the King of Gods; in this myth, Jupiter led his siblings in a rebellion against their tyrannical father, Saturn, the ancient god of time. Jupiter was able to overthrow Saturn and then divide the universe among his brothers.

Another popular story tells of Jupiter's defeat of the giant Typhon, a terrifying creature that threatened all gods and humans. Using his mighty lightning bolts, Jupiter battled Typhon. After a fierce fight, Jupiter trapped the giant under Mount Etna. This story was a favorite among Roman children, much like superhero tales are today!

Jupiter's Legacy

Jupiter's influence was seen everywhere in Roman culture, such as in public festivals like the spectacular Games of Jupiter. These events featured athletic competitions, chariot races, and theatrical performances, all held in his honor. Today, when we look up at the vast sky or watch a storm, we can remember Jupiter, the Roman King of Gods. His stories of bravery, leadership, and protection remind us of the values the Romans held dear—strength, justice, and the care for the community.

Juno: The Queen of Roman Gods

High above the busy streets of ancient Rome, in the mystical realm of the gods, reigned Juno, the revered Queen of the Gods. Juno, who had a majestic presence and offered wise counsel, was not just any goddess—she was the protector of the Roman state and the divine symbol of marriage and childbirth.

Imagine a powerful and graceful queen, draped in beautiful robes, her eyes filled with wisdom and care. This is Juno, the daughter of Saturn. Juno was also the sister and wife of mighty king Jupiter. As the queen of the gods, Juno held a special place in the hearts of the Roman people. She was revered not only as a goddess of marriage but also as a guardian of the Roman state, offering protection and advice to her followers.

Juno, the Goddess of Marriage

Juno's role as the goddess of marriage was central to her identity. She watched over married couples and families, blessing marriages with happiness and prosperity. The

Romans believed that Juno's favor was crucial for a harmonious family life.Many would offer prayers and sacrifices to her on their wedding day, hoping to receive her blessings.

Every year, Roman women celebrated the festival of *Matronalia* in honor of Juno. This special day was dedicated to happiness and well-being in married life. Wives received gifts from their husbands, and prayers were offered to Juno asking for strong, loving relationships. It was a day filled with joy and festivities, reflecting Juno's importance in the lives of Roman families.

Juno, the Protector of the State

Juno's role, however, extended beyond personal and family life; she was also the protector and counselor of the Roman state. This responsibility was a vital aspect of her divine duties. The Romans believed that Juno watched over their city, safeguarding its people and its leaders. Leaders and soldiers alike would seek her guidance and protection before making important decisions or going into battle.

The Temple of Juno, *Moneta*, located on the Capitoline Hill alongside the Temple of Jupiter, was a testament to her importance. *Moneta* comes from the Latin word for "warn" or "advise," which reflects Juno's role as an advisor. Interestingly, her temple was not just a religious site, but also the place where Rome's mint was located. This was symbolic of Juno's protective watch over the city's wealth and well-being.

Myths and Stories Involving Juno

Juno appears in many myths and stories. In these stories, she often shows her protective nature, but sometimes her jealousy and rivalry with other gods and mortals who crossed her or her loved ones came out. Despite these challenges, Juno was always respected by the other gods and goddesses, and her wisdom was unmatched.

One famous story involves Juno's peacock. According to legend, Juno transformed Argus, her hundred-eyed servant, into a peacock. Argus's many eyes were transformed into the bird's stunning feathers. This story highlighted her ability to watch over many things at once, always keeping a close eye on the affairs of gods and humans.

Juno's Legacy

Today, when we think of Juno, we remember her legacy as one of nurturing care and wise counsel. These qualities made her a beloved figure in Roman mythology. As you explore the tales of the Roman gods and goddesses, think of Juno not just as a figure of power, but also as a beacon of protection and wisdom. Her stories teach us the importance of how we should care for others and guide them with wisdom, just as she did for the ancient Romans from her high throne in the heavens.

Neptune: The Mighty God of the Sea

Deep beneath the sparkling waters of the Mediterranean, past the rolling waves and the ocean's blue mysteries, lived Neptune, the Roman god of the sea. With his powerful trident in hand, Neptune ruled over all the waters of the world—from the tiniest freshwater stream to the vast and stormy Atlantic Ocean.

Neptune was one of the most powerful gods of Roman mythology, known for his command over water in all its forms. He was the brother of Jupiter, the king of the gods, and Pluto, the god of the Underworld. Together, these three brothers ruled the heavens, the Earth, and the Underworld, maintaining balance in the world.

The Worship of Neptune

All Romans had deep respect for Neptune, especially those whose lives were closely tied to the sea. Sailors and fishermen prayed to Neptune for safe voyages, especially before embarking on long and perilous journeys. Temples dedicated to Neptune were often located near the coast. During his festivals, Romans celebrated him with games, horse races, and offerings thrown into the sea as a tribute to his power.

One of the biggest celebrations in honor of Neptune was the *Neptunalia*, held during the heat of summer. People would build temporary shelters from branches, where they then feasted and drank spring water and wine to cool down. They thanked Neptune for providing relief from the summer heat.

Neptune in Mythology

In mythology, Neptun's mood could change quickly. He was quick to anger but also capable of great kindness. When Neptune was calm, the seas were peaceful and the sailors safe. But when he was angry, the oceans would churn and waves would crash fiercely against the shores, reflecting his stormy moods.

Like Juno and Jupiter, Neptune was also part of many famous mythological stories. He often appeared as a mediator in disputes among gods or as a formidable opponent to those who dared to challenge him. Much like his brother Jupiter as well, Neptune's romantic escapades were legendary and involved various nymphs and goddesses.

Neptune's Legacy

Today, Neptune's image is still very much alive in both art and literature. He represents the majesty and mystery of the ocean—a world that is beautiful and bountiful, yet fierce and unforgiving. He teaches us about the power of nature and the need to respect the seas and all bodies of water on our planet.

As you think about Neptune, imagine the vast blue seas, where rhythmic waves are controlled by the trident of a mighty god. He serves as a reminder to us of the ancient Romans' deep respect for the powers that govern the natural elements. Additionally, Neptune's stories encourage us to be just as mindful today of the natural world's strength and beauty.

Mars: The Mighty God of War and Agriculture

Mars was the son of Jupiter and Juno, the king and queen of the gods. With such powerful parents, Mars was bound to be a significant figure among the gods. Though many know him as a god of battle, he was more than that. Mars was also integral to agricultural success. These two aspects of his power made Mars immensely important to the Romans—both in their survival and in their conquests.

In war, Mars was the emblem of strength and bravery. He was often depicted in shimmering armor, ready to lead soldiers into battle. In times of peace, he was a symbol of fertility and growth, showing a softer side that brought life to crops and prosperity to the Roman people.

Mars and the Protection of Rome

Mars held a special place in the hearts of the Romans because he was seen as the protector of Rome itself. He watched over the city's military and its borders, ensuring that peace prevailed. His presence was invoked during various festivals and rituals, especially before embarking on military campaigns.

One of Mars's most famous legacies was fathering Romulus and Remus, the legendary founders of Rome. According to myth, Mars fell in love with a Vestal Virgin named Rhea Silvia, who gave birth to the twins. The twins were raised by a she-wolf and eventually established the city of Rome. Mars's involvement in the story of Romulus and Remus underscored his integral role in the foundation of the city.

Celebrations in Honor of Mars

Mars was celebrated throughout the Roman calendar, but his most prominent festivals were held in March (named after him) and October. These festivities marked the beginning and end of the military campaign season. The festivals were filled with ceremonies that included parades of soldiers, offerings of the first fruits of harvest, and prayers for successful farming and safekeeping of the troops.

The month of March began with the Festival of Mars, known as *Martius*. During *Martius,* the *Salii,* or dancing priests of Mars, moved through the city carrying sacred shields and singing hymns to invoke the god's protection and blessings. It was a vibrant and robust start to the year, filled with the promise of protection and bounty.

Mars in Roman Culture

Mars was more than a deity to the Romans; he was a central figure in their cultural identity. His dual role as a god of both war and agriculture reflected the Romans' values of courage and productivity. Like Mars, they Romans saw themselves as a strong people, capable of defending their republic and making the land fruitful.

Statues and images of Mars were common in Roman homes. These representations of Mars served not just as decorations, but also as symbols of safety and assurance. His temples were also places of refuge and strength, drawing people who sought the god's intervention in their lives.

Mars's Legacy

Today, Mars continues to be a symbol of "martial" prowess and defense. His name lives on in our word, "martial," which relates to war and military life. Even the planet Mars that glows in our night sky is named after this god because of its blood-red color. The planet Mars helps remind us of the god of war's enduring presence.

Venus: The Goddess of Love and Beauty

Imagine a goddess so beautiful she made flowers spring up wherever she walked, and everyone around her smiled. This is how one could imagine Venus, the Roman goddess whose very presence brought joy and love. In Roman myths, Venus was not only the goddess of romantic love, but also a symbol of fertility and the beauty of nature and humans alike.

Venus's influence was seen in gardens bursting with life, love that united couples, and any art form that celebrated beauty. Her powers were so vast that the Romans believed they affected everything from personal relationships to the growth of crops in the fields.

Venus and Her Famous Myths

Venus was central to many stories and myths that often involved romance and its struggles, as well as adventure. One of the most famous tales featuring Venus describes her relationship with Mars, the god of war. As they were opposites in every way—Venus, the emblem of love and beauty, and Mars, the symbol of war and aggression—their story highlights how love can unite the most unlikely characters.

Another beloved myth involves Venus's role in the tale of Aeneas. Aeneas was a Trojan hero who survived the Trojan War. He then traveled to Italy, where he became one of the ancestors of the Romans. Venus, as Aeneas's mother, guided and protected him throughout his journeys, showcasing her role not just as a goddess of beauty but as a mother and protector.

Celebrations in Honor of Venus

The Romans had a lot of respect for Venus. As such, they celebrated her through various festivals and rites. One particularly important celebration was the *Veneralia*. On this day, women would seek Venus's assistance in their love lives and marriages, praying for happiness and fidelity.

Temples dedicated to Venus were decorated with the finest flowers and artworks, turning them into places of incredible beauty that mirrored the goddess's attributes. Romans would visit these temples to pay tribute to Venus and ask for her blessings in their romantic endeavors and family life.

Venus in Roman Culture

Venus's impact on Roman culture was profound. She was often depicted in sculptures and paintings, which emphasized her attributes of ideal feminine beauty and grace. These artworks not only served as religious icons but also as cultural symbols of what were considered the greatest aesthetic and moral qualities.

Furthermore, Venus was a patron of the arts. Many believed she inspired artists, poets, and musicians to create works that celebrated love and beauty. Her influence even spread to Roman fashion, jewelry, and even personal grooming.

Venus's Legacy

Today, Venus is still synonymous with beauty and love. Her legacy survives in the arts, literature, and the names of flowers and other natural wonders (like the Venus flytrap). The planet Venus, shining bright and beautiful in the night sky, is also named after her. It serves as a testament to her enduring presence as a symbol of allure and splendor.

As you think about Venus, remember her not only as the goddess of love but as a symbol of the beauty in the world and in ourselves. Her stories teach us about the power of love and the cultivation of beauty in all its forms—whether in nature, relationships, or the arts.

Vulcan: The God of Fire and the Forge

Imagine a god with a strong, muscular figure, covered in soot from his forge (a place where blacksmiths create weapons and armor), working tirelessly by the glow of molten metal. This was how one could imagine Vulcan. He was a god whose skilled hands could craft anything from thunderbolts for Jupiter to armor for heroes and gods. Though he was another one of Jupiter and Juno's sons, he was quite different from his celestial siblings. Vulcan preferred the heat of his forge over the enchanting Mount Olympus.

Vulcan's Realm and Powers

Legend has it that Vulcan's workshop was located underneath Mount Etna in Sicily. Mount Etna is a real volcano whose eruptions were said to be caused by Vulcan working in his forge. Here, amid rivers of lava and fiery pits, Vulcan crafted masterpieces. He created everything from weapons that could win wars to delicate jewelry that could win hearts.

As the god of fire, Vulcan's role extended beyond mere craftsmanship. He was also associated with the destructive and renewing power of fire. In agriculture, he was seen as a figure who could prevent fires from damaging crops. On the other hand, in city life, people prayed to Vulcan for protection against accidental fires.

The Festivals of Vulcan

Vulcan was honored by the Romans during the *Vulcanalia*, a festival celebrated on August 23rd each year. On this day, Romans would hang their clothes and fabrics out in the sun, hoping that Vulcan would prevent these goods from catching fire throughout the year. It was a day to respect the power of fire. The festival served as a reminder of not only how dangerous fire could be, but also how necessary it was for Roman civilization.

Vulcan in Mythology

The mythology behind Vulcan's character and history is filled with themes of resilience and transformation. According to myth, he was born weak. This deformity caused Juno to cast him out of heaven. He fell for a whole day and night, eventually landing in the sea where he was raised by sea nymphs. This tough beginning gave Vulcan a uniquely sympathetic perspective among the gods, as he treasured underdogs and hard workers.

Vulcan went on to marry Venus This was an odd match, but symbolized the union of very different forces—fire and beauty with craftsmanship and grace.

Vulcan's Legacy

Today, Vulcan still symbolizes the art of smithing and metalworking. He is often thought of as the patron of various modern crafts that involve fire, such as welding and firefighting.

Vulcan teaches us the importance of using our skills to create and protect. His legacy reminds us that even the most humble craftsman can achieve greatness through hard work and dedication.

Mercury: The Swift Messenger God

Among the many fascinating Roman gods and goddesses came Mercury, who zipped through the skies as the quickest of the gods. He was also the most clever of all. Known as the messenger of the gods, Mercury carried news and commands throughout the heavens and to the world below. But his talents didn't stop there—Mercury was also the god of translators and interpreters, making him a key figure in the communication between gods and mortals.

Imagine a young god wearing winged sandals and a winged hat, darting through the skies with the speed of light. This was how many depicted Mercury (aka Hermes for the Greeks), the son of Jupiter and Maia, a Pleiades nymph and daughter of Atlas. With his quick wit and ability to move between worlds, Mercury was indispensable to the other gods.

The Role of Mercury

Mercury had several important jobs among the gods. His primary role was to deliver important messages between the gods, or from the gods to humans. This wasn't an easy job, considering it involved traveling great distances and often carrying secrets of great importance.

But Mercury's role extended beyond just carrying messages. As the god of translators and interpreters, he helped bridge the gap between different languages and cultures. This job was crucial while the Roman Empire was expanding and encompassing many different peoples. Mercury enabled understanding and unity through translation, helping to maintain peace and order.

Mercury and His Cleverness

Mercury was celebrated not only for his speed but also for his mind. He was known for his shrewdness and ability to solve problems that stumped others. One famous myth tells the story of how Mercury invented the lyre. As a newborn, he stole cattle from Apollo. Since Apollo was not happy about this, Mercury had to make amends. So, he crafted the lyre from a tortoise shell and gave it to Apollo, charming the sun god and earning his forgiveness.

Mercury also showed his cleverness through his role as the guide of souls to the underworld. In many myths, Mercury used his wit and diplomacy to guide souls safely to the realm of Pluto, navigating the complexities of the afterlife.

Celebrations and Honors

Mercury was honored throughout the Roman world. Those involved in commerce and trade were particularly prone to worship Mercury, as he was also considered the god of merchants. His ability to move swiftly and negotiate made him a patron deity for traders and businessmen.

The Romans celebrated the festival of *Mercuralia* on May 15th to honor Mercury. On this day, merchants would sprinkle their goods and their heads with water from a sacred well dedicated to Mercury, seeking his blessings for success in their ventures and protection in their travels.

Mercury's Legacy

Today, Mercury is remembered not only as a mythological figure but also as a symbol of communication. His legacy lives on in the term "mercurial," often used to describe someone who is witty, clever, and quick in thought and action. His influence is also evident in the medical symbol of the *caduceus*. The *caduceus* reflects Mercury's role as a healer and mediator.

All in all, Mercury's tales inspire us to be both quick in our actions and thoughtful in our decisions. Like Mercury, we should use our abilities to help and inform others.

Pluto: The Mysterious God of the Underworld

Now, let's head to the Underworld, where you can imagine a kingdom hidden beneath the earth filled from glittering minerals to the souls of the departed. All are kept safe under the watchful eye of Pluto. Pluto is a god often pictured with a stern face who holds the keys to the underworld. He is normally accompanied by Cerberus, the three-headed dog who guards the gates of his kingdom.

Like Jupiter, Pluto was the son of Saturn, the god of time, and Ops, the goddess of wealth. As such, he was also the brother of Jupiter and Neptune. While his brothers ruled the sky and the sea, Pluto's domain was the Underworld. There he reigned supreme, ensuring that the natural order of life and death was maintained.

Pluto's Kingdom

The Underworld was not just a place of darkness and gloom as many imagine. As the king of the underworld, Pluto was responsible for ensuring that the spirits of the dead found their rightful place, whether that was the peaceful fields of Elysium or the depths of Tartarus, depending on their deeds during life. This meant that the Romans believed that all spirits of the dead traveled to the Underworld after death.

In addition to being the god of the dead, Pluto was also associated with wealth, specifically the mineral riches of the earth like gold and silver. This connection likely came from the fact that these precious metals were mined underground. These minerals were considered gifts from Pluto himself. He also played a role in agriculture, which was tied to the belief that the seeds planted in the earth die to bring about new life. This belief mirrors the cycle of death and rebirth overseen by Pluto in the Underworld.

Pluto in Roman Myths

Pluto is featured in several Roman myths, most notably in the story of Proserpina (Persephone in Greek mythology). According to the myth, Pluto fell in love with Proserpina, the beautiful daughter of Ceres (goddess of agriculture). He abducted Proserpina to make her his queen in the Underworld. This act brought about the changing of the seasons. The myth attributes these changes to Ceres who, in her grief, caused all crops to wither until her daughter was allowed to return to the surface for part of the year.

Pluto's Legacy

Today, Pluto's name lives on in the dwarf planet Pluto, which was discovered in 1930. This small planet is a symbol of the fact there are mysterious and distant places in our solar system. Pluto's story also helps us understand the ancient Romans' views on life, death, and the natural world.

As you learn about Pluto, think of him not just as a dark, foreboding figure, but as a necessary part of the natural cycle of life. He reminds us that endings are just as important as beginnings, and that wealth and abundance can come from even the darkest of places.

Bellona: The Fierce Goddess of War

We end our journey through the action-packed world of Roman mythology, filled with gods and goddesses that oversaw various aspects of life and nature, with Bellona. This figure stood out as the formidable goddess of war. Known for her bravery and battle prowess, Bellona was a figure of strength and determination, inspiring soldiers and commanders as they headed into combat.

Bellona was closely associated with Mars, the god of war. As such, she was sometimes even considered to be his wife or sister. Together, they represented the full terror and valor of military conflict. While Mars was more broadly recognized as the deity of war strategy and masculinity, Bellona specifically symbolized actual warfare and its combative spirit. Before Roman soldiers went off to fight, they would often invoke her name in hopes she would grant them courage and victory. Bellona's temples served as places not only for worship, but also for planning military tactics and meetings among commanders.

Celebrating Bellona

Bellona was honored with several festivals and rituals, particularly by those about to embark on military campaigns. One of her most important celebrations was the Bellona Festival, held in June, which included parades and military displays. During this festival, soldiers and commanders gathered to pray for strength and victory in their upcoming battles.

Bellona's symbols, such as the helmet and weapons, underscored her "martial" nature. She also carried a torch or whip, which represented the harsh realities of war—destruction and discipline, respectively. These symbols made her a relatable and revered figure among those who faced the uncertainties of battle.

Bellona's Legacy

Today, Bellona's legacy can be seen in how we depict and remember female figures of war. Bellona embodies the idea that bravery and courage are not limited by gender, and that the spirit of battle resonates with the concept of the defense of one's home and values.

Chapter conclusion

Together, we've journeyed through the incredible legends and history of the Roman gods and goddesses. We have explored the powers and adventures of Jupiter, Juno, Neptune, and many others. Each story has shown us how these divine figures were thought to have influenced everything in Roman life, from the weather to the fate of the mighty Roman Empire. They weren't just characters in stories; they were symbols of strength, wisdom, and guidance, inspiring the people of ancient Rome.

CHAPTER 5: HEROES, LEGENDS & MYTHS THAT SHAPED ROME

In this last chapter, we'll dive into the captivating stories, myths and legends that helped shape ancient Rome. These myths served as more than just simple stories to the Romans. Rather, they were the backbone of Roman identity, offering lessons on morality, bravery, and the laws of the land. These stories have been passed down through generations, each one packed with drama, intrigue, and wisdom. Get ready to explore how these ancient myths influenced the great city of Rome and its people. Let's embark on this mythical journey together!

The Founding of Rome by Romulus and Remus

Long ago, in the misty realms of ancient history, legend has it that two twin brothers founded one of the greatest cities the world has ever known; Rome. This is the tale of Romulus and Remus, which mixes adventure, danger, and the fierce bonds of family. It is a myth that captures the imaginations of all who hear it.

The story begins with a princess named Rhea Silvia. She was the daughter of Numitor, the king of *Alba Longa*, a city near where Rome was eventually established. Numitor was overthrown by his cruel brother Amulius, who forced Rhea Silvia to become a Vestal Virgin (or, as mentioned previously, a priestess for the goddess of the home, Vesta). This new role meant she wasn't allowed to marry or have children. Mars, however, fell in love with her. So, she soon gave birth to twins, Romulus and Remus.

Fearing the boys would grow up to challenge him, Amulius ordered them to be thrown into the River Tiber. But destiny had other plans for these children, as the river god Tiberinus calmed the waters to save them. Because of Tiberinus, the basket carrying the twins came safely to rest in the soft mud of the riverbank.

Raised by a Wolf

Here, something wonderful happened. A she-wolf, hearing the cries of the infants, came to their rescue. She gently cared for them with her warm milk, a scene so touching that it would be remembered forever in the statues and paintings of Rome.

Later, a kind shepherd named Faustulus found the boys and brought them home. He and his wife, Acca Larentia, raised the boys as their own.

As the twins grew, they became natural leaders. Strong, brave, and fair, they attracted a band of loyal followers. As they learned of their royal heritage, however, the boys decided to overthrow Amulius and restore their grandfather, Numitor, to the throne of Alba Longa. After achieving this, Romulus and Remus set out to build a city of their own.

Founding a New City

The brothers chose a spot near the River Tiber, where they had been saved as infants, to establish their new city. But soon, a fierce argument broke out between them. Both wanted to rule the city and to decide its location and name. To resolve this problem, Romulus and Remus agreed to seek the gods' favor through a contest of *augury* (which was how Romans interpreted the will of the gods by looking at how birds flew).

As ancient Rome was said to have been built on seven hills, each brother chose one to stand on. Romulus stood on Palatine Hill and Remus on Aventine Hill. They chose these hills to practice *augury* and looked for flying birds. Where Remus only saw six birds, Romulus saw twelve. Thus, the supporters of Romulus claimed this as a sign that the gods favored him as the new ruler, and that the Palatine Hill should be the site of the new city.

The dispute over the omens led to more arguments. One day, in a fit of anger, Romulus killed Remus. Though he was heartbroken, Romulus went on to build the city. He named it Rome after himself, becoming its first king and establishing many of its laws and traditions.

Rome grew rapidly under Romulus. He invited people from all walks of life to become its citizens, creating a melting pot of cultures that made the city strong and vibrant. He also formed the Roman Senate, laying the foundations for what would become a great republic and then an even greater empire.

Conclusion

The tale of Romulus and Remus is more than just an origin story for Rome; it's a narrative about destiny, leadership, and the complexities of human nature. It teaches us that actions have consequences, being compassionate is important, and strong foundations have an enduring impact. The story of these twin brothers continues to fascinate and remind us that great beginnings often come from humble origins.

The Horatii and Curiatii: A Tale of Honor and Sacrifice

After the establishment of Rome, the city thrived alongside its neighbor, Alba Longa. As often happens between neighbors, tensions rose, and soon they were on the brink of war. But instead of leading their people into a bloody battle, the leaders decided that the conflict should be settled by a duel between two sets of triplets; the Horatii brothers from Rome and the Curiatii brothers from Alba Longa.

The Horatii and the Curiatii were chosen as the strongest and bravest young men in their respective cities. Each was determined to bring victory to their respective city.. On the day of the duel, the six young men met on the battlefield. They would fight under the watchful eyes of their fellow citizens, who gathered to witness this unusual contest that would decide their fate.

The Battle Begins

The battle was fierce and evenly matched at first. As the brothers' swords clashed,tension among the spectators was noticeable. Before long, however, the tide of battle turned. Two of the Horatii were struck down, while all three Curiatii were wounded. It seemed that Alba Longa was destined to win, as only one Horatius brother remained standing against three injured Curiatii.

A Clever Strategy

But the last Horatius, knowing he couldn't defeat all three Curiatii in a direct flight, came up with a clever plan. He pretended to flee, hoping to separate his slower, wounded opponents. As expected, the Curiatii, hindered by their injuries, chased after him at different speeds. This caused them to spread out across the field. Turning swiftly, Horatius faced them one by one in single combat, using his full strength against their weakened states. This strategy was successful; he defeated each Curiatius brother separately, securing a dramatic and hard-won victory for Rome.

After the Battle

When Horatius returned to Rome, he was hailed as a hero. However, the story took a tragic turn when he discovered his sister weeping. She had been betrothed to one of the Curiatii, and her grief overwhelmed her. In a moment of anger and sorrow, Horatius killed his sister, declaring that no Roman should mourn an enemy of the state. This act shocked the city. As such, Horatius was put on trial for his sister's murder.

In the end, he was set free, largely due to his recent service to Rome. The Horatius brother, however, was required to pass under a yoke as a symbol of atonement for his crime. The yoke served to remind him of the heavy burden of his actions.

The Legacy of the Horatii and Curiatii

The duel between the Horatii and Curiatii became a legendary part of Roman heritage, teaching lessons about the gravity of war and the honor of warriors. It showed that sometimes, the greatest battles are not won by strength alone, but by cleverness, courage, and a deep sense of duty.

Aeneas's Big Journey: The Founding Hero of Rome

Aeneas was a Trojan prince that was known for his strength and bravery. As previously mentioned, he was also said to be the son of Venus. That meant he was half-human, half-god. During the Trojan War, Aeneas fought valiantly to defend his city. Troy, however, was destined to fall. As the city burned, Aeneas gathered his family and a group of followers and fled. To make sure everyone escaped, Aeneas carried his elderly father on his back and led his son by the hand.

After escaping Troy, Aeneas and his followers began a long and perilous journey across the sea in search of a new home. This mission was not just about survival; it was a divine quest assigned to Aeneas by the gods. They told him that he would establish a new city that would one day grow into a great empire. Unsurprisingly, this city was Rome.

Aeneas's voyage was filled with challenges and adventures. One of his first stops was at a city called Carthage, where a beautiful queen named Dido fell in love with him. They shared a brief, happy time together, but Aeneas knew he couldn't stay. After the gods reminded Aeneas of his destiny, he left Carthage with a heavy heart, also causing Dido to be heartbroken.

As Aeneas continued his journey, he and his crew faced many dangers, including a terrifying encounter with a cyclops and a journey to the Underworld. In the Underworld, however, Aeneas met the spirit of his father. His father showed Aeneas the long line of descendants who would follow him and the great city they would build.

The Arrival in Italy

Finally, after many years of traveling, Aeneas and his followers reached the shores of Italy. But, their trials were not over yet. They had to fight several fierce battles against local tribes who did not welcome the newcomers. Still, with his leadership and the help of the gods, Aeneas was able to secure a piece of land where they could settle.

Aeneas's journey did not just lead to the founding of a new city; it set the stage for the creation of the Roman Empire. Aeneas was seen by the Romans as a model of piety and duty, always putting his obligations above his personal desires. His story was immortalized by the poet Virgil in the epic poem "The Aeneid," which became a national epic of Rome.

Aeneas's big journey teaches us about the importance of perseverance and following one's destiny. It shows that even when the path is filled with obstacles, determination and faith can lead to great things. Finally, Aeneas's adventures remind us that even from small beginnings, great empires can grow.

Cincinnatus: The Farmer Who Saved Rome

Though many heroes shaped the city of Rome's destiny with their courage and wisdom, Lucius Quinctius Cincinnatus stands out as a true model of selflessness and duty. His story is not just a tale of heroism in battle, but also a lesson in humility and the virtues of simplicity. Let's explore how this humble farmer came to save Rome and became one of its greatest legends.

Cincinnatus was a simple Roman farmer who lived in the early days of the Roman Republic, around the 5th century BC. He owned a small plot of land, which he tended with his own hands. He lived a simple life, but those who knew him for his integrity and wisdom respected him greatly.

A City in Crisis

The story of Cincinnatus begins with a crisis in Rome, as the city was under threat from neighboring tribes.At that moment, the Roman army was trapped and the enemy was closing in. It was apparent that Rome needed a leader who could guide them through this perilous time. The Roman

Senate knew exactly whom to call upon – Cincinnatus, known for his previous service as a consul and his unquestionable moral character.

According to legend, messengers sent by the Senate found Cincinnatus at his farm, plowing the fields. They approached him with great reverence and told him that Rome needed him to become dictator. This was a powerful role given only in times of emergency and allowed the leader to have complete control over the city to handle the crisis. Cincinnatus accepted the responsibility without hesitation, leaving his plow in the fields and heading to the city to take command.

Once in power, Cincinnatus acted swiftly. He organized the troops, devised a brilliant plan, and led the army to battle himself. With cunning strategy and fearless leadership, he defeated the enemy. Then, Cincinnatus rescued the trapped Roman soldiers and returned triumphantly to Rome—all within a mere 15 days.

A True Hero's Choice

What Cincinnatus did next is what truly made him a legend. Instead of using his power to enrich himself or extend his rule, he did something almost unheard of—he resigned and returned to his farm. Cincinnatus had been granted absolute power to save Rome, but once he had done so, he willingly gave that power up. This act of selflessness and devotion to the Republic made him a symbol of civic virtue and duty.

Cincinnatus's Legacy

Cincinnatus became a hero not only for his military deeds but also for his character. His story has been told throughout the centuries as an example of leadership at its best—power used wisely and relinquished willingly for the common good. Cincinnatus teaches us that true leadership involves putting the needs of one's community or country before their own desires.

The Legend of the Capitoline Geese

Throughout Roman history, many humans have been recognized as heroes. Atop the Capitoline Hill, however, appears a different tale—or, that of few feathered heroes whose vigilance saved the city from disaster.

This is the story of the Capitoline geese. These birds were not a flock not of mighty eagles or a pride of fierce lions, but rather a group of simple, watchful geese who became unsung heroes of Rome. Their legend is a delightful blend of how small creatures can make a big difference and that even the most unlikely heroes can save the day.

A City Under Siege

The story takes us back to a time when Rome was under siege by the fierce Gauls in 390 BC. The Gauls were led by their chieftain Brennus. The Romans were struggling to defend their city against these powerful invaders who had already captured much of the city. The only place left unconquered was Capitoline Hill, a fortified area and the last refuge for the city's defenders.

The Gauls knew that taking the Capitoline Hill would mean victory. So, they tried every trick to capture it. At first, the Gauls fought hard during the day but could not break through the Roman defenses. So, they devised a cunning plan to climb the hill's cliffs under the cover of night and catch the Romans off-guard while they slept.

The Night of the Climbing Gauls

So, one dark night, the Gauls began their silent climb up the steep cliffs of Capitoline Hill. The Roman guards, weary after days of siege, didn't notice the silent shadows inching closer to the city's last stronghold. It seemed that nothing could stop the Gauls from overrunning the hill and sealing Rome's fate.

The Geese Spring into Action

One important detail of Capitoline Hill was forgotten, however, which were : the sacred geese of Juno. This flock was housed in her temple on the hill. As these were not ordinary geese (they were devoted to Juno, the goddess who watched over the city), they perhaps had a touch of her divine awareness.

As the Gauls neared the top, the geese sensed something amiss. They began honking furiously, flapping their wings and creating a racket that no human guard had managed. Startled by the noise, Marcus Manlius, a former consul and a vigilant defender of Rome, woke up. He quickly gathered other soldiers to rush towards the noise.

The Battle on the Hill

The Romans arrived just in time to see the shadowy figures of the Gauls reaching the top of the cliffs. Thanks to the geese's warnings, the Romans were prepared and fought fiercely. They managed to push the surprised Gauls back down the hill, thwarting their night attack. The geese had saved Capitoline Hill—and Rome itself—with their watchful eyes and loud warning.

The next day, as the story of the night's events spread throughout the remaining Roman forces. The geese were hailed as heroes as they had succeeded in detecting the silent approach of the Gauls even when the guards had failed to do so. The grateful Romans saw this as a sign that Juno herself was protecting the city through her sacred birds.

Legacy of the Legend

The Legend of the Capitoline Geese became a cherished tale among the Romans. As such, Juno's geese were celebrated in sculptures and stories, and they became a symbol of watchfulness and protection in Roman culture.

This is a tale that encourages us to be vigilant and courageous. Most importantly, however, it teaches us to appreciate the everyday heroes in our lives, whether they have feathers, fur, or two hands.

The Tale of Mucius Scaevola: The Brave, Left-Handed Hero

Though Juno's geese were essential to Rome's survival of the Gauls, let's get back to human heroes. Long ago, a young man named Mucius, who would come to be known as Mucius Scaevola (which means "Mucius the Left-Handed"), made his mark on ancient Rome. This legend not only thrilled the people of Rome, but also taught them the value of courage and conviction.

A City Under Siege

Mucius's story begins when the city of Rome was under siege by a fierce king named Lars Porsena and his people, the Etruscans. Due to the king's mighty army, Rome seemed on the brink of defeat. This worried the Romans, who feared their beloved city might fall into the hands of the enemy. But amid these dark times, young Mucius, a mere citizen with no great title or rank, decided he would do something to save his city.

Mucius came up with a bold plan: he would sneak into the enemy camp and assassinate King Lars Porsena himself. He believed that without their leader, the enemy army would be thrown into chaos and retreat. With his heart set on saving Rome, Mucius bid farewell to his family and friends and slipped into the enemy camp, disguised as an Etruscan soldier.

The Mistake and the Test

Mucius tried to find the king in the bustling camp. In a fateful mix-up, however, he mistook the king's scribe for the king himself. Mucius killed the scribe instead, meaning he was immediately captured by the soldiers and brought before King Porsena. The king was furious and demanded to know why Mucius had attempted such a bold act.

Standing before the king, Mucius showed no fear. He declared proudly that he was a Roman and that many other brave Romans were ready to risk their lives to protect their city just as he had. To prove his courage and that fear had no hold on him, Mucius thrust his right hand into a nearby fire. He burned it without showing any signs of pain, shocking everyone including King Porsena.

The King's Response

Moved by Mucius's courage and realizing the determination of the Roman people, King Porsena decided to negotiate peace rather than continue the war. He was impressed by the young Roman's bravery and saw that the spirit of Rome was stronger and more resilient than he had thought. Mucius was freed without harm, and he returned to Rome a hero.

Upon his return, Mucius was given the nickname "Scaevola," meaning "left-handed," because his right hand had been disabled by the fire. He was honored by all of Rome, and his deed became a symbol of the bravery that every Roman was expected to embody. Mucius's story was told and retold, inspiring countless others to be courageous in the face of danger.

The tale of Mucius Scaevola is more than just a story of a young man who dared to defend his city; it's a lesson in the power of courage and the strength of conviction. It teaches us that sometimes, one brave act can change the course of history. Mucius reminds us that true heroism comes from standing firm for what we believe in, no matter the odds.

The Story of Cloelia: The Brave Roman Girl

Though many heroes woven into the rich tapestry of Roman legends were men, let's talk about a brave young girl named Cloelia. Unlike tales of warriors and kings, Cloelia's story is a remarkable testament to the bravery and resourcefulness of youth. Her adventure not only inspired the hearts of ancient Romans but continues to teach us about courage and cleverness today.

A City in Peril

This tale begins during the same troubling time for Rome as when Mucius had lived. The city was at war with a neighboring state, Clusium, ruled by the fierce King Lars Porsena. In an attempt to secure peace, the Romans agreed to send hostages to King Porsena. Among these hostages was a young girl named Cloelia.

Cloelia, along with other Roman youths, was taken to the enemy camp across the Tiber River. While life in the camp was safe and the hostages were treated well, the idea of being prisoners weighed heavily on them. They longed for their freedom and their beloved city, but escape seemed impossible. The hostages were closely guarded and surrounded by the wide, rushing river.

Cloelia's Bold Plan

Cloelia was not one to sit by idly. She devised a daring plan to escape and lead her fellow hostages back to Rome. With a spirit as fierce as any warrior's, Cloelia rallied the other young Romans and led them to the river's edge. Under the cover of darkness, they made their bold move.

Cloelia was aware that the river served as a formidable barrier, but she also knew it was the hostages' only path to freedom. With courage in their hearts, Cloelia and the hostages plunged into the Tiber and began to swim across its swift currents. It was a perilous journey and not all were strong swimmers. Still, Cloelia urged them on with unyielding determination.

Against all odds, Cloelia and her companions reached the far bank of the river. Wet and weary, but excited by their success, the hostages made their way back to Rome. Their return was met with joy and astonishment. Cloelia was hailed as a heroine and all of Rome celebrated her bravery.

King Porsena was furious when he learned of the hostages' escape. He demanded that Cloelia be sent back to him, as per the terms of the peace treaty. The Romans, bound by honor, agreed. So, Cloelia returned to the Clusian camp, bravely facing the consequences of her actions.

Impressed by her courage and integrity, King Porsena did something unexpected—he forgave Cloelia and praised her bravery. As a token of his admiration, he allowed Cloelia to choose half of the remaining hostages to take back with her to Rome. So, Cloelia chose the youngest, and once again, she returned to her city. This time, however, she was not an escapee, but rather a negotiator of freedom.

The story of Cloelia teaches us that bravery comes in many forms, and even the youngest among us can change the course of history with acts of great courage. Her tale reminds us to stand up for what we believe in. Cloelia reminds us that the greatest heroes are those who act not only for themselves but for the good of others.

Wisdom from the Waters

After the fierce and mighty Romulus established Rome, there came a king who was his opposite in nearly every way. This king was Numa Pompilius, a wise and thoughtful ruler who sought to enrich Rome with laws and rituals instead of expanding the city through battle. One of the most enchanting tales from his reign is that of his secret advisor, Egeria. This story is a beautiful example of how ancient

Romans revered both wisdom and nature, and the tale speaks to the power of knowledge and peace.

As the story goes, Numa would often wander the forests near Rome, seeking solitude and space to think about the laws he was creating for his people. During one of these walks, he encountered the nymph Egeria. Egeria was a wise and beautiful nymph who lived in a sacred grove with springs and streams that were said to have healing properties.

Egeria, impressed by Numa's dedication to his city and his kind heart, decided to help him. She became his advisor, meeting him in the grove where she lived. To hide her existence, she counseled Numa under the cover of night. During their talks, Egeria shared her divine knowledge of rituals, laws, and governance with Numa. With Egeria's counsel, Numa established many of the religious customs and institutions that would shape Roman society for centuries to come.

Thanks to Egeria's wisdom and Numa's leadership, Rome enjoyed a long period of peace and prosperity. Numa set up colleges for priests, including the Vestal Virgins, and created the Pontifex Maximus. The Pontifex Maximus was the high priest who oversaw all religious ceremonies to ensure that the gods continued to support Rome.

Numa's laws were just and aimed at maintaining peace and fairness in Roman society. He believed this structure pleased the gods and brought stability. The king's focus on law and rituals deeply ingrained the importance of religion in Roman public life, and taught the Romans that peace was just as honorable as war.

The Legacy of Numa and Egeria

The tale of Numa Pompilius and the nymph Egeria teaches us that it is important to seek knowledge from those who can share it. It shows that true leadership involves listening, learning, and respecting both the people and the world around us. Their story is a beautiful reminder of how peace can lead to a society's prosperity and how nature can inspire the best in us all.

Chapter Conclusion

Now, we have ventured through the captivating myths that not only entertained the citizens of ancient Rome and grounded them in values and principles that defined their civilization. These stories, rich with heroes and moral lessons, have painted a vivid picture of the societal ideals and spiritual beliefs that influenced everything from daily life to grand policy in ancient Rome.

As we close this chapter, we carry with us the timeless wisdom and enduring spirit of these ancient legends. The tales of courage, sacrifice, and innovation continue to inspire us and remind us of how myth has the power to shape societies and moral landscapes.

CONCLUSION

As we reach the end of our journey through "Roman Legends for Kids," we remember the grandeur, the triumphs, and the eventual fall of one of the most iconic civilizations in history—the Roman Empire. Its decline, marked by the relentless Barbarian invasions, severe economic troubles, and the division into East and West, teaches us about the vulnerability of even the mightiest powers when faced with internal and external pressures.

Throughout the book, we have traveled back in time to explore bustling marketplaces, stood in the shadows of colossal aqueducts, and heard the roaring crowds of the Colosseum. We met formidable emperors who strategized Rome's expansions, brave gladiators who fought for glory and freedom, and inventive gods and goddesses who shaped the fates of people and cities alike.

Each legend and historical figure has taught us about courage, wisdom, and the complexities of human nature. From the strategic prowess of Julius Caesar to the architectural innovations that still influence modern engineering, the legacy of Rome is a testament to the empire's lasting impact on law, language, and governance that still resonates in our world today.

But, you should consider this book as only the beginning of your adventure into the past. History is filled with mysteries waiting to be solved and stories yearning to be heard. By exploring archaeology, engaging with storytelling, and studying the histories of ancient civilizations like Rome, you can discover how the past shapes our present and influences our future.

So, keep the spirit of curiosity alive! Visit museums, read more books, and discuss what you've learned with friends and family. Perhaps one day, you will add your own stories to the rich tapestry of history.

Remember that every chapter of history offers insights that can inspire and guide us. Let these tales of Rome remind you that you, too, can build something enduring that might one day inspire future generations. So, turn the page and start creating your own chapter to add to the book of history! Whether you're just getting started or you're ready to challenge yourself further, remember to keep discovering new things and bringing history to life!

Congratulations on completing your grand tour through the legends of ancient Rome! Head over to the quiz section and see how much you've learned. Can you answer all the questions and prove yourself to be a young historian of Rome?

TEST YOUR KNOWLEDGE

Hey young explorers! Now that you've journeyed through the grand stories of ancient Rome, met mighty emperors and courageous gladiators, learned about powerful gods and legendary heroes, how much can you remember? It's time to put your knowledge to the test with this fun quiz. Ready to prove that you're a true historian of ancient Rome?

Let's get started!

Chapter 1: Mighty Emperors of Rome

Who was known as the founder of the Roman Empire?

- A) Caligula
- B) Nero
- C) Augustus
- D) Tiberius

Which emperor is famous for his philosophical writings and being a "Philosopher-Emperor?"

- A) Nero
- B) Julius Caesar
- C) Marcus Aurelius
- D) Vespasian

Name the emperor who famously made his horse a senator.

- A) Nero
- B) Caligula
- C) Claudius
- D) Diocletian

Who was the emperor during the Great Fire of Rome in AD 64?

- A) Vespasian
- B) Titus
- C) Nero
- D) Domitian

Which emperor divided the Roman Empire into the Eastern and Western Roman Empires?

- A) Constantine the Great
- B) Julian
- C) Diocletian
- D) Theodosius I

Chapter 2: Powerful Women of Rome

Who was Livia Drusilla?

- A) The mother of Nero
- B) The confidante and advisor to her husband, Emperor Augustus
- C) A famous Roman poet
- D) The last queen of Rome

Name the queen who allied with both Julius Caesar and Mark Antony.

- A) Agrippina the Younger
- B) Julia Domna
- C) Cleopatra VII
- D) Livia Drusilla

Which warrior queen led a revolt against Roman invasion in her territory?

- A) Julia Domna
- B) Boudica
- C) Fulvia
- D) Cleopatra VII

Who was the mother of Emperor Nero and a prominent figure in Roman politics?

- A) Agrippina the Younger
- B) Cleopatra VII
- C) Livia Drusilla
- D) Julia Domna

Name the Roman empress known for her philosophical interests and support of her son's reign.

- A) Agrippina the Younger
- B) Julia Domna
- C) Cleopatra VII
- D) Boudica

Chapter 3: Brave Gladiators of the Colosseum

Who was the gladiator that led a major slave uprising against Rome?

- A) Tetraites
- B) Commodus
- C) Spartacus
- D) Crixus

What type of gladiator was known for using a net and trident?

- A) Murmillo
- B) Retiarius
- C) Secutor
- D) Thraex

Which two gladiators were known for their battle that ended in a draw, earning them both their freedom?

- A) Flamma and Crixus
- B) Spartacus and Commodus
- C) Priscus and Verus
- D) Tetraites and Secutor

What was the name of the gladiator who refused to win his freedom, choosing to remain in the arena instead?

- A) Commodus
- B) Flamma
- C) Crixus
- D) Spartacus

Chapter 4: Mighty Gods & Goddesses of Rome

Who was the king of the Roman gods?

- A) Mars
- B) Saturn
- C) Jupiter
- D) Neptune

Name the god of the sea in Roman mythology.

- A) Mars
- B) Mercury
- C) Neptune
- D) Pluto

Which goddess is associated with love and beauty?

- A) Juno
- B) Vesta
- C) Bellona
- D) Venus

Who was the Roman god of war, also associated with agriculture?

- A) Mars
- B) Vulcan
- C) Mercury
- D) Saturn

Chapter 5: Heroes, Legends & Myths that Shaped Rome

Which is the legendary story of the founding of Rome?

- A) The journey of Aeneas
- B) The tale of Mucius Scaevola
- C) The founding by Romulus and Remus
- D) The legend of Cincinnatus

Who was the hero believed to have journeyed from Troy to establish the city ofRome?

- A) Julius Caesar
- B) Romulus
- C) Aeneas
- D) Remus

Name the Roman hero who is known for sticking his hand in a fire to prove his bravery.

- A) Cincinnatus
- B) Mucius Scaevola
- C) Numa Pompilius
- D) Gaius Mucius Cordus

Which Roman figure is celebrated for returning to his farm after saving Rome from invasion?

- A) Cincinnatus
- B) Aeneas
- C) Gaius Mucius Cordus
- D) Romulus

Who were the twin brothers who fought against each other to settle a war between Alba Longa and Rome?

- A) Aeneas and Ascanius
- B) Romulus and Remus
- C) The Horatii and Curiatii
- D) Priscus and Verus

ANSWERS

Chapter 1: Mighty Emperors of Rome

Who was known as the founder of the Roman Empire?

Answer: C) Augustus

Which emperor is famous for his philosophical writings and being a "Philosopher_Emperor?"

Answer: C) Marcus Aurelius

Name the emperor who famously made his horse a senator.

Answer: B) Caligula

Who was the emperor during the Great Fire of Rome in AD 64?

Answer: C) Nero

Which emperor divided the Roman Empire into the Eastern and Western Roman Empires?

Answer: C) Diocletian

Chapter 2: Powerful Women of Rome

Who was Livia Drusilla?

Answer: B) The confidante and advisor to her husband, Emperor Augustus

Name the queen who allied with both Julius Caesar and Mark Antony.

Answer: C) Cleopatra VII

Which warrior queen led a revolt against Roman invasion in her territory?

Answer: B) Boudica

Who was the mother of Emperor Nero and a prominent figure in Roman politics?

Answer: A) Agrippina the Younger

Name the Roman empress known for her philosophical interests and support of her son's reign.

Answer: B) Julia Domna

Chapter 3: Brave Gladiators of the Colosseum

Who was the gladiator that led a major slave uprising against Rome?

Answer: C) Spartacus

What type of gladiator was known for using a net and trident?

Answer: B) Retiarius

Which two gladiators were known for their battle that ended in a draw, earning them both their freedom?

Answer: C) Priscus and Verus

What was the name of the gladiator who refused to win his freedom, choosing to remain in the arena instead?

Answer: B) Flamma

Chapter 4: Mighty Gods & Goddesses of Rome

Who was the king of the Roman gods?

Answer: C) Jupiter

Name the god of the sea in Roman mythology.

Answer: C) Neptune

Which goddess is associated with love and beauty?

Answer: D) Venus

Who was the Roman god of war, also associated with agriculture?

Answer: A) Mars

Chapter 5: Heroes, Legends & Myths that Shaped Rome

Which is the legendary story of the founding of Rome?

Answer: C) The founding by Romulus and Remus

Who was the hero believed to have journeyed from Troy to establish the city of Rome?

Answer: C) Aeneas

Name the Roman hero who is known for sticking his hand in fire to prove his bravery.

Answer: B) Mucius Scaevola

Which Roman figure is celebrated for returning to his farm after saving Rome from invasion?

Answer: A) Cincinnatus

Who were the twin brothers who fought against each other to settle a war between Alba Longa and Rome?

Answer: C) The Horatii and Curiatii

REFERENCES

This book was created using sources including books, academic journals, educational websites, encyclopedias, documentaries, and museum collections to provide a thorough and engaging exploration of ancient Roman history, culture, and mythology.

Books:

- "The History of Rome" by Titus Livius (Livy)
- "SPQR: A History of Ancient Rome" by Mary Beard
- "The Oxford Classical Dictionary"
- "Encyclopedia Britannica"

Academic Journals and Articles:

- Journal of Roman Studies
- Classical Antiquity
- JSTOR
- Google Scholar

Educational:

- BBC History
- National Geographic Kids
- TED-Ed videos on Roman history, which are often created and vetted by educators and can provide both inspiration and factual content.
- The British Museum
- The Metropolitan Museum of Art

EGYPTIAN LEGENDS FOR KIDS

Mummies, Pharaohs, Queens, Gods & Myths from Ancient Egypt

History Brought Alive

FREE BONUS FROM HBA: EBOOK BUNDLE

Greetings!

First of all, thank you for reading our books. As fellow passionate readers of History and Mythology, we aim to create the very best books for our readers.

Now, we invite you to join our VIP list. As a welcome gift, we offer the History & Mythology Ebook Bundle below for free. Plus you can be the first to receive new books and exclusives! <u>Remember it's 100% free to join.</u>

Simply scan the QR code to join.

https://www.subscribepage.com/hba

<u>Keep up to date with us on:</u>

YouTube: History Brought Alive

Facebook: History Brought Alive

www.historybroughtalive.com

CONTENTS

INTRODUCTION

Welcome, young adventurers, to the enchanting world of "Egyptian Legends for Kids!" Under the golden sands of the Nile River valley lie mysteries and wonders waiting to be discovered. Are you ready to embark on an unforgettable journey through time, where ancient pharaohs, mighty gods, and legendary heroes await?

In this captivating book, we will delve deep into the heart of ancient Egypt. This land is steeped in history, mythology, and intrigue. From the majestic pyramids of Giza to the mystical rituals of mummification, each chapter is filled with tales of valor, wisdom, and adventure that will spark your imagination and ignite your curiosity.

Chapter 1: The Mighty Pharaohs

Our journey begins with the mighty pharaohs. These characters were the revered rulers of ancient Egypt who wielded power and authority over the land. You will meet Tutankhamun, the boy king whose golden tomb held secrets beyond imagination. You will also discover Djoser, the visionary pharaoh who built the very first pyramid, and Ramses II, the great and powerful ruler whose reign stretched across the ages.

But our adventure doesn't stop there! You'll learn about Akhenaten, the heretic king who challenged tradition with his radical religious revolution, and Khufu, the builder of the Great Pyramid of Giza. Join us as we unravel the stories of these legendary figures and uncover the mysteries of their reigns.

Chapter 2: Queens of the Nile

In this chapter, we'll turn our gaze to the powerful queens who stood alongside the pharaohs. These women shaped the destiny of Egypt with their grace and strength. From Nefertiti, the beautiful queen who captured the hearts of her people, to Cleopatra, the last queen whose Roman ties changed the course of history, these remarkable women left a long-lasting mark on the sands of time.

Chapter 3: The Mysterious Mummies

Next, prepare to journey into the realm of the afterlife as we explore the ancient art of mummification. You'll learn about the intricate process of preserving a body for eternity and uncover the secrets hidden within the tombs of Egypt's illustrious pharaohs. From beliefs about the afterlife to the exploration of Egyptian graves, this chapter will unravel the mysteries of mummification and its significance in ancient Egyptian culture.

Chapter 4: Gods and Goddesses

After discovering the mysteries of the afterlife, you'll step into the realm of the gods and goddesses. These were the mighty deities who ruled over the heavens and the earth.

From Ra, the radiant sun god, to Osiris, the benevolent ruler of the dead, each deity holds a unique place in the pantheon of Egyptian mythology. Join us as we unravel the stories of these divine beings and explore the ancient mysteries of those who worshiped them.

Chapter 5: Myths of Ancient Egypt

When you've discovered the secrets of the gods and goddesses of ancient Egypt, you'll continue by embarking on a journey through the myths and legends of ancient Egypt. These stories describe heroic sailors who braved the seas, wise scribes who recorded their adventures, and ancient artifacts that revealed the secrets of the past. From the creation myth of Heliopolis to the legendary adventures of Sphinx, each tale is a window into the rich tapestry of Egyptian folklore and tradition.

Chapter 6: Heroes and Legends

In our final chapter, we'll celebrate the heroes and legends that shaped the course of Egyptian history. Meet Imhotep, the architect who became a god, and Sinuhe, the adventurous scribe (someone who copied books and worked as a professional writer) whose tales captivate the imagination. Discover the wisdom of Ptah-hotep, the wise vizier (government official), and journey with Moses as he leads his people to freedom. From Ibn Khaldun, the great philosopher, to Muhammad Ali, the father of modern Egypt, these remarkable figures inspire us with their courage, wisdom, and resilience.

So, young adventurers, are you ready to embark on this extraordinary journey through the land of the pharaohs? Prepare to unlock the secrets of ancient Egypt! Let's embark on an adventure that will leave you spellbound and eager for more.

Now, let the magic of "Egyptian Legends for Kids" ignite your imagination and transport you to an ancient world of wonder!

CHAPTER 1:
THE MIGHTY PHARAOHS

Welcome, dear readers, to the first chapter of our journey through the sands of ancient Egypt—a land where gods and mortals walked side by side and mighty pharaohs ruled with divine authority. In this chapter, we will dive into the world of the pharaohs. We will explore their roles, stories, and those legacies which have echoed through the corridors of time.

The pharaohs were more than just kings; in fact, they were respected as living gods that were entrusted with the sacred duty of maintaining order, harmony, and prosperity throughout their kingdom. Because they acted as a divine messenger between the mortal realm and the gods, pharaohs wielded unparalleled power and authority. They commanded loyalty and devotion from their subjects. Our journey begins with tales of some of the most renowned pharaohs of ancient Egypt, whose names have been whispered on desert winds throughout centuries of history.

Tutankhamun: The Boy King and His Golden Tomb

In the land of ancient Egypt, where the mighty Nile River flows and the pyramids touch the sky, there once lived a young king named Tutankhamun. Though his name might be a mouthful, you can simply call him King Tut. His story is one of mystery and treasure. It began over 3,000 years ago!

The Young King

King Tut became pharaoh when he was about nine years old—imagine being a king in third or fourth grade! He was so young that people often called him the "Boy King." During a time when Egypt was filled with splendid palaces and grand monuments, young Tutankhamun had a very big role. But what is really fascinating wasn't just his age; rather, it's the incredible story of how he was discovered many years later.

A Tomb Lost and Found

For thousands of years, the sands of Egypt hid King Tut's tomb from the world. It's true that many pharaohs had grand tombs filled with treasures, but over time, robbers had taken almost all of them. King Tut's tomb, however, was different. It lay hidden under the sands, keeping its secrets and treasures safe, waiting to be discovered.

It wasn't until 1922 that a British explorer named Howard Carter found a step cut into the rock of the Valley of the Kings. After some careful digging, he uncovered a doorway, and behind it was the tomb of King Tut! Imagine finding a secret door that no one had opened for over 3,000 years!

Treasures Galore

When Howard Carter opened the tomb, he couldn't believe his eyes. There was treasure everywhere! He saw golden statues, jewelry, chariots, and even King Tut's throne. But the most amazing of the treasures was King Tut's coffin that was made of solid gold. Inside, the young king's mummy wore a magnificent golden mask that showed his youthful face, calm and serene.

Carter found rooms filled with things a king might need in the afterlife. There were clothes, weapons, and even toys from Tut's childhood—things he loved when he was probably about your age! Because Egyptians believed that life after death was very similar to life on earth, they buried their dead with everything they thought they might need.

The Curse of the Pharaohs

However, this wouldn't be a good treasure story without a bit of mystery. When Carter found King Tut's tomb, rumors started about a "curse" that would affect anyone who entered the tomb. Newspapers told spooky stories of bad luck and strange occurrences that happened to those who visited the tomb. But, don't worry, these stories are just myths. In fact, many people involved in the tomb's discovery lived long and happy lives.

Why King Tut is Famous

So, why is King Tut so famous if he was so young and did not stay pharaoh for very long? Well, it's because his tomb gives us a glittering window into Egypt's past. As previously mentioned, most royal tombs were emptied by robbers long ago. Tut's tomb, however, was full of treasures that help us understand how the ancient Egyptians lived, what they believed, and how they celebrated their kings.

King Tut teaches us that you don't have to be the biggest or the oldest to be remembered. Sometimes, being a part of a great discovery is enough to make you famous forever, like King Tut—the Boy King whose golden tomb helped us discover the wonders of ancient Egypt.

Djoser: The Visionary Pharaoh

After discovering the mysteries of the afterlife through King Tut, next we'll delve deep into the life and legacy of a pharaoh who ushered in an era of progress and innovation to ancient Egypt. This extraordinary ruler's name was Pharaoh Djoser.

Pharaoh Djoser's most enduring legacy is undoubtedly the magnificent Step Pyramid. This pyramid is located in the sprawling necropolis (or, a cemetery filled with elaborate tombs) of Saqqara. This awe-inspiring structure, which rises majestically from the desert sands, stands as a testament not only to Djoser's vision but also the ingenuity of ancient Egyptian craftsmanship. Built under the guidance of Djoser's brilliant architect, Imhotep, the Step Pyramid revolutionized funerary architecture and laid the foundation for future pyramid construction.

Economic Revitalization

Djoser's accomplishments, however, extended far beyond the realm of monumental construction. He was a forward-thinking ruler who recognized that economic development was vital to ensure the prosperity of his kingdom. Djosein began ambitious mining expeditions across Egypt to tap into the nation's rich natural resources. His copper mines yielded precious metal for tools and weapons, while turquoise mines provided gemstones for beautiful jewelry. Furthermore, Djoser understood trade dynamics, which enabled him to negotiate profitable deals with neighboring regions.

Agricultural Innovation

In addition to his efforts in mining and trade, Djoser implemented groundbreaking reforms in agriculture, which was essential to Egypt's prosperity. Djoser recognized that the Nile River was vital to the kingdom's agricultural success. So, he oversaw the construction of irrigation canals and reservoirs to ensure the water was distributed to farmland. These innovative irrigation systems transformed desert landscapes into fertile fields. These systems also enhanced crop yields and ensured food security for Egypt's growing population.

Legacy of Leadership

Pharaoh Djoser's reign was characterized by bold initiatives and forward-thinking policies that propelled Egypt to new heights of prosperity and influence. His unwavering commitment to innovation and progress left a permanent mark on the ancient world, which went on to inspire future generations of rulers and visionaries. Today, as we marvel at the incredible Step Pyramid and reflect on Djoser's enduring legacy, we are reminded of the importance of imaginative leadership and the potential of human achievements.

Ramses II: The Great and Powerful Ruler

After exploring the impressive innovations and architectural achievements of Djoser, we will visit one of the most remarkable kings of ancient Egypt, Ramses the Great. This pharaoh was famous not just for his power in battle, but also for building some of the most awe-inspiring monuments that we can still see today!

Ramses II, or Ramses the Great, was a pharaoh of the Nineteenth Dynasty. He ruled Egypt for an impressive 66 years—from his teenage years all the way into his nineties! During his reign, Egypt enjoyed peace and prosperity. People were happy, crops grew well, and there was plenty of food for everyone. But Ramses, however, didn't just want to be remembered for that; he wanted to be remembered forever.

A King and His Monuments

So, Ramses began building incredible temples and statues to leave his mark on Egypt forever. If you've ever seen pictures of giant statues with faces that look like they're gazing down at you, you may have been looking at some of Ramses' work!

The Temple of Abu Simbel

One of his most famous projects is the Temple of Abu Simbel. This temple was carved out of a mountainside, and has four huge statues of Ramses himself. Each statue is about as tall as a house!

Inside the temple, the walls are decorated with carvings that tell the story of Ramses's victories in battle and blessings from the gods. Twice a year, the sun shines directly into the heart of this temple, lighting up the sculptures on the back wall. Only one statue remains unlit, which displays the god of the underworld. This magical event shows how knowledgeable the ancient Egyptians were in relation to astronomy and architecture.

The Ramesseum

Another amazing building project by Ramses is the Ramesseum, his funerary temple in the Valley of the Kings. This massive temple was not just a place for worship, but also a place to celebrate his reign and achievements. It once featured a gigantic statue of Ramses that weighed over 1,000 tons—that's as heavy as 200 elephants!

Ramses the War Hero

Ramses wasn't just good at building; he was also a brave warrior. One of his most famous battles was the Battle of Kadesh. Ramses led his army against the Hittites, a powerful group of people that wanted to take over Egyptian territories. The battle was fierce, and though both sides claimed victory, Ramses used this event to boost his image as a strong and invincible leader. At his command, the story of the battle was carved on temples all across Egypt so everyone knew about Ramses's bravery.

Why We Remember Ramses the Great

Today, we don't only remember Ramses because he was a powerful king. Ramses also left us with some of the most incredible Egyptian monuments that we can still visit today. These constructions tell us a lot about the ancient Egyptians—how they lived, what was important to them, and their worldview.

Ramses also made sure that his deeds and stories were carved on the walls of these temples. Because of this, we know about his battles, his family, and even his favorite hobbies! It's like he made a stone time capsule for us to discover thousands of years later.

Ramses the Great, his grand monuments, and thrilling battle stories, now teach us an important lesson: what we create and do in our lives can tell our story long after we're gone. Thanks to Ramses' efforts, we can still walk through the halls of his temples today and marvel at the same scenes he looked upon thousands of years ago. He made sure he would be remembered as more than a king of Egypt; rather, he made sure he was remembered as a legend.

Next time you build something—whether it's a sandcastle, a Lego tower, or a drawing—think about what story you want it to tell. Just like Ramses, you're creating something that tells your story!

Akhenaten: The Heretic King and his Religious Revolution

You'll soon learn that Ramses was not the only one who wanted to permanently shape Egyptian history. This pharaoh's name was Akhenaten, and he was one of the most unusual pharaohs in Egyptian history. Instead of worshiping lots of gods like everyone else, Akhenaten chose to worship just one god. Let's dive into the story of this bold king and his big changes!

Who Was Akhenaten?

Akhenaten was not always known by this name. When he became pharaoh, he was called Amenhotep IV. As time went on during his reign, Akhenaten decided he was going to be different. About five years into his rule, Amenhotep changed his name to Akhenaten, which means "He who is of service to Aten." Aten was the sun disk, and according to Akhenaten, the only god that should be worshiped.

The City of the Sun

Akhenaten's first big move as pharaoh was to build a brand-new city in honor of his favorite god, Aten. He named this city Akhetaten, which means "Horizon of Aten." This city was located in the middle of Egypt, and it was where Akhenaten said Aten's (the sun's) rays were the strongest. Imagine a whole city built just to honor the sun!

In Akhetaten, big open-air temples were built so that everyone could feel the sun's rays. Akhenaten designed the temples this way because he believed that Aten's spirit was in the sunlight. So, unlike other dark, mysterious temples of Egypt, these were bright and filled with sunshine.

A New Art Style

Akhenaten also made another bold move by changing the way art was made in Egypt. Before Akhenaten, art in Egypt was formal and strict. Humans were usually shown in perfect, idealized forms. But Akhenaten liked art that was more relaxed and realistic. As such, art from his time shows him and his family in ways no one had ever seen pharaohs before—playing with their children, showing affection, and even looking less-than-perfect with long, exaggerated features.

Trouble with the Change

Not everyone liked these changes. Many people were upset because they loved their gods and did not want to worship only Aten. The priests who served other gods were especially unhappy because they lost a lot of power and money when people stopped worshiping their gods.

Because of all these changes, some people started calling Akhenaten the "Heretic King," which means he was someone who went against what everyone else believed. This was a big deal because, in ancient Egypt, keeping the gods happy was very important. People believed that if the gods were unhappy, bad things like famine or disease began.

After Akhenaten

Akhenaten ruled for about 17 years. After he died, things in Egypt quickly went back to the way they had been before. For example, the capital was moved back to the city of Thebes, and the temples of Aten were closed. The new pharaohs, including Tutankhamun (who was thought to be Akhenaten's son) decided it was better to go back to worshiping many gods instead of just one.

Why Akhenaten is Remembered

Even though his ideas didn't last, Akhenaten is one of the most famous pharaohs today because he dared to be different. His attempt to change the Egyptian religion was a big deal. His decision shows us that sometimes, being a leader means making hard decisions that not everyone will like.

Akhenaten's story helps us understand that history isn't just about what works; it's also about experiments and ideas that may not succeed but certainly make a mark. His city, art, and ideas tell us a lot about how one person tried to change the world around him. His story is about shining a light on new ideas, just like the sun's rays shining down on his city of Akhetaten.

Snefru: The Pyramid Builder

Long before the Great Pyramid of Giza stood tall, there was a pharaoh named Snefru. Snefru loved building pyramids so much that he built not one, not two, but three massive pyramids that transformed Egyptian architecture forever. Let's journey back to the time of Snefru, the king who set the stage for all pyramids that came after his.

Who Was Snefru?

Snefru was the first pharaoh of the Fourth Dynasty of Egypt, around 4,600 years ago. He is known as one of

Egypt's most effective and ambitious builders. Unlike other pharaohs who were mostly remembered for their battles, Snefru was famous for his peaceful reign and his passion for giant building projects. In fact, he was so good at building that he is often called the "Pyramid King."

Snefru's Pyramid Adventures

The Meidum Pyramid

Snefru's first pyramid was actually at Meidum, which was originally a step pyramid built by his predecessor. Snefru converted it into a true pyramid by filling in the steps with limestone. However, this pyramid didn't turn out as well as he hoped—over time, it collapsed into a heap of rubble. But from this failure, Snefru learned many lessons about pyramid-building that he would use in his later constructions.

The Bent Pyramid

At Dahshur, you'll find Snefru's first big project called the Bent Pyramid. But, why is this pyramid bent? Well, it's because halfway through building it, the architects realized the angle was too steep, and the whole thing would collapse if they didn't make some quick changes. So, they changed the angle to make the pyramid rise more gently, which gave it a unique bent shape. They were practically learning how to build a pyramid while actually doing it!

The Red Pyramid

Not far from the Bent Pyramid, Snefru built another pyramid. This one was known as the Red Pyramid because of the reddish hue of its stones. This pyramid was the first successful attempt at building a smooth-sided pyramid (which is what most of us think of when we imagine a pyramid). This great success made Snefru very proud, and it set the standard for all future pyramids in Egypt, including the most famous ones at Giza.

Snefru's Legacy

Snefru's pyramids were not just big piles of stones; they were marvels of engineering and symbols of divine kingship. They showed the power and glory of the pharaoh and ensured that Snefru would be remembered for millennia. Each pyramid was an improvement on the last, demonstrating Snefru's growing understanding of architecture and determination to perfect his craft.

Snefru's efforts paved the way for his son, Khufu, who would go on to build the Great Pyramid of Giza, which is one of the Seven Wonders of the Ancient World. Thanks to Snefru's innovations, Khufu had the knowledge and tools he needed to construct a pyramid that would stand as the tallest structure made by humans for thousands of years.

Why Snefru is a Hero

In the storybooks of Egyptian history, Snefru might not battle monsters or lead giant armies into war, but he still teaches us something very important: that failure is just a step on the path to success. Though his first pyramid didn't quite work out, and his second one needed a big change halfway through, Snefru never gave up. He kept improving, and eventually, he achieved his dream of building Egypt's first smooth-sided pyramid.

So, remember Snefru not just for his pyramid building, but also for his problem solving and as a pioneer, who turned his dreams into reality through persistence and ingenuity. His story encourages us all to keep trying, learning, and building, no matter how challenging our goals may seem. Just like Snefru, you too can build something wonderful, one stone at a time!

Khufu: The Builder of the Great Pyramid

Our next ancient Egyptian king, Khufu (known to the Greeks as Cheops), was the second pharaoh of the Fourth Dynasty of ancient Egypt. He ruled over 4,500 years ago and is most famous for constructing the Great Pyramid of Giza. But Khufu was more than just a builder; he was also a powerful leader whose reign brought significant achievements in art and architecture.

The Great Pyramid of Giza

Imagine a structure so massive and that it was the tallest man-made structure in the world for nearly 4,000 years. This was the title that the Great Pyramid of Giza held until the Lincoln Cathedral was built in England in the 14th Century! This pyramid was originally built to be Khufu's tomb, meaning that it would've been a huge monument meant to display his power and ensure his journey to the afterlife. This pyramid is truly a marvel of engineering and architectural planning.

How Was It Built?

The Great Pyramid is made up of millions of limestone blocks, each weighing several tons. How the ancient Egyptians transported and assembled these blocks remains one of history's great mysteries. Some believe they used ramps, while others suggest a series of pulleys might have been involved. Despite modern technology and archaeological advances, the exact methods of construction still puzzle scientists and historians today.

Khufu believed that his great pyramid was not just his final resting place but also a staircase to heaven. This belief highlights the deep spiritual and religious significance of the pyramids, serving as a bridge between the earthly realm and the divine.

The Pyramid's Interior

Inside the Great Pyramid, the corridors and chambers are arranged with precision. The most famous room is the King's Chamber, which lies at the heart of the pyramid. Here, the walls are smooth, and the ceiling is made of large granite slabs. Those who have studied this pyramid believe these slabs relieved the weight from the layers of stone above them.

Visitors who tour the pyramid today will feel a direct connection to Egypt's distant past via the cool, narrow passages that lead to these ancient rooms.

Khufu's Legacy

Although not much is known about Khufu's reign beyond his pyramid, his legacy is monumental. His pyramid not only symbolizes the architectural achievements of ancient Egypt, but also how fascinating Egypt is in the collective imagination of people around the world.

Today, the Great Pyramid of Giza continues to be a symbol of Egypt's grandeur and has inspired countless tales, studies, and even replicas around the globe. It attracts millions of tourists each year, all eager to glimpse the majesty of the past.

Thutmose III: The Warrior Pharaoh

Though many ancient Egyptians are known for building the pyramids, other pharaohs are known for accomplishments in military strategy. Thutmose III was one of these successful pharaohs. He was part of the powerful Eighteenth Dynasty. He took the throne while he was still very young after the death of his stepmother, Hatshepsut, who had been his co-ruler for many years. So, once he became the sole ruler, Thutmose III proved himself as one of the most ambitious and successful military leaders in ancient history.

The Rise of a Warrior

Even as a young prince, Thutmose III showed great promise in military strategy and combat skills. When he took full control of the throne, Thutmose III wasted no time in expanding Egypt's empire. He led numerous military campaigns into lands such as Syria, Nubia, and the Near East, bringing these vast territories under Egyptian control.

One of Thutmose III's most famous military exploits was the Battle of Megiddo. This battle is considered one of the first to be well-documented in history, with detailed accounts recorded on the walls of the Temple of Karnak. Thutmose's army faced a large allied army of rebellious states led by the king of Kadesh. Instead of taking the easy routes to Megiddo, Thutmose chose a narrow pathway, surprising his enemies with his bold and risky move. His strategy was a success, and the victory at Megiddo was a turning point that solidified his reputation as a brilliant military leader.

The Empire Builder

Through his numerous campaigns, Thutmose III greatly expanded the borders of Egypt. He created an empire that stretched from northern Syria to deep into Nubia. His conquests also brought wealth and resources to Egypt, making it the most powerful and prosperous nation in the ancient world at that time. Thutmose III ensured that Egypt had control over crucial trade routes and demanded that his conquered lands supplied Egypt with gifts, which filled Egypt's coffers with gold, ivory, and precious woods.

Thutmose the Administrator

Thutmose III was not only a great warrior; he was also a skilled leader. He made sure that the empire he built was well-managed and organized. He appointed loyal officials to govern the new territories and established supply storerooms to support his army. He also built great temples and monuments to celebrate his victories and honor the gods, particularly Amun, whom he credited with his military success.

The Festival Temple of Thutmose III

Among his architectural achievements, the Festival Temple of Thutmose III at Karnak is especially notable. This temple was unique because it served as both a place of worship and a memorial of Thutmose's reign and military triumphs. The walls of the temple were decorated with inscriptions that detailed his military campaigns and celebrated his victories. This temple served as a historical record for future generations.

His Legacy

Thutmose III ruled Egypt for almost 54 years, during which he transformed the empire into an international superpower. His reign is often seen as a golden age of prosperity and power for ancient Egypt. After his death, he was worshiped as a god by the people he had ruled, a rare honor that only a few pharaohs received.

Thutmose III, the Warrior Pharaoh, was a ruler whose military genius and visionary leadership left a lasting mark on the world. His story teaches us about courage, strategy, and the importance of strong leadership. As we close this chapter on Thutmose III, remember that his battles and triumphs are not just ancient stories, but lessons on how determination and wisdom can lead to greatness.

Xerxes I: The Persian Pharaoh

Now we'll travel beyond the familiar borders of ancient Egypt to meet a ruler from a land far away—Xerxes I, also known as Xerxes the Great. He was not just any ruler; he was the "Achaemenid king" of Persia who also became known as a pharaoh of Egypt during the 27th Dynasty. Let's dive into the story of this intriguing figure!

Xerxes I ruled from 486 BC to 465 BC and was one of the most famous kings of the Achaemenid Empire. This empire was based in Persia, which is now modern-day Iran. His empire was huge, stretching from India to the edges of Greece. This included Egypt, which had been conquered by the Persians in 525 BC under his predecessor, Cambyses II.

Xerxes as Pharaoh

When Xerxes I took the throne, he inherited not just the Persian Empire but also its territories, including Egypt. As ruler of Egypt, he was recognized as a pharaoh, but his reign was markedly different from those of native Egyptian kings. Xerxes was seen by many Egyptians as an outsider, and his rule was characterized by a lack of respect for local Egyptian traditions.

A Tyrant in the Eyes of Many

Xerxes I's approach to governance caused the Egyptian people to dislike him. He was often described as a tyrant because he imposed Persian customs and ignored Egyptian religious and cultural practices. This disregard for local tradition made him unpopular, and many Egyptians longed for the return of a native ruler. The Greeks also did not like him. They thought he was a harsh ruler, especially because of his attempts to invade Greece.

The Invasion of Greece

One of Xerxes I's most ambitious military campaigns was when he attempted to conquer Greece. He mobilized a massive army and navy, and in 480 BC, he personally led these forces into Greece. There were many famous battles, such as those at Thermopylae and Salamis. Although initially successful, his campaign ultimately failed, and this defeat marked a turning point in his reign. It also cemented his reputation among the Greeks as a classic "bad guy" in their stories of heroism and resistance.

Despite his negative reputation, Xerxes I's rule had significant impacts on the regions he governed. In Egypt, his reign incorporated the Egyptian territory into the Persian

Empire's administrative and economic systems. This period highlighted the complexities of empire-building and the challenges of managing diverse cultures within a single government.

Xerxes's Legacy

Xerxes's legacy is complicated. In Persia, he was remembered as a mighty king who tried to expand the boundaries of his empire, even if not always successfully. In Egypt, his legacy is more controversial because he didn't care about local customs and governance. His attempts to impose Persian authority on Egypt without embracing its rich cultural traditions left a lasting stain on the historical memory of his rule.

Xerxes I, the Persian Pharaoh, teaches us about the challenges and intricacies of ruling over a diverse empire. His story helps us understand that respect for local traditions and cultures is crucial in maintaining harmony within a society.

Chapter Conclusion

As we draw the curtain over the tales of these mighty pharaohs, we find ourselves immersed in the timeless beauty of ancient Egypt—a world where gods and mortals danced in the flickering light of eternity, and the echoes of greatness echoed through the ages.

From the golden treasures of Tutankhamun's tomb to the towering monuments of Ramses the Great, each pharaoh left their mark in the sands of time. But beyond the gold and granite lies a deeper truth—a testament to the resilience, intelligence, and boundless ambition of the human spirit. The pharaohs, with their towering monuments and divine authority, remind us of how humans share an enduring quest for immortality that transcends the boundaries of time.

As we bid farewell to the pharaohs and their timeless legacy, let us carry their stories in our hearts, like precious jewels gleaming in the darkness of the night. For in the heart of the desert, amidst the whispers of the gods, the spirit of the pharaohs lives on.

CHAPTER 2:
QUEENS OF THE NILE

After taking a peek into the fascinating lives of the pharaohs, in this chapter, we will delve into the lives of the influential queens whose legacies burn brightly in Egyptian history. From the iconic beauty of Nefertiti to the mysterious reign of Queen Merneith, each queen's story offers a glimpse into the rich tapestry of Egyptian civilization. Their tales reveal the complexities of leadership, the pursuit of justice, and the enduring legacy of female empowerment in the ancient world.

Join us as we journey through the corridors of history to uncover the triumphs and challenges faced by these remarkable women who reigned as queens of the Nile. Prepare to be captivated by the tales of these extraordinary women who dared to defy convention and add their names into the sands of time.

Nefertiti: The Beautiful One Has Come

Long ago, in the sunny land of Egypt, there lived a queen so beautiful and wise that her story has been told for over 3,000 years. Her name was Nefertiti, which means "The Beautiful One Has Come," but she was also as clever as she was pretty. Let's dive into her powerful story!

Who Was Nefertiti?

Nefertiti was the wife of Pharaoh Akhenaten (remember this pharaoh who was obsessed with the sun god?), and together they ruled Egypt during a time of big changes. She is famous not just for her stunning beauty but also for her powerful role in Egypt's cultural and religious revolution. Nefertiti wasn't born a royal, but she became one of the most influential queens Egypt ever saw.

A Queen and Her King

Nefertiti and her husband, Akhenaten, did something extraordinary when they became the rulers of Egypt. As previously mentioned, they decided that instead of worshiping many gods, as people in Egypt had done for centuries, they would worship only one god, Aten, the sun disk. This was a huge change! Akhenaten and Nefertiti moved the capital to a new city called Akhetaten (now known as Amarna), dedicated to their new god.

Nefertiti didn't just sit around looking pretty; she shared power with Akhenaten. She took on roles that were usually reserved for kings. In artwork created in that time, Nefertiti is often shown driving a chariot or cutting down Egypt's enemies. This proved that Nefertiti was more than just a wife; she was a co-ruler.

The Famous Bust of Nefertiti

One of the reasons we remember Nefertiti so well is because of a stunning piece of art. During a German archaeologist's dig in 1912, a beautifully painted bust (a type of sculpture that displays the head and face of an important person) of Nefertiti was found. This bust, now in Berlin, shows her with a long, graceful neck, a perfectly symmetrical face, and a colorful crown. It's so lifelike that it almost seems like she could start talking at any moment!

Nefertiti's Mysterious End

Towards the end of Akhenaten's reign, Nefertiti disappears from historical records. So, what happened to her remains a mystery. Some believe she might have died, while others think she may have ruled Egypt on her own as the Pharaoh Neferneferuaten after her husband's death. This mystery makes her story even more fascinating.

Why Nefertiti is Important

Nefertiti is an icon of beauty and power. She shows us that ancient queens were not just royal wives but could also be influential leaders and reformers that ruled empires and made history. Her life tells a story of courage, change, and mystery that captures the imagination of people all around the world, even today.

The story of Nefertiti also teaches us about the importance of art, leadership, and innovation. She and her husband tried to change Egyptian society in ways that were far ahead of their time. Though not all these changes lasted, their attempt shows us that it's okay to think differently and try new things, even if they don't turn out as expected.

So, as you flip through the pages of history, remember Nefertiti, the beautiful queen who left a lasting mark. Her story isn't just about ancient Egypt; it's about the timeless beauty and strength that lives in all of us, waiting to be discovered.

Queen Merneith: The Mysterious Ruler of the Nile

Meet one of the most puzzling figures of ancient Egypt—Queen Merneith. Her story takes us all the way back to Egypt's First Dynasty, around 2920 BCE. Let's uncover the secrets of this possibly first female ruler of Egypt, whose life is shrouded in mystery.

Queen Merneith may have been one of the earliest women to rule ancient Egypt, but much about her life remains a puzzle. Unlike famous pharaohs whose stories fill the pages of history books, Merneith's tale is pieced together from small clues left behind over millennia. She lived so long ago that only a few records of her name survive, mainly on some artifacts and a tomb that might be hers.

A Queen or a Regent?

Historians are not entirely sure if Queen Merneith was a pharaoh or a regent, which means she might have ruled on behalf of her young son, Den, who was too young to govern. This situation wasn't uncommon in ancient times—often, when a king died and his heir was too young, a trusted family member, usually the mother, would rule until the child was old enough.

Her Powerful Role

What we know about Merneith suggests that she was a woman of significant power and status. She is listed among the kings of the First Dynasty in a document from much later times, which hints that she was not just a caretaker but a ruler. Her burial site also supports this idea. Merneith was buried in a large and richly furnished tomb at Abydos, one of ancient Egypt's most sacred burial grounds. Her tomb was surrounded by those of other pharaohs, a place of honor that suggests she was much more than just a royal family member.

Queen Merneith's tomb is especially remarkable because it shows how respected she was. Archaeologists found that she was buried alongside 50 servants, who were laid to rest with her to serve her in the afterlife. This was a royal privilege, underscoring her high rank and the respect she commanded within the kingdom.

Because there are so few records, much about Queen Merneith's reign is left to our imagination. Did she lead battles? Did she oversee the construction of monuments? Did she make laws? These are questions that might never be answered. However, the fact that she was buried among kings tells us that her people valued her leadership and likely saw her as a capable and strong ruler.

Why Her Story Matters

Queen Merneith's story is important because it shows us that women in ancient Egypt could rise to the highest levels of power. Her legacy helps us understand the role of women in ancient Egyptian society, where people could respect and honor a woman as a leader. Her story also excites historians and archaeologists who continue to search for clues about her life and reign.

So, dear friends, as we close this chapter on Queen Merneith, remember that history is often like a puzzle. With every small piece we find, we get a clearer picture of the past. Queen Merneith reminds us that even those from long ago, whose names are barely remembered, can still have stories worth telling.

Hatshepsut: The Queen Who Became King

Unlike Merneith, other ancient Egyptian women are more understood via artifacts and other records. Hatshepsut was one of these women. She was a princess that was born into a family of pharaohs. Her father was Thutmose I, so she grew up surrounded by the riches and power of the Egyptian court. But Hatshepsut was no ordinary princess; she had great ambition and intelligence that set her apart from others.

After her father's death, Hatshepsut didn't follow the typical path expected for women at the time. Instead, she became Egypt's queen by marrying her half-brother Thutmose II (this was a custom for royals). But when he died young,

Hatshepsut did something extraordinary—she declared herself pharaoh instead of a queen. She even began to dress like a king and wear a false beard, symbols of pharaonic power. This was nearly unheard of in the male-dominated world of ancient Egyptian royalty!

Her Reign as Pharaoh

As pharaoh, Hatshepsut was not just playing dress-up; she was a powerful and effective leader. She ruled for about 22 years and brought great prosperity to Egypt. Her reign was a time of peace and economic flourishing. She increased trade with distant lands and built magnificent temples that still stand today as a testament to her reign.

The Expedition to Punt

One of Hatshepsut's most famous achievements was her trading expedition to the mysterious land of Punt, which is thought to have been near the Red Sea or along the coasts of East Africa. This expedition brought back loads of treasures, such as gold, exotic spices, and ivory. Live myrrh trees were also brought back and planted in the temple gardens. The success of this voyage was celebrated in carvings and paintings on her temple walls, which still amaze people today.

Building Projects

Hatshepsut was also known for her ambitious building projects. She constructed a stunning temple at Deir el-Bahri, near the Valley of the Kings. This temple, with its elegant terraces and pillars, is considered one of the architectural wonders of ancient Egypt. Its walls tell the story of her divine birth and successful reign.

Her Legacy

Hatshepsut's success as a pharaoh was so profound that after her death, attempts were made to erase her from history. Her successor, Thutmose III, might have felt overshadowed by her achievements and ordered her images and name to be removed from temples and monuments. But despite these efforts, Hatshepsut's legacy endured. Modern archaeologists and historians have pieced together her story, and she is now recognized as one of Egypt's most successful and intriguing rulers.

Hatshepsut's story teaches us about the courage to defy expectations. She shows us that leadership and wisdom are not bound by gender. Hatshepsut took on the role of pharaoh not just to wield power, but to serve her people and guide her country to prosperity. Her story is a powerful reminder that with determination and intelligence, anyone can achieve greatness, no matter the obstacles. Hatshepsut not only carved her monuments into the stone of Egypt but also her legacy into the history of its great rulers.

Sobekneferu: The First Confirmed Female Pharaoh

Hatshepsut was not the only woman from ancient Egypt who was remarkable. Our next character's name was Sobekneferu, who became the first confirmed female pharaoh of Egypt. Her story is not just about ruling a kingdom but also about breaking down barriers and setting a precedent for future generations.

Sobekneferu, whose name means "the beauty of Sobek," was the daughter of Pharaoh Amenemhat III, who was one of the great rulers of the Twelfth Dynasty. After the death of her brother, there were no other male heirs to take the throne, so Sobekneferu stepped forward to lead Egypt. She thus became Egypt's first known female pharaoh.

Becoming Pharaoh

Imagine a time when most rulers were men, but along came Sobekneferu, a princess with the courage to become a queen and then a pharaoh. When she took the throne, she faced the enormous task of leading one of the most powerful and sophisticated civilizations in the world. Sobekneferu not only took on this role but also embraced it fully, using both traditional and innovative ways to show that she was a capable ruler.

Though Sobekneferu ruled Egypt for almost four years, which was a relatively short time, her impact was significant. She continued the building projects started by her father, showing her skills in maintaining the prosperity and stability of the kingdom. Her reign demonstrated her ability to govern a nation, manage extensive architectural projects, and uphold religious traditions, which were critical aspects of being a pharaoh.

Symbols of Power

To assert her authority, Sobekneferu used many of the same symbols and titles as male pharaohs. She wore the traditional false beard, which was a symbol of pharaonic power. Her statues were also made to show her both in female and traditional male pharaoh attire. This blending of gender symbols in representations of Sobekneferu showed her subjects that she possessed all the qualities needed to rule Egypt, regardless of her gender.

The Legacy of Sobekneferu

Although Sobekneferu's reign was brief, she opened the door for other women to rule Egypt. The most famous of these was Cleopatra, who would rule about 1,400 years later. Sobekneferu proved that a woman could take on the role of pharaoh and lead with strength and wisdom. Her legacy exists not only in what she built with stone, but also in the ideas she cemented about leadership.

Sobekneferu shows us that history is full of pioneers, or people who dare to do things differently and challenge the norms of their times. Her story is a lesson in bravery and the ability to lead in the face of uncertainty. It teaches us that leadership is not about gender but about the courage to stand up and take responsibility when it is needed most.

Sobekneferu's Influence on History

Today, when we talk about Sobekneferu, we remember her not only as a pharaoh but as a trailblazer who helped to redefine possibilities for women in power. She is an inspiration to all of us, showing that you can be a leader by being yourself and embracing the roles you choose to take on.

So, as we turn the pages of history books and uncover the stories of great leaders, let us remember Sobekneferu, the first confirmed female pharaoh of Egypt. Her reign may have been short, but her impact on history was monumental. She teaches us that sometimes, it's not the length of time we have but what we do with it that truly counts.

Queen Nitocris: The Legendary Ruler of the Nile

Let's move from the iconic Sobekneferu to the puzzling and enigmatic Queen Nitocris.. While some scholars debate her very existence, arguing she may have been a mythical or symbolic figure, other ancient texts mention that she was a real ruler. She is often remembered as a fair and wise leader who ascended to the throne under dramatic circumstances—following the untimely death of her brother, the last pharaoh of their dynasty.

Her Rule and Reign

Legend has it that Nitocris was more than just a ruler; she was also a reformer who brought prosperity back to a faltering Egypt. Her reign was marked by a series of bold initiatives intended to restore the stability and richness of her kingdom. It's said that she ruled with both wisdom and benevolence, implementing policies that improved the lives of her people and ensured the kingdom's prosperity.

Architectural Achievements

Queen Nitocris is credited with several ambitious architectural projects that showcased her foresight and brilliance in engineering. Among these were the construction of dams and canals that helped control the flooding of the Nile. These projects were crucial for improving irrigation (making water accessible for crops) and agriculture, which were the backbone of Egypt's economy. Additionally, she strengthened Egypt's defenses, preparing the kingdom against potential invasions.

A Reputation for Justice

One of the most enduring aspects of Nitocris's legacy is her commitment to justice. She is said to have been a fair and strict ruler, creating laws that ensured order and fairness within her kingdom. Her wisdom and fairness earned her the respect and admiration of her subjects.

Her Mysterious Legacy

Despite the tales of her great deeds, concrete historical evidence of Nitocris's reign has not been discovered. This lack of definitive records has fueled ongoing debates among historians and archaeologists (people who study humans and societies) about whether she existed. Some suggest that Nitocris may have represented a combination of the qualities and achievements of several lesser-known female rulers of her time.

Regardless of the debates surrounding her existence, the story of Queen Nitocris has left a lasting mark on Egyptian folklore and the narrative of ancient civilizations. She is a symbol of female empowerment and leadership, inspiring tales and scholarly discussions that span centuries. Like Sobekneferu and Hatshepsut, Queen Nitocris's legend proves that women in ancient governments could have an impact in societies traditionally dominated by men.

Queen Nitocris's legendary wisdom and just rule remains a fascinating subject in the study of ancient Egypt. Whether she walked the earth as a pharaoh or sprang from the imagination of later generations, her story encourages us to think about the roles women played in ancient history and the legends we still remember.

Tiy: The Powerful Matriarch

Though Queen Nitocris may have been a real queen or just the combination of many less influential but equally important female rulers, our next character, Tiy, was a real and powerful matriarch whose wisdom and influence shaped the future of Egypt. Let's dive into the incredible life of Queen Tiy and learn how she became one of the most influential figures in Egyptian history.

Queen Tiy was the wife of Pharaoh Amenhotep III and the mother of Akhenaten (who worshiped only the sun god), one of Egypt's most controversial pharaohs. She was not from a royal background, which makes her rise to prominence even more remarkable. Tiy was not only a queen but a true partner to her husband, involved deeply in the political and cultural life of Egypt.

A Queen with Many Roles

Unlike many other queens of her time, Tiy was depicted almost as an equal to her husband in statues and paintings, which was quite rare in ancient Egypt. This proves that she was both respected and powerful. She wore crowns and headdresses that usually only pharaohs could use and was often shown participating in ceremonies and important state functions.

Queen Tiy was known for her sharp mind and political skills. She played a significant role in maintaining relationships with other powerful kingdoms. Letters between Queen Tiy and foreign dignitaries have been found, meaning she was actively involved in Egypt's foreign affairs. This would have normally been a task reserved for the pharaoh himself.

Mother of a Revolutionary

As the mother of Akhenaten, Queen Tiy had a significant influence on her son, who would go on to challenge Egypt's traditional religious beliefs through his worship of one god over many. Her guidance and support were crucial as her son navigated these radical ideas, which also reshaped Egyptian religion and art.

Queen Tiy was so loved and respected that her husband, Amenhotep III, built several temples and statues in her honor. This was quite unusual for a queen at the time. One of the most famous statues of Queen Tiy, which can be seen in museums today, shows her with a serene yet strong face, wearing a tight-fitting gown and a heavy wig decorated with a floral diadem (a special headband that showed the importance of the person wearing it).

Legacy in Art and Culture

Tiy's legacy is also found in the art of her time. Both her and her family's influence caused a shift in Egyptian art towards realism. The artistic styles developed during her time set the stage for what would come during her son's reign. Her impact on Egyptian art and culture was profound, setting trends that would continue for generations.

Queen Tiy's story teaches us about the power of influence and intelligence. As a matriarch, she shows that leadership comes in many forms—for example, in guiding a family, advising a ruler, or managing a kingdom's most important relationships. Her life reminds us that behind every great leader are advisors and family members who play crucial roles in their decisions and lives.

Tiy's Influence on History

Tiy was a queen who stood out not because she sought power, but because she wielded her influence with wisdom and kindness. She supported her husband and son, managed her family's legacy, and contributed to the prosperity of her nation. Her story is a testament to the important roles women have played throughout history as leaders and pioneers.

So, as we look back at the tales of ancient Egypt, let's remember Queen Tiy. Do not remember her as just a queen, but as a matriarch who used her position to guide her family through times of transformation. She shows us that being a leader isn't just about having power; it's about how you help others and make a lasting impact.

Cleopatra: The Last Queen and Her Roman Ties

Long ago, in the ancient land of Egypt, there lived a queen with a story so fascinating that people still talk about her today. Her name was Cleopatra VII, the last queen of Egypt. Cleopatra was not just a ruler; she was also a scholar, a diplomat, and a savvy political strategist. Her life was full of drama, romance, and intrigue, especially when related to the mighty Roman Empire.

Who Was Cleopatra?

Cleopatra was born into the Ptolemaic dynasty, a family that came from Greece but ruled Egypt for many centuries. She became queen at the young age of 18. Right from the start, it was clear that Cleopatra had big plans for her kingdom. Unlike other rulers of her time, she was also known for being incredibly smart; she spoke many languages and was educated in mathematics, philosophy, and astronomy.

Cleopatra's Roman Connections

Cleopatra's reign was marked by her close ties with Rome, the superpower of her time. She knew that keeping a good relationship with Rome was key to keeping her throne. This led to famous alliances between Egypt and some of the most powerful Roman leaders.

Julius Caesar

The first of these famous Roman leaders was Julius Caesar, a mighty Roman general. Cleopatra met him when she was in a bit of a pickle because she was fighting her brother for control of Egypt. Cleopatra had herself wrapped in a rug (though say it was a sack) and smuggled into Caesar's presence to ask for his help. Caesar was charmed by the young queen's bravery and intelligence, so he helped her regain her throne. Thus, during Caesar's stay in Egypt, they became allies and even had a son together named Caesarion.

Mark Antony

After Caesar was tragically killed, Cleopatra found another Roman ally in Mark Antony, a dashing Roman leader. Theirs is one of the greatest love stories ever told. Antony and Cleopatra fell deeply in love, causing Antony to spend a winter in Egypt. This period was known as the Winter of Discontent due to the great political tensions in Rome caused by their union. Still, they had three children together and dreamed of creating a new empire that would combine the powers of Rome and Egypt.

However, not everyone in Rome liked the idea of a Roman leader teaming up with an Egyptian queen. Antony's rival, Octavian (who would later become Emperor Augustus), used their relationship to stir up trouble in Rome. This rivalry led to a great naval battle at Actium, where Cleopatra and Antony were defeated.

The End of an Era

After their defeat, Antony and Cleopatra returned to Egypt. Knowing that they could not win against Octavian, they both chose to end their own lives. Antony fell on his sword, and Cleopatra, ever the queen, was bitten by a venomous snake.

Why Cleopatra is Remembered

Cleopatra was the last pharaoh of Egypt. Her death marked the end of Egyptian rule and the beginning of Roman control over Egypt. But, Cleopatra's legacy isn't just about how she died; it's also about how she lived. She was a ruler who used her intelligence, charm, and political savvy to try to restore Egypt to greatness.

Cleopatra's story shows us that history is not just about battles and territories, but also about the power of personality and the impact one person can have on the world around them. We can learn about the importance of courage and determination from Cleopatra's story. Her life as a leader, mother, and scholar continues to inspire people around the world today.

Chapter Conclusion

These remarkable Egyptian queens ruled over the sun-drenched land of ancient Egypt, amidst the grandeur of pyramids and the mystique of the Nile, with dignity, strength, and wisdom. As we draw the curtains on this captivating chapter, we reflect on the profound impact these remarkable women had on history and their legacy.

From the splendor of Nefertiti's court to the intrigue of Cleopatra's alliances, each queen's story offers a window into an ancient kingdom, where power and influence were wielded both gracefully and cunningly. Their reigns were marked by innovation, diplomacy, and the pursuit of greatness.

But beyond the glitz and glamor of the royal court, the queens of the Nile also embodied timeless virtues that transcend centuries. They exemplified courage, wisdom in times of uncertainty, and compassion for their people's welfare. Theirs were tales of resilience, determination, and unwavering resolve, inspiring generations to come.

As we bid farewell to these magnificent queens, let us carry their legacy forward by honoring their memory and embracing the timeless ideals they embodied. May their stories serve as inspiration for all who dare to dream. Let these rulers also remind us that the spirit of queenship lives on in the hearts of all those who dare to lead with the same grace and dignity.

CHAPTER 3:
THE MYSTERIOUS MUMMIES

Before we dive into the fascinating world of mummification, let's take a moment to imagine how ancient Egyptians would have felt and what they believed—Egypt was a place where everyday things were filled with special meaning, and where people believed in magic and mystery. So, in this ancient land, when someone passed away, it wasn't the end of their story but the start of a new adventure.

Picture yourself by the great Nile River, surrounded by towering pyramids and golden temples. Here, the ancient Egyptians had a unique way of preparing their loved ones for the afterlife. They didn't just bury them in the ground; they turned them into mummies—bodies that stayed preserved for thousands of years.

Mummies were preserved so they wouldn't rot or decompose like a normal body would. To follow this method of preservation, the Egyptians used special salts and wrapped the body in linen.

Why Did Egyptians Make Mummies?

You might be thinking, "Why would anyone want to keep old bodies around?" Well, for the ancient Egyptians, making someone into a mummy was very important because they believed in life after death. They believed that when you die, your spirit goes on a journey to another world, where it can live forever in happiness. But there's a catch! To reach this wonderful afterlife, the spirit needed its body. That's why they preserved the bodies, so the spirit could recognize and use it in the next world.

The Mummification Process: A Step-by-Step Adventure

Imagine you are an ancient Egyptian embalmer, a special kind of "magician" who turns people into mummies. Here's what you would do:

- **The Purification**: First, you would clean the body with a palm wine (which smells great) and rinse it with Nile water. It's similar to preparing the body for a royal bath!

- **Removing the Insides:** Next, you would carefully take out the stomach, intestines, lungs, and liver. Don't worry; they didn't throw these away! They preserved these in special jars called "canopic jars," and each one was protected by a god.

- **Taking Care of the Heart:** The heart was believed to be a human's center of thought and emotion, so that was left inside the body. Egyptians thought it would be needed in the afterlife to help when the gods judged the deceased.

- **Drying Out the Body:** After removing the other organs (and leaving the heart alone), you would use a special salt called "natron" and pack it around the body. This salt dried out the body completely, which took about 40 days. This step stopped the body from rotting.

- **Wrapping Up:** After the body was fully dried, you would wrap it in hundreds of yards of linen strips, almost like bandages. Sometimes, embalmers placed amulets or small magical charms between the layers for protection on the journey to the afterlife.
- **The Final Touches:** Finally, you would place the mummy in a decorated coffin. This meant the mummy was ready to be taken to its tomb, which served as a safe house for the mummy where it could rest peacefully and the person's spirit could enjoy the afterlife.

So Why All The Effort?

Egyptians went through all this trouble because they believed that mummification was a way to keep the person alive in the world of the gods. Becoming a mummy was their ticket to eternity, ensuring that person would continue to exist and enjoy the pleasures of life after death. Every step in the process of mummification was filled with care, respect, and lots of magic spells to protect the deceased on their journey to the afterlife.

From Mummies to Mysteries: Exploring Egyptian Tombs

Now that we understand how and why the ancient Egyptians preserved their dead, let's take the next step to experience the incredible structures built to house these mummies—their tombs. Grab your explorer hats and flashlights, because we're about to go on a thrilling journey.

Imagine being an archaeologist, which you could compare to being a type of treasure hunter. You must dig through the sands of time to discover secrets hidden for thousands of years. What treasures and tales lie within these sacred spaces? Let's see what these tomb explorers have found inside!

What is a Tomb?

First, let's talk about what a tomb really is. In ancient Egypt, a tomb was not just a grave (or a place to bury bodies); it was a house for the afterlife. The Egyptians believed that when you died, you went on to live in another world where you would need all the things you had and enjoyed while you were alive. So, they built tombs to be safe places where they could keep the person's treasures, favorite snacks, and even their beds!

The Discovery of Tombs

Archaeologists are not only treasure hunters, because they also act like detectives. They use clues from old writings and the landscape to find where the tombs are hidden. Most of these tombs are found in special places called "necropolises," which are like cities for the dead. These cities are often located in the desert, where the dry sand helps keep everything inside the tombs safe and sound for thousands of years.

Inside the Tombs

When archaeologists first enter a tomb, they find passages that lead to different rooms, just like in a house. These rooms are filled with amazing things:

- **Mummies**: Of course, the most important thing in a tomb is the mummy lying in its coffin, which is often decorated with gold and colorful pictures that tell stories about the person's life.
- **Treasures**: Tombs can be treasure chests filled with gold, jewelry, and precious stones. These were not just to show off, but to help the person in the afterlife. Egyptians believed gold was the skin of the gods!
- **Wall Paintings and Carvings**: The walls of tombs are covered with paintings and carvings as well. These are not just decorations, as they tell stories of the person's life. These images show the person

hunting, fishing, and partying with their family. They also include spells from the Book of the Dead to help them in the afterlife.

- **Daily Life Items:** Imagine finding toys, clothes, furniture, and even makeup in a tomb. Egyptians included these small belongings so the person in the tomb could use them forever.
- **Food and Drink**: Egyptians also included pots of beer, wine, bread, and meat in tombs. Why? Because even after death, Egyptians wanted to feast!

Famous Tomb Discoveries

Remember King Tut? His tomb was one of the most famous discoveries of archaeologists. His tomb was found almost untouched in 1922 by the archaeologist Howard Carter. Inside, there were over 5,000 items, including a golden throne, a chariot, and even King Tut's sandals! His coffin was made of solid gold, and his mask is one of the most famous treasures in the world.

The Mystery and Magic of Tombs

Every time a tomb is discovered, it's like opening a time capsule. These tombs help us understand how the ancient Egyptians lived, what they believed, and how they saw the world. These Discoveries are not just about finding gold or mummies; they're also about uncovering stories from the past.

Why Are These Discoveries Important?

Finding these tombs teaches us more than just history; it shows us the creativity and beliefs of ancient people. It helps us see that even though cultures are different, we all share similar dreams and hopes. It connects us to the past and teaches us to respect other ways of life. Each tomb is like a puzzle box waiting to be solved, full of history, treasures, and tales of old. There are still many tombs hidden under the sands, waiting for the next generation of archaeologists—maybe even you—to uncover their secrets.

As we continue our exploration, we now turn to a fundamental question that has guided much of ancient Egyptian spiritual and practical life; what did the Egyptians believe about the life that awaited them after death?

The Afterlife

Having uncovered the treasures and secrets within ancient Egyptian tombs, let's delve deeper into one of Egypt's most fascinating beliefs; the afterlife. The reason that Egyptians made mummies in the first place ties back to their hopes and dreams for life after death. Join us as we unravel this ancient mystery and learn about the spiritual beliefs that shaped an entire civilization!

What is the Afterlife?

Imagine a place where you could do all your favorite things forever. No school, no chores—just fun, games, and feasts! The ancient Egyptians believed that such a place existed. They thought that after they died, they would go on to live in this wonderful world as long as they did.

Why Make a Mummy?

To the Egyptians, the body was a home for the soul. So, if the body was damaged or disappeared, the soul might get lost and therefore never reach the afterlife. That would be a disaster! So, they developed mummification to keep the body safe and intact. Making a mummy was like packing a suitcase for a long trip, ensuring you had everything you needed to travel to the afterlife.

The Journey to the Afterlife

The Egyptians believed that the journey to the afterlife was full of challenges and adventures. To help the deceased on their way, they included spells and magical items with the mummy. As previously mentioned, one famous collection of spells is known as the "Book of the Dead." These spells were like a map that helped the soul navigate the tricky parts of their journey.

The Fields of Reeds

So how did the Egyptians imagine the afterlife? They pictured it as a lush and beautiful place called the Fields of Reeds. They thought it looked a bit like the best parts of Egypt—full of green fields, flowing rivers, and lots of food. In this heavenly place, people would do the things they loved, like fishing, farming, and feasting, all day long.

Judgement Day

But, getting into the Fields of Reeds wasn't easy. The Egyptians believed that you had to pass a test called the "Weighing of the Heart." On this day, the god of the dead, Osiris, and some other gods would judge the deceased. Together they would weigh the person's heart on a giant scale against a feather, which represented truth and justice. If your heart was as light as the feather, it meant that you had lived a good life and could enter the afterlife. But if your heart was heavy with bad deeds, a terrifying creature called Ammit would gobble it up, and you would vanish forever!

Preparing for Eternity

Because the afterlife was so important, Egyptians spent a lot of time and effort preparing for it. They filled their tombs with food, tools, and even statues called "shabtis" that could come to life and work for them in the afterlife. The richer and more powerful you were, the bigger and more elaborate your tomb would be. So, naturally the pharaohs' tombs were massive pyramids.

What an amazing belief system, right? As we close this chapter, think about the incredible lengths the Egyptians went to in order to secure their eternal happiness.

But our journey through the mysteries of ancient Egypt is far from over. There are still countless secrets waiting to be unearthed, stories waiting to be told. So, as we conclude this chapter, let's keep our explorer spirit alive and ready for the adventures that lie ahead. Who knows what wonders we'll discover next in the timeless sands of Egypt's past?

CHAPTER 4:
GODS AND GODDESSES

Welcome to a new chapter of our journey through ancient Egypt! In this chapter, we'll dive into the exciting world of Egyptian gods and goddesses. These divine beings were super important to the ancient Egyptians. They were like important celebrities, but with special powers!

Imagine a world where gods and goddesses ruled the sky, the earth, and everything in between. That's ancient Egypt! The Egyptians believed in many gods and goddesses, each with their own jobs and superpowers. These gods were like big stars in the sky, and people looked up to them for help and protection.

Religion was a big deal in ancient Egypt. For them, it was more than going to temples and saying prayers; in fact, it was a way of life. The Egyptians believed in balance, and felt it was the gods who made sure the sun rose every day and the crops grew well. They thought that if they pleased the gods, everything would go smoothly.

Each god and goddess had a special job to do. For example, Ra was the sun god, so he made sure the world had light and warmth every day. Osiris looked after the dead, guiding them to the afterlife. And Hathor brought joy and happiness to everyone she met. These gods and goddesses were like superheroes, each with their own powers and responsibilities.

As we learn about the gods and goddesses of ancient Egypt, we're not just exploring stories from the past; we're discovering important lessons about kindness, bravery, and the wonders of the world. So get ready to journey back in time and uncover the secrets of Egypt's magical pantheon!

Ra: The Sun God

Ra is one of the most important and powerful gods in ancient Egyptian mythology. Because he is the god of the sun, his job was a big deal because the sun is very important—it provides light, warmth, and life to the whole world. The Egyptians believed that every morning, Ra's golden sun chariot rose in the east, traveled across the sky, and set in the west. Egyptians believed that Ra's journey brought daylight to the world and that he defeated darkness every day.

The Look of a Sun God

Imagine a god with the head of a falcon and a sun disk resting on his head. That's Ra! This sun disk was a powerful symbol glowing with fiery light, and showed that Ra was the king of all gods. His falcon head, sharp and majestic, helped him watch over the world from high above, making sure everything was in order.

Ra's Daily Journey

Each day was an epic adventure for Ra. His job was to drive the sun across the sky in his magical chariot. But it wasn't a peaceful trip; Ra had to fight off the monster of chaos,

Apophis, who was a giant snake that tried to swallow the sun every night. This battle happened in the underworld, the mysterious realm below the earth, during the night. By winning this fight every night, Ra made sure that the sun would rise again the next day, bringing light and life back to the world.

Ra and the Creation of the World

Ra was not just the god of the sun; he was also a creator of the world (according to one ancient story)!! It all started when Ra spoke the names of things, and poof! They came into being. He named the mountains, the seas, the plants, animals, and even humans. This story shows just how powerful words and names were to the ancient Egyptians.

Ra's Family

Ra was at the center of a big family of gods and goddesses. He was thought to be the father of many gods, but his most famous children are Shu, the god of air, and Tefnut, the goddess of moisture. These two gods represented how essential air and water are for life, also demonstrating that Ra's power extended to all parts of creation.

The Temples and Worship of Ra

The Egyptians built great temples to honor Ra, and people worshiped him through music, singing, and celebrations. The priests at these temples performed daily rituals to help keep Ra strong in his battle against chaos. They offered him beautiful prayers, sang hymns, and presented offerings of food and treasures. They believed these rituals were very important to keep the universe in balance and ensure that Ra continued his journey across the sky each day.

The Legend of Ra's Secret Name

One of the most fascinating tales about Ra is about his secret name. It was believed that Ra had a hidden name that held all his power. If anyone ever learned this secret name, they would have control over Ra and his powers. Legend has it that the clever goddess, Isis, wanted to know this secret name. Through a clever trick, she managed to learn it from Ra, gaining immense wisdom and power.

Why Ra Matters

Ra was more than just a sun god to the Egyptians; he was a symbol of life, order, and power. By understanding Ra, we get a glimpse into how the ancient Egyptians saw the world. They saw the universe as a beautiful, ordered place where every day was a victory of light over darkness, and life over chaos.

Anubis: Guardian of the Underworld

Now let's imagine another god with the body of a man and the head of a sleek, black jackal (an animal related to dogs). That's Anubis! In ancient Egyptian mythology, Anubis is known as the God of Mummification and the Afterlife.

The Role of Anubis

Anubis had a very important job. He was the protector of the dead, making sure they were safe on their journey to the afterlife. But his duties didn't stop there. Anubis was also in charge of mummification—the special process of preserving bodies to make mummies as we talked about in the previous chapter. Imagine him as a divine embalmer, ensuring that the mummies were ready for their eternal life.

The Ceremony of Mummification

Anubis was the master of ceremonies when it came to mummification. He watched over the embalmers' work, guiding their hands as they prepared the body. Once the body was wrapped up as a mummy, Anubis performed the "Opening of the Mouth" ceremony. This ritual was believed to bring the mummy back to life so it could eat, drink, and speak in the afterlife.

Anubis and the Weighing of the Heart

One of the most thrilling moments in the journey to the afterlife was the Weighing of the Heart ceremony, and Anubis played a starring role. In the great Hall of Maat, Anubis would place the heart of the deceased on the giant scale that was only balanced with a feather.

If the heart was lighter than the feather, it meant the person had led a good life and could go on to the paradise of the afterlife. But if the heart was heavier, it was eaten by Ammit and their soul would disappear forever.

Why a Jackal Head?

You might be wondering, why did Anubis have a jackal head? Well, jackals were common in the deserts around Egypt, often seen lurking around cemeteries at night. The Egyptians thought that Anubis, in the form of a jackal, was protecting the dead. So, Anubis's jackal head is a sign of his role as a protector and guardian.

Temples and Worship

While Anubis was a very popular god, he didn't have as many temples dedicated to him as some of the other gods. Instead, places where mummification and rituals for the dead were carried out were considered his sacred spaces. People would also offer prayers and gifts to Anubis to ask for his protection for their loved ones who had passed away.

Anubis's Legacy

Anubis is one of the coolest and most unique gods in Egyptian mythology. His appearance captures our imagination and takes us back to a time when people saw the world in a magical way. He helps us understand how the ancient Egyptians felt about death and the afterlife—it wasn't something to be scared of, but a journey to be prepared for. Anubis was the guardian watching over it all.

Anubis shows us the importance of caring for those who have passed and protecting them on their way to the next life. As we continue our journey through the legends about the Gods And Goddesses of Egypt, keep the image of

Anubis in your mind—the kind and powerful protector who watches over the night.

Osiris: Ruler of the Dead

After discussing the guardian of the dead, let's move onto their ruler, Osiris. Osiris was one of the most important gods in ancient Egyptian mythology. He was the god of the afterlife, the underworld, and rebirth. Imagine him as the king who looks after everyone who has passed away, making sure they have a safe journey in the world beyond. Osiris is often shown as a mummy holding a crook and flail (symbols of kingship). He has distinctive green or black skin, which represents rebirth and the fertile Nile soil.

The Story of Osiris

The story of Osiris is a tale of jealousy, betrayal, and the power of love. Osiris was a beloved king of Egypt who taught the people how to farm and make laws. His brother, Set, was jealous of his power and popularity. In a wicked plot, Set tricked Osiris by offering him a beautiful chest at a banquet. He said he would give the chest to anyone who could fit perfectly inside it. When Osiris lay down in the chest, Set slammed it shut, sealed it, and threw it into the Nile River.

But the story doesn't end there! Osiris's wife, Isis, who was a powerful goddess herself, searched everywhere for her husband. She found his chest and brought it back to Egypt. Sadly, Set found the chest again, stole Osiris's body, and chopped it into pieces, scattering them across Egypt. The determined Isis gathered all the pieces, and with her magic, brought Osiris back to life long enough to conceive their son, Horus. Afterward, Osiris became the god of the underworld, ruling over the dead and offering them the chance of rebirth.

Osiris and the Afterlife

As the Ruler of the Dead, Osiris's job was to welcome the souls into the underworld. Here, he would judge them in the Hall of Truth. As previously mentioned, in this mystical room the hearts of the dead were weighed against the feather of Maat, the goddess of truth and justice.

Celebrating Osiris

Osiris was not only the god of death but also of resurrection and life. Every year, the Egyptians celebrated the mysteries of Osiris. These were special ceremonies that reenacted the story of his death and rebirth. They believed these rituals would renew the fertility of the land and help the dead be reborn in the afterlife. Villages across Egypt had their own versions of these rituals, showing just how beloved and central Osiris was in their lives.

Osiris's Influence

Osiris had a huge impact on Egyptian culture. He was a symbol of hope, promising a peaceful and blessed existence in the afterlife for those who lived a virtuous life. His story encouraged the people to follow the values of truth and righteousness.

Osiris's tale teaches us about the values that were important to the ancient Egyptians—justice, truth, and loyalty. As the Ruler of the Dead, Osiris reassures us that there is always a chance for renewal and rebirth, no matter the challenges we face. So, as we close this chapter on Osiris, remember the lessons he brings: that goodness and justice can triumph over evil, and that love and determination can overcome any obstacle.

Isis: Goddess of Magic

Now let's talk about Osiris's wife, Isis, who was a goddess that could do it all. She was known as the goddess of magic, motherhood, healing, and even the protector of the kingdom. Egyptians pictured her as a beautiful woman wearing a throne-shaped crown, because she was also considered the queen of the gods. Her powerful wings could spread far and wide to protect those in need.

The Story of Isis

The story of Isis is one of adventure, love, and magic. Because Isis was married to Osiris, who was originally the king of Egypt, they ruled the land together. But when Osiris was betrayed and killed by his jealous brother, Set, the kingdom fell into darkness. However, like mentioned in the previous section, Isis gathered the pieces of her husband's body and used her magic to bring him back to life.

Isis also used her wits and magic to protect her son, Horus, from Set. She raised Horus in secret swamps and marshes where Set couldn't find them. With her guidance, Horus grew strong and wise, and he eventually defeated Set. Horus thus became the new king of Egypt. So, Isis's magic and cleverness were key to restoring balance and peace.

Isis's Magical Powers

Isis was known for her incredible magical abilities. She could heal the sick, protect the dead, and even control the fate of the skies. One of her most famous tales involves tricking the sun god Ra. Remember that Ra was very powerful and had a secret name that held the source of his strength. Using her wits, Isis crafted a snake from the earth that bit Ra. After the snake had bit him, Isis offered to heal him if he told her his secret name. Ra eventually gave in, meaning that Isis gained even more magical powers.

The Worship of Isis

Isis was worshiped all over Egypt and even beyond its borders. She had many temples dedicated to her, where people would come to ask for her blessings and protection. The priests and priestesses who served her performed rituals to harness her magical powers, hoping to bring healing and protection to their communities. The festival of Isis was also a grand celebration connected to the Nile flooding, which was a crucial event for farming. People thanked Isis during this festival for bringing fertility and life to their fields.

Isis's Legacy

The influence of Isis spread far beyond the sands of Egypt. After the time of the pharaohs, people in the Roman Empire and beyond worshiped her. She became a symbol of the ideal mother and wife, as well as a protector of nature and the people. Her image has inspired countless generations, and her stories continue to fascinate people around the world.

Isis, the Goddess of Magic, shows us the power of love, protection, and clever thinking. Her magical adventures and caring nature teach us about the strength that comes from caring for others and standing up for what's right. As we close this chapter, remember Isis as a symbol of the magical possibilities all around us.

Horus: The Falcon God of Protection

Horus is one of the most important gods in ancient Egyptian mythology. He's usually shown as a man with the head of a falcon that wears a crown with red and white colors, which represent Egypt. As the god of the sky, Horus's eyes are literally the sun and moon, where the sun occupies his right eye and the moon his left. Imagine having the whole sky as your kingdom!

The Birth of Horus

Horus's story begins with his parents, Isis and Osiris. After Osiris was betrayed by Set, Isis used her magical powers to bring Osiris back to life long enough to conceive Horus. Horus was born in secret, hidden in the marshes of the Nile Delta to keep him safe from Set, who wanted to prevent him from claiming the throne.

Horus's Battle for the Throne

As Horus grew, he was determined to avenge his father's death and reclaim the throne from Set. This led to a series of epic battles between Horus and Set, which are among the most famous stories in Egyptian mythology. These battles were not just physical fights but also involved clever tricks and magical contests. In the end, with the help of the other gods, Horus won, and he became the ruler of Egypt, symbolizing the triumph of good over evil.

Horus as the God of Protection

As the ruler of Egypt, Horus had a very special role: he was the protector of the pharaohs. The pharaohs were considered to be the 'living Horuses,' meaning they were earthly embodiments of the god himself. This is why you often see statues and images of Horus standing behind a pharaoh, spreading his wings protectively. It was believed that Horus watched over the pharaohs as their divine guardian, ensuring they had the wisdom and strength to rule wisely.

The Eye of Horus

One of the most famous symbols associated with Horus is the "Eye of Horus," also known as the "wedjat eye." It's a symbol that looks a bit like a stylized eye with a twisty tail coming out of it. This symbol was a powerful amulet used for protection against evil and illness. It was worn by the living and placed on the dead to protect them during their journey through the underworld.

The Worship of Horus

Temples dedicated to Horus dotted the landscape of ancient Egypt. The most famous temple was the Temple of Horus at Edfu, which also happens to be one of the most well-preserved temples in all of Egypt. Inside, walls adorned with carvings tell the story of Horus's epic battles and his victory over Set. Priests in these temples performed daily rituals to honor Horus, asking for his protection and favor.

Horus's Legacy

Horus remained one of the most significant gods in ancient Egyptian religion throughout the history of the civilization. His image as a falcon-headed man represents strength, vigilance, and the rule of law, all of which were central values to the ancient Egyptians. His connection to the pharaohs also underscored the divine right to rule that was vital to maintaining order and stability in ancient Egyptian society.

Horus teaches us about courage, justice, and the protective power of leadership. As we continue our journey through Egyptian Legends, keep your eyes on the sky—maybe you'll spot Horus watching over you too!

Set: God of Chaos and Disorder

Though he might sound a bit scary, Set's story is full of wild adventures. So, let's find out why Set is one of the most fascinating characters in ancient Egyptian mythology!

Set is a god with a look as unique as his role in Egyptian myths. He's often shown with an animal head that's hard to identify—it looks a bit like an aardvark, a donkey, and a jackal all mixed together! This mysterious animal is called the "Set animal" and it's just as wild and unpredictable as Set himself. Set was the god of chaos, storms, and war. But even though he represents chaos, Set also played a crucial part in protecting the sun god, Ra, from his nightly battles against the serpent Apophis.

Protector of the Sun God

Despite his reputation for chaos and disruption, Set was not just a villain. He had a very important job every night as one of the protectors of Ra's solar barge. Ra sailed through the underworld each night. Every evening, Set fought against Apophis, a giant serpent who tried to swallow the sun. This battle was crucial because it ensured that the sun rose each morning. In this way, Set's destructive power was also used to protect the world from eternal darkness.

The Worship of Set

Set was worshiped in various parts of ancient Egypt, particularly in places where storms and harsh weather were common. People believed that honoring Set could protect them from natural disasters and help them in battles. His temples were places where people prayed for strength and resilience in the face of chaos.

Set in Egyptian Culture

Even though Set was associated with violence and disorder, he was also a symbol of strength against adversity. The ancient Egyptians understood that chaos and order were two sides of the same coin. They believed both were necessary for the balance of the universe. Set's stories remind us that even in chaos, there is space for structure and protection.

So, young explorers, now you know about Set, the God of Chaos and Disorder. His tales are a mix of thrilling battles, family drama, and the essential balance between order and chaos. Set shows us that every story has many sides and that even a stormy character can display heroism.

Hathor: Goddess of Love and Joy

After exploring the story of the god of chaos, let's meet his opposite, Hathor, the ancient Egyptian Goddess of Love and Joy. She is one of the most loved and celebrated goddesses from ancient Egypt, and was thought to spread happiness and music wherever she went. So, let's dance along with Hathor and discover her delightful world!

Hathor is depicted as a beautiful woman with the ears of a cow. Sometimes though, she was even depicted as a whole cow. She wore a headdress with horns and a sun disk nestled between them. Why a cow, you might wonder? In ancient Egypt, cows were seen as nurturing animals, providing the essential milk and meat that sustained life. Thus, Hathor's connection with cows symbolizes her role as a nurturing goddess who provides love, protection, and joy to all.

The Many Roles of Hathor

Hathor was known as the goddess of many things—love, beauty, music, dancing, fertility, and motherhood. She was like the ancient version of a superstar, bringing joy and celebration wherever she was worshiped. Hathor's presence was said to bring peace and happiness to homes and temples alike.

The Joyful Protector

Hathor was also a protective goddess. Mothers and children would pray to her for health and happiness. She was especially important to women, who looked up to her as a symbol of femininity and strength. But more than just a protector, people also believed in her power to bring them happiness. So, Hathor's temples were places where music and dance filled the air, creating an atmosphere of joy and festivity.

Hathor and the Sky

One of Hathor's most fascinating roles was as the goddess of the sky. The ancient Egyptians believed she welcomed the rising sun each day with joyous music. She flew around her domain, the sky, as a cow, spreading light and happiness. She was also thought to be the Eye of Ra, meaning she was the sun god's protective female counterpart. As such, she helped Ra fight off enemies and bring the sun across the sky.

Celebrations in Hathor's Honor

The most famous festival celebrated in Hathor's honor was the "Feast of Drunkenness." This might sound strange, but it was actually a joyful and sacred festival! It celebrated a myth in which Hathor, as the Eye of Ra, saved humanity from destruction. People danced, sang, and even drank to excess to imitate and honor the overwhelming joy and love that Hathor brought back to the world after her rage was calmed. It was a way for everyone, from the simplest farmer to the highest priest, to feel connected to the goddess and each other.

Hathor's Temples

Hathor's main temple was at Dendera, which is another one of the most beautiful and well-preserved temples in all of Egypt. This temple was her special home on Earth, and was decorated with magnificent images of her as both a woman and a cow. Pilgrims traveled from far and wide to visit and pay their respects, hoping to gain her favor and enjoy her blessings of joy and love.

Hathor's Legacy

Hathor's legacy is one of love, happiness, and nurturing care. Her stories and the celebrations in her honor show us how the ancient Egyptians cherished and upheld the ideals of love and joy in their culture. Hathor's role goes beyond just myths and legends; she represents the celebration of life itself.

As we finish our chapter on Hathor, the Goddess of Love and Joy, remember that like Hathor, you can bring happiness and love into the lives of those around you. Whether through a smile, a song, or a dance, sharing joy is something that everyone can do, just like Hathor did for the ancient Egyptians.

Thoth: The Wise God of the Moon and Magic

Thoth was her another one of the most important deities in ancient Egyptian mythology. He was often depicted in art as a man with the head of an ibis. An ibis is a type of bird with a long, curved beak. Other times Thoth was depicted with the head of a baboon. Either way, both animals were considered sacred to him. These unique looks made Thoth stand out among the gods and were symbols of his connection to the natural world.

The Roles of Thoth

Thoth wore many hats among the gods. He was not just the god of the moon but also the god of wisdom, knowledge, writing, hieroglyphs, science, magic, art, and judgment. This made him one of the busiest deities on the Egyptian pantheon's payroll!

- **Moon God**: As the god of the Moon, Thoth measured and kept time. The ancient Egyptians believed that Thoth's light in the night sky helped them calculate the days and months.
- **God of Wisdom and Knowledge**: Thoth was believed to hold all the knowledge in the world. He gave the gift of hieroglyphs, which were the Egyptian's system of writing, to humanity. This made him the patron god of scribes (people who wrote or copied books and other texts), who were very respected in ancient Egypt.

- **God of Science and Magic**: Thoth wasn't just about book-smarts; he was also the god of magic and science. As such, he knew secrets that other gods didn't, which made him a powerful figure in myths and capable of solving problems that stumped others.

Thoth's Family

In the rich tapestry of Egyptian mythology, Thoth's feminine counterpart was Seshat, the goddess of writing and measurement. Seshat helped him with his duties. His wife was Ma'at, the goddess of truth and justice, which fit perfectly with his role as a god of wisdom and judgment. Together, they were a powerful pair who maintained the universe's balance and order.

Thoth in Egyptian Art and Culture

Thoth was a popular subject in Egyptian art. He was often shown holding a writing palette and a reed pen, ready to record the deeds of the dead in the underworld—another of his important jobs. This depiction as a record-keeper highlighted his role in the judgment of the dead, where he made sure that justice was carried out correctly.

Thoth's Legacy

Thoth's influence extended beyond just religion; he was a cultural icon that represented the intellectual achievements of ancient Egypt. As such, temples dedicated to Thoth were centers of learning, similar to universities today. His legacy encouraged enlightenment and the pursuit of knowledge.

Thoth teaches us about the value of knowledge and the power of words. His story reminds us that learning and wisdom are treasures that can lead to better understanding and harmony in the world. Thoth's role in Egyptian mythology as a mediator and wise counselor shows us the importance of fair judgment and truth in maintaining order and peace. His fascinating story helps us appreciate the ancient Egyptians' deep respect for knowledge and justice, which are both values that are still important today.

Bastet: The Feline Goddess of Protection

Now let's meet Bastet, the cat goddess. Known for her protective powers and gentle nature, Bastet was a figure that had been worshiped and adored since the Second Dynasty. Let's paw our way into the world of this fascinating goddess.

Bastet, also known as Bast, is an ancient Egyptian goddess who appears as a fierce lioness or a gentle cat. Her names, which include B'sst, Baast, Ubaste, and Baset, reflect her attributes as a deity of home, fertility, and protection. In ancient Greek culture, she was known as Ailuros, meaning "cat."

Bastet was originally depicted as a lioness, which symbolized her role as a protector and warrior. However, over time, her image softened to that of a domestic cat, highlighting her nurturing aspects. This transformation mirrors her dual roles:

- **Protector**: As a fierce lioness, Bastet was seen as a defender of the pharaoh and the nation, warding off enemies and evil spirits. Temples dedicated to Bastet often featured her as a lioness, emphasizing her strength and majesty.

- **Goddess of Home and Fertility**: As a gentle cat, Bastet represented domestic bliss and fertility. She was thought to bring joy and protect homes from evil spirits. Many Egyptian families had statues of Bastet to ensure their household was safe and happy.

Worship of Bastet

Bastet was especially popular in the city of Bubastis, which became her cult center. Here, grand festivals were held in her honor, attracting devotees from across Egypt who came to celebrate her with music, dance, and feasting. The festivals were so lively and joyous that they were famous throughout ancient Egypt.

The Temple of Bastet in Bubastis was one of the most magnificent in all of Egypt. It was a place of pilgrimage and celebration, and people went there to pay homage to the goddess. Archaeologists have found many statues and artifacts in this temple that show how deeply loved and revered Bastet was among the ancient Egyptians.

Bastet and Her Symbolism

The image of Bastet as a cat has a special significance in Egyptian culture. Cats were highly revered animals, valued for their grace and their ability to catch and kill snakes and rats. By associating Bastet with cats, the Egyptians highlighted her protective qualities—she kept away both physical and spiritual vermin that could harm their homes.

The Legacy of Bastet

Today, Bastet is still a symbol of protection and motherly care. Her statues, which show her as both a fierce lioness and a gentle cat, remind us of the dual nature of her powers. She embodies the balance between strength and kindness, which the ancient Egyptians greatly respected. Her story teaches us about the values of protection, joy, and the comforts of home. Bastet's legacy shows us that caring and courage can go hand-in-hand, providing safety and happiness to those we love.

Concluding Our Journey

As we wrap up our exploration of the gods and goddesses of ancient Egypt, we remember the treasure trove of stories, lessons, and wonders we've uncovered. From Ra's journey across the sky to Hathor's joyful celebrations, each deity has left a mark on history and our hearts.

Through the tales of these divine beings, we've learned about the values and beliefs that shaped ancient Egyptian society. We've seen how religion was more than just rituals; it was a guiding force that brought people together and gave meaning to their lives.

But our journey doesn't end here. As we step away from the temples and tombs of ancient Egypt, we carry with us the wisdom left behind by these legends. The lessons of kindness, courage, and the pursuit of knowledge will guide us on our own adventures, helping us navigate the challenges of the modern world.

So let's keep our curiosity alive, always seeking to learn more about the wonders of the past and the mysteries of the universe. Who knows what other ancient secrets are waiting to be uncovered? Remember to keep your hearts open to the magic of history and the beauty of the world around us as we continue into our next chapter.

CHAPTER 5: MYTHS OF ANCIENT EGYPT

In this chapter, we'll continue our thrilling adventure as we unravel captivating tales that have enchanted people for thousands of years. From the creation of the world to epic battles between gods and monsters, these ancient Egyptian stories are filled with magic, mystery, and timeless wisdom.

Our expedition begins with an introduction to the mythical tales and characters that populate the rich tapestry of Egyptian mythology. These stories not only entertain but also offer insights into the values and beliefs of ancient Egyptian society. As we delve deeper, we'll discover how these myths provide explanations for the natural world and prove to be important moral lessons to generations from the past and present.

The Creation Myth of Heliopolis: Atum and the Ennead

Gather around, young explorers, as we dive into one of the most fascinating tales from ancient Egypt—the Creation Myth of Heliopolis! This story isn't just about how the world began, it's also about the adventures of the god named Atum and his family, known as the Ennead. So, let's set sail on this ancient river of myths and discover how the Egyptians believed the world was created.

The Beginning of Everything

In the very beginning, there was nothing but endless darkness and swirling chaos. This was a silent, empty place called Nun. But within this nothingness, something incredible happened—a mound of land magically appeared! According to the Egyptians, this was the first piece of land ever to exist, and it was called the Benben. On this mound, the first god, Atum, came into being all by himself. Imagine being the first and only one alive in a vast, dark space!

Atum: The First God

Atum was a special god because he possessed the amazing ability of creation. His power meant he was not born the usual way; rather, he created himself out of the chaos. As he stood on Benben, he felt lonely in the endless darkness. So, Atum decided he wanted some company. But how could he create other beings? Well, Atum had a unique way of creating things—by spitting or sneezing! When he did this, he created the first pair of gods—Shu, the god of air, and Tefnut, the goddess of moisture.

The Adventures of Shu and Tefnut

Shu and Tefnut were the children of Atum. They were very important because they brought air and moisture into the world, which are essential for life. But one day, they wandered off into the darkness and got lost. Atum was so worried about his children that he sent his eye out into the chaos to find them. When Shu and Tefnut finally returned with the eye, Atum was so happy that tears streamed down his face. What's amazing is that where his tears fell, humans sprang up! That's how the first people were created according to this myth.

The Ennead: The Great Family of Gods

As the family grew, Shu and Tefnut had two children of their own—Geb, the god of the earth, and Nut, the goddess of the sky. But their father, Shu, separated his children, as he didn't think the sky should mix with the earth. So, Geb lay below while Nut arched over him, creating the world as the ancient Egyptians knew it.

Geb and Nut also had children—Osiris, Isis, Seth, and Nephthys, who became key figures in many other Egyptian myths. Together, these nine gods (Atum, Shu, Tefnut, Geb, Nut, Osiris, Isis, Seth, and Nephthys) are called the Ennead, which means a group of nine. They were worshiped and loved across Egypt.

Why This Myth Matters

The Creation Myth of Heliopolis explains how the Egyptians understood the world around them. It showed them that even in chaos, there can be order and life, and that families—just like the Ennead—were at the heart of everything. This myth also taught them that everyone and everything has a place in the world, from the air they breathed (Shu) to the ground they walked on (Geb).

So, the story of Atum and the Ennead is just one of the endless wonders of ancient Egypt. Remember, every myth and legend carries a spark of the magic and mystery of the times gone by. As you dream tonight, imagine what it would be like to stand on the first mound of earth and watch a whole world being created!

The Legend of Osiris and Isis: The Story of Resurrection

Now that we've talked about Earth's creation, let's discuss what happened on Earth. We will now revisit the tale of Osiris and Isis in more detail. Remember this story about love, betrayal, and the power of hope? Get ready for a journey into the world of gods, magic, and miracles!

Osiris and Isis were both brother and sister, a husband and wife, which was common for Egyptian gods. They were rulers of the gods and very much in love. Osiris was the god of agriculture and the afterlife, teaching people how to grow crops and live well. Isis was a powerful goddess of magic, known for her wisdom and kindness.

The Jealous Brother

But, not everyone was happy with Osiris. Remember his brother, Set, who was very jealous of Osiris's power and popularity? As we have learned, Set was the god of chaos and the desert. He plotted to take over as the ruler of Egypt.

The Evil Plot

As you already know, Set held a feast and brought a beautiful wooden chest with him. He said that whoever could fit perfectly in the chest would win a competition! All the guests tried their luck, but the chest seemed to fit no one—until Osiris stepped in. As soon as he laid down, Set slammed the lid shut, sealed the chest, and threw it into the Nile River. Remember that Set then declared himself king, and chaos began to spread across Egypt.

The Search for Osiris

We already know that Isis was heartbroken when she learned about Osiris's fate. She couldn't accept his death and set out on a long journey to find him. Her journey led her through many dangers, but her magical powers and determination helped her along the way. Finally, she found the chest containing Osiris's body in a distant land, where it had been caught in a tree's branches.

The Magic of Isis

Isis used her powerful magic to bring Osiris back to life. She breathed new life into Osiris with her wings and spells. For a brief moment, Osiris was alive again, and the two were reunited. Horus was born at this time as well. But Osiris couldn't stay in the world of the living. He became the ruler of the underworld, where he would judge the souls of the dead.

The Birth of Horus and the Revenge

As previously mentioned, Isis hid her son, Horus, in the marshes. She raised Horus to be strong and wise so that he could challenge Set and reclaim his father's throne. The two battled and Horus eventually became the king of Egypt, restoring order and justice.

The Legacy of Osiris and Isis

The story of Osiris and Isis had a huge impact on Egyptian culture. It was a tale of resurrection that promised life after death to ordinary Egyptians, not just the pharaohs and nobles. The promise of being reborn in the afterlife gave them hope and a reason to live a good life according to the laws of Ma'at.

The legend of Osiris and Isis teaches us about the power of love and the enduring nature of the soul. It shows us that even in the face of the greatest trials, courage and perseverance can restore balance and harmony. Remember, like Isis and Horus, you can overcome challenges with determination and support from those you love.

The Tale of the Shipwrecked Sailor: The Serpent King

After reviewing the epic tale of Horus, Isis, and Osiris, let's move onto distant waters. We start this story with a brave

Egyptian sailor who set out on a ship with his fellow crewmen. They were on a mission to find precious treasures for the Pharaoh. The sun was shining, and the sea was calm, but suddenly, a fierce storm came out of nowhere! The winds howled, the waves crashed, and in the chaos, our sailor was thrown overboard.

When the storm finally calmed, the sailor found himself washed up on the shore of a mysterious island. He was all alone, scared, and unsure of what to do next. But he didn't give up. Instead, he started to explore the island, hoping to find food, water, or maybe a way back home.

The Discovery of the Serpent King

As he explored, the sailor stumbled upon a strange and marvelous sight—a huge, shimmering serpent with scales of gold and eyes like the brightest of emeralds. This was no ordinary serpent; it was the Serpent King, a magical creature who ruled over the island. The sailor was terrified at first, but the Serpent King spoke to him in a calm and regal voice, asking him how the sailor came to his island.

The Serpent King's Tale

The Serpent King was not always a serpent. He told the sailor that he used to be a prince of a rich and lush kingdom. But a curse had turned him into a serpent and his subjects vanished, leaving him alone on the island with only his treasures. Despite his fearsome appearance, the Serpent King was kind and wise. He comforted the sailor and promised that no harm would come to him during his stay.

A Promise of Rescue

The Serpent King, moved by the sailor's plight, made a surprising promise. He told the sailor that soon a ship would come to rescue him and take him back to Egypt. Before the sailor's departure, the Serpent King gave him treasures—precious stones and spices—as gifts to take back to his pharaoh. But he also gave a warning: that he couldn't speak of the island to anyone except the pharaoh, for its secrets were not for the ears of ordinary men.

The Return Home

True to the Serpent King's word, a ship arrived. The sailor returned to Egypt with his arms laden with treasures. When he reached home, he went straight to the pharaoh to tell him of all that had happened. The pharaoh was amazed by the story and the riches the sailor brought back. He praised the sailor for his bravery and wisdom in dealing with the Serpent King.

The Lesson of the Tale

The story of the shipwrecked sailor teaches us about courage and kindness in unexpected places. It shows us that even when you feel lost and alone, there can be magical moments and new friends in surprising forms. It's a tale that encourages us to be brave in our adventures and wise in our dealings with the unknown.

The Legendary Adventures of Sphinx

Now from the sea we will move to the sands of Egypt, where a hero known as Sphinx lived. The Sphinx had the body of a lion and the head of a human, making him a powerful and majestic figure. He was revered by all who knew his name. But his strength didn't come from mere muscles—it came from the Orb of Ra, a mystical artifact gifted to him by the ancient god himself.

The Orb of Ra

The Orb of Ra wasn't just any magical object—it was a source of immense power. The Orb was bestowed upon Sphinx to aid him in his quest against darkness. When Sphinx held the orb, he could feel its energy coursing through his veins, filling him with courage and strength. With the orb by his side, Sphinx became the greatest hero Egypt had ever known.

The Quest Against Apep

So, when the land of Egypt was threatened by Apep, a fearsome serpent of chaos who sought to plunge the world into darkness, the Sphinx had to fight. Apep was a formidable foe, with powers that rivaled even the gods themselves. But Sphinx, armed with the Orb of Ra and his unwavering bravery, was determined to stop him.

The Battle of Light and Darkness

The battle between Sphinx and Apep raged across the sands of Egypt, echoing through the ancient temples and pyramids. With every strike of his sword and blast of his magic, Sphinx fought valiantly against the forces of darkness. Apep, however, was cunning and relentless, using his powers to twist the very fabric of reality.

Victory and Triumph

But Sphinx, fueled by the power of the Orb of Ra and his unyielding spirit, refused to back down. With a final, mighty blow, he struck Apep down, banishing the serpent back into the depths of the underworld. The people of Egypt rejoiced, celebrating Sphinx as their savior and protector.

Legacy of Sphinx

Sphinx's victory over Apep became a legend and was retold for generations to come. Temples were built in his honor, and festivals were held in his name, celebrating his bravery and heroism. Sphinx's legacy lived on, inspiring all who heard his story to stand up against darkness and fight for what is right.

And so, dear adventurers, we conclude our tale of Sphinx, the legendary hero of ancient Egypt. Remember, just like

Sphinx, each of us has the power to stand up against darkness and make a difference in the world. So, let your courage shine bright, and may your adventures be as legendary as those of Sphinx himself!

The Marvelous Tale of the Ogdoad

Now let's move beyond Egypt's sky and sands to the vast expanse of the universe, to a time before the sun touched the sky or the rivers flowed with life. In this space the Ogdoad existed—the "Eight" who stood at the dawn of creation. These ancient deities existed when the world was but a swirling chaos of darkness and void. It was from their divine essence the cosmos was born.

The Eight Primordial Deities

The Ogdoad consisted of four divine couples, each representing fundamental aspects of existence. These pairs of gods and goddesses were:

- **Nun and Naune**t: This couple represented the primordial waters (sacred waters that were bel, symbolizing the boundless expanse of the universe.

- **Heh and Hauhet**: These gods represented infinity and eternity. They embodied the endlessness of time and space.

- **Kek and Kauket**: These two represented darkness and obscurity, as well as the mysterious depths of the cosmos.

- **Amun and Amaunet:** Finally, these gods represented hiddenness and concealment, and they hid the secrets of creation from mortal eyes.

Together, these eight deities formed the foundation upon which the world was built, each contributing their divine essence to shape the universe.

The Role of the Ogdoad

As the first generation of deities, the Ogdoad played a crucial role in the creation and maintenance of cosmic order. They were also revered as the guardians of Ma'at (truth, balance, and harmony). Their power helped keep the forces of chaos in check, allowing life to flourish and thrive.

The Legacy of the Ogdoad

Though the Ogdoad faded into obscurity as Egypt's religious beliefs evolved over time, their legacy endured in the hearts and minds of the people. They were honored in temple rituals and revered as the ancestors of all the subsequent gods and goddesses. Even as newer deities gained importance, the Ogdoad remained a symbol of the ancient and eternal forces that govern the cosmos.

And so, dear adventurers, we conclude our tale of the Ogdoad. As we journey through the sands of time, let us remember the ancient wisdom of these divine beings and the profound impact they had on the creation and the world around them.

The Story of Sinuhe: Exile and Return

Lets move from the gods back into the mortal world to embark on a journey with an Egyptian official named Sinuhe. Sinuhe experienced a life full of adventure, danger, and eventually, a heartwarming return to his homeland. So, fasten your seatbelts, as we travel back in time to accompany Sinuhe on his adventures.

Who Was Sinuhe?

Sinuhe was a nobleman who served at the Egyptian court during the reign of Pharaoh Amenemhat I. He was a trusted and loyal servant, living a life of comfort and respect within the palace walls. But Sinuhe's life soon took a dramatic turn that led him on a journey across foreign lands.

One day, while on a military campaign, Sinuhe received shocking news: Pharaoh Amenemhat I had been assassinated. Fearing that he too might be in danger, Sinuhe panicked and fled Egypt. With a heavy heart, he left behind everything he knew and loved. His quick departure was not out of disloyalty to his king, but out of fear for his own life.

Sinuhe's Life in Exile

Sinuhe's escape led him to the land of Canaan, where he sought refuge among strangers. Despite his fears and the uncertainty of living in exile, Sinuhe adapted to his new life. He married a local woman and was welcomed by the chief of a tribe, who admired Sinuhe's Egyptian wisdom and skills. Sinuhe even fought battles alongside his new companions, earning respect and wealth in his adopted land.

A Warrior in a Foreign Land

As years passed, Sinuhe became a celebrated warrior and a man of status among his new community. He was given land and servants, and he built a life that many would envy. However, despite his success and the peace he had found, Sinuhe's heart remained in Egypt. He missed his home and dreamed of returning to serve under the new pharaoh.

The Pharaoh's Invitation

One day, a message arrived from Egypt. The new Pharaoh, Senusret I, had heard of Sinuhe's plight and invited him to return to Egypt. The pharaoh offered Sinuhe forgiveness and promised him a place of honor back home. Overwhelmed with emotion, Sinuhe prepared to leave his life in Canaan behind to return to the land of his birth.

The Return to Egypt

Sinuhe's return to Egypt was triumphant and emotional. He was received with honors and given estates (a lot of land and servants) by the pharaoh. The people celebrated his return. Now back in his homeland, Sinuhe was overwhelmed with joy. He visited the tomb of his old king, Amenemhat I, and paid his respects, feeling that he had completed the circle of his life.

Sinuhe's Reflections

In his old age, Sinuhe wrote down his story, reflecting on his adventures and the lessons he had learned. He spoke of the value of humility, the importance of home, and the kindness of strangers. Sinuhe's story became a legendary tale in Egypt, told and retold as a testament to the strength of the human spirit in the face of adversity.

Today, Sinuhe's story teaches us that though life can take unexpected turns, courage and adaptability can help us overcome challenges. It also reminds us of the power of forgiveness and the importance of treasuring where we come from.

Unearthing the Past: Archaeological Discoveries and Their Global Fascination

In reality, these myths from ancient times have been brought back to life through the fascinating work of archaeologists. Today, let's put on our explorer hats and delve into the world of archaeology, where every discovery helps to piece together the vast, intricate puzzle of human history. In this section, we're going to explore how modern adventurers unearth secrets that have been buried for millennia. From magnificent tombs to the mysterious Rosetta Stone, each discovery has helped us connect with a past that, though ancient, feels closer with every brushstroke. So, let's start digging!

What is Archaeology?

Archaeology is the study of old things left behind by people from the past, such as bones, pots, tools, buildings, or even entire cities buried under the ground! Archaeologists are like detectives, but instead of solving crimes, they solve mysteries about how people lived long ago.

Discovering Ancient Egypt

Egypt is a treasure trove for archaeologists because it was one of the most advanced civilizations of its time. The dry desert climate of Egypt helped preserve many of these treasures in amazing condition, giving us clear snapshots of the past.

So, why do people find Egyptian archaeology so fascinating? Well, it's like putting together a giant puzzle of human history. Each discovery tells us more about how people lived, what they believed, and what they valued. Egypt's pyramids, mummies, and golden treasures tell tales of a world that seems almost magical.

These discoveries don't just help us learn; they also bring people together. Museums around the world display Egyptian artifacts, allowing everyone to share in their wonder. When archaeologists uncover something new, it can be headline news around the globe, sparking the imaginations of kids and adults alike.

Even today, new discoveries in Egypt are being made all the time. Just recently, archaeologists found new tombs, statues, and even entire workshops where ancient Egyptians made artifacts for the afterlife. Each new find helps fill in the blanks of history and teaches us more about this fascinating culture.

It is important to protect these exciting discoveries. Archaeologists work hard to make sure that ancient artifacts can be studied without damage. They are like guardians of history, making sure that future generations can also learn and be amazed by these treasures. Remember, the past is like a book waiting to be read, and archaeology is how we turn the pages.

The Rosetta Stone and the Decoding of Hieroglyphs

One of the most remarkable pages ever turned in the history of archaeology involves the Rosetta Stone, an artifact that unlocked the long-lost language of the ancient Egyptians. Imagine finding a huge puzzle piece that helps solve a puzzle that's been mixed up for thousands of years. That's what the Rosetta Stone is! It's a big slab of black rock called granodiorite, and it was found by French soldiers in Egypt in 1799 near a town called Rosetta (Rashid). What makes this stone super special is that it has the same message written in three different scripts: Greek, Demotic, and Ancient Egyptian Hieroglyphs (their written language).

Why Was the Rosetta Stone Important?

For many years, nobody knew how to read ancient Egyptian hieroglyphs. They were a complete mystery! People could see beautiful symbols on tomb walls and artifacts, but didn't know how to read them. When the Rosetta Stone was discovered, it was like finding a secret key because one of the languages written on it—Greek—was already well-known. This meant that if you could read Greek, you could figure out what the Egyptian hieroglyphs were saying too!

The Challenge of Decoding

Decoding the hieroglyphs wasn't easy. It was trickier than trying to solve the hardest crossword puzzle in the world because the hieroglyphs were pictures that could represent either sounds or whole ideas. Many smart scholars tried to decode them, but the real hero of our story is a man named Jean-François Champollion.

Jean-François Champollion Cracks the Code

Champollion was a French scholar who loved languages. He was fascinated by the Rosetta Stone and worked very hard to understand the hieroglyphs. In 1822, after years of studying, Champollion finally figured it out! He realized that some of the hieroglyphs represented the sounds of the Egyptian language, much like letters in the alphabet. This breakthrough was huge—it meant that at last, people could read the ancient words written thousands of years ago by the Egyptians.

Champollion used the Greek text on the Rosetta Stone as a guide. He knew that all the texts would say the same thing, so he compared them. By looking at names of rulers like Ptolemy and Cleopatra, which appeared in both the Greek and hieroglyph sections, he started to match sounds to symbols. Slowly but surely, he unlocked the language of the ancient Egyptians.

The Impact of Decoding Hieroglyphs

Once Champollion cracked the code, a whole new world opened up. Scholars could finally read the texts on temple walls, in tombs, and on ancient scrolls. They learned about Egyptian history, religion, and everyday life in incredible detail. It was like listening to the voices of people who had lived thousands of years ago.

Today, the Rosetta Stone is one of the most famous artifacts in the world, and it now lives in the British Museum in London. People from all over the world come to see it because it represents a great human achievement: the power of curiosity and intelligence to unlock the secrets of the past.

So, thanks to this incredible discovery and the genius of Champollion, we can now understand the messages left behind by the ancient Egyptians. The story of the Rosetta Stone shows us that with persistence and clever thinking, no mystery is too great to solve.

Egyptian Mythology in Modern Media

Thanks to the Rosetta Stone and Champollion's discovery, the exciting Egyptian tales from long ago haven't stayed in the past; instead, they've traveled all the way into today's movies, books, and video games! In this section we're going to see how ancient Egyptian myths have influenced some of your favorite stories and games. Let's jump on a magical carpet ride and discover how these old legends are still sparking fun and adventure in our modern world!

Egyptian Mythology in Movies

One of the most exciting ways Egyptian mythology comes to life is through movies. Filmmakers have long been fascinated by the rich stories and colorful characters of ancient Egypt. Have you ever seen a movie where a mummy comes to life? Many of these films are inspired by tales of curses and magic from Egyptian myths.

For example, the movie series "The Mummy" showcases adventures that blend real myths with fictional stories. These movies often feature exciting explorations of pyramids and encounters with creatures from Egyptian lore, like the fearsome god Anubis and various mummies. While these films take a lot of creative liberties, they also encourage audiences to learn more about the actual stories behind the characters.

Egyptian Gods in Books

Many authors have been inspired to write books that bring Egyptian mythology into the lives of their characters. Rick Riordan, for example, wrote a series called The Kane Chronicles, where modern-day kids discover they are connected to powerful Egyptian gods like Horus and Set. These books mix action-packed adventures with fun facts about ancient Egypt, making learning about mythology exciting and relatable.

Books like these help young readers imagine what it would be like to interact with the gods and goddesses of Egypt. They also explore themes of bravery, family, and destiny, which are all common elements in ancient myths.

Video Games and Egyptian Mythology

Video games also offer a dynamic way to experience the world of Egyptian mythology. One popular game, "Assassin's Creed: Origins," takes players on a journey through a digital recreation of ancient Egypt, where they can explore detailed environments that look like the real historical sites. Players meet characters from Egyptian history and mythology and engage in quests that involve famous myths and legends.

These games are not just about having fun; they're also about stepping into the shoes of someone from ancient times and experiencing their world. This helps players learn history in an immersive way.

Why Is Egyptian Mythology So Popular in the Media?

One reason Egyptian mythology is so popular in modern media is because of how vibrant and visual these myths are. The stories are full of dramatic conflicts, heroic deeds, and mystical creatures, which make them perfect for creative adaptations. The gods and goddesses, with their animal heads and fantastic powers, capture our imaginations and offer endless possibilities for storytelling.

Learning from Myths in Modern Media

While enjoying these modern adaptations, it's good to remember that they are often not entirely accurate to the historical myths. They are meant to entertain and inspire, leading to a deeper interest in learning about the real stories and history of ancient Egypt. This is why it's fun and useful to read books, visit museums, or even watch documentaries about ancient Egypt alongside enjoying its mythology in movies and games.

Chapter Conclusion

As our journey through the myths of ancient Egypt draws to a close, let us pause to reflect on the wonders we have encountered and lessons we have learned. From the epic tales of creation to the heroic exploits of gods and mortals, these stories have captivated our imaginations and illuminated the mysteries of a bygone era.

Through exploring the myths of ancient Egypt, we have uncovered timeless truths about the human experience, such as love and loss, courage and sacrifice, and the enduring quest for meaning. Through the lens of mythology, we have glimpsed the rich tapestry of human existence, woven with threads of hope, resilience, and the boundless potential of the human spirit.

But our journey does not end here. The legacy of ancient Egypt lives on, not only in the stories we have encountered but also in the archaeological wonders that continue to inspire awe and wonder. From the towering pyramids to the enigmatic hieroglyphs, each artifact is a testament to the ingenuity and creativity of a civilization that flourished millennia ago.

As we bid farewell to the myths of ancient Egypt, let us carry with us the wisdom and wonder they impart. Let us remember the lessons of the gods and goddesses, the triumphs of heroes, and the enduring power of storytelling to illuminate the human condition. And let us be inspired to seek out our own adventures, to uncover the mysteries that lie hidden in the sands of time, and to embrace the legacy of ancient Egypt as a beacon of hope and inspiration for generations to come.

CHAPTER 6:
HEROES AND LEGENDS

Now that we've covered some of ancient Egypt's most interesting legends, get ready to meet some of the most amazing people from the past. These heroes did incredible things and became legends because of their bravery, smarts, and kindness. We'll explore exciting stories about an architect who designed a giant pyramid, a scribe who went on a wild adventure, and a wise advisor who shared important lessons with everyone. Each story is full of surprises and big dreams!

So, grab your explorer's hat and let's set off on an adventure to discover the incredible lives of these legendary figures. Are you ready to find out what makes someone a hero? Let's go!

Imhotep: The Architect Who Became a God

Long ago, in the dusty sands of ancient Egypt, lived Imhotep, whose name means "he who comes in peace." He did not start out as a pharaoh or a prince, but rather was born as a commoner in the city of Memphis. Despite his status as a commoner, Imhotep was incredibly smart and talented. He served under the Pharaoh Djoser as an architect, priest, engineer, and physician.

The Architect of the First Pyramid

Imhotep's most famous achievement was designing the Step Pyramid at Saqqara. This pyramid was the very first of its kind—it was a structure so magnificent and unique that it set the standard for all future pyramids. The Step Pyramid was originally built as a simple tomb for Pharaoh Djoser, but Imhotep had a grand vision. He expanded it into a towering six-layered structure that stretched up to the heavens, unlike anything ever seen before.

Imhotep the Physician

Imhotep was also a pioneering physician that wrote medical texts. His writings were used for centuries after his death to help with treatment of diseases and injuries. The texts described treatments with such skill that people believed Imhotep was blessed by the gods. In fact, Imhotep's approach to medicine was so advanced that he is often called the "Father of Medicine," long before Hippocrates ever was!

A Man of Wisdom and Knowledge

Imhotep was also known for his wisdom and deep knowledge of the arts, science, and literature. He served as the high priest of the sun god Ra, which was a position of great honor. His wise sayings and proverbs were famous among the Egyptians, and his advice was sought by many. He was a true polymath, which means he knew a lot about many different subjects!

Imhotep's Legacy

Because of his brilliant contributions to Egyptian society, Imhotep was deified, which means he was turned into a god after his death. This was a rare honor usually reserved only for pharaohs. As a god, Imhotep was worshiped as the patron of scribes and the healer of the sick. People prayed to him for wisdom, health, and guidance. Many temples were also built in his honor.

Today, thousands of years later, Imhotep's legacy still shines bright. He is remembered not only as a great architect and physician but also as a symbol of human potential. His journey from a common man to a god demonstrates that with talent, hard work, and kindness, anyone can achieve greatness.

Ptah-hotep: The Wise Vizier and His Maxims

Now, let's move on to meet Ptah-hotep, an ancient Egyptian vizier who was famous for his wisdom. His teachings have been passed down through the ages, and today we'll discover why his words still matter. Get ready to learn from a master of ancient wisdom!

Ptah-hotep served as a vizier—the highest official to serve the king—under the Pharaoh Djedkare Isesi during Egypt's Fifth Dynasty, around 2400 BCE. This was a time when Egypt was flourishing, so wise counsel was highly valued. Ptah-hotep was not only a political advisor but also a revered sage (very intelligent person) whose ideas on ethics and proper conduct were written down in a collection known as "The Maxims of Ptah-hotep."

The Maxims of Ptah-hotep

The "Maxims of Ptah-hotep" is one of the oldest books in the world. Here, Ptah-hotep wrote down advice on how to live a good life, based on principles of justice, kindness, and respect for others. His maxims teach us how to handle conflicts, be good leaders, and find harmony in our lives.

Here are a few of his wise sayings:

- "Be a good listener—it is a source of strength."
- "If you are a leader, listen calmly to the speech of one who pleads."
- "Do not be proud of your knowledge, consult the ignorant and the wise."

Ptah-hotep's Role as Vizier

As vizier, Ptah-hotep's job was to ensure that the kingdom ran smoothly. This meant overseeing the administration, legal matters, and the treasury. His role required wisdom, fairness, and a deep understanding of people. So, his maxims were not just philosophical thoughts but practical advice for dealing with daily responsibilities in ways that promoted peace and fairness.

Teaching Through Stories

Ptah-hotep often used simple stories and parables to illustrate his points. This made his lessons easy to understand and remember, even for young people. He believed that wisdom came from listening carefully and thinking deeply, which were both qualities that he tried to instill in others through his teachings.

Why Ptah-hotep Matters Today

Ptah-hotep's teachings are still relevant because they speak to universal truths about human behavior and social justice. His call for humility, thoughtful listening, and respectful communication are qualities that help us build better relationships and stronger communities even today.

The story of Ptah-hotep, the Wise Vizier, teaches us that true wisdom comes from understanding and respecting one another. His life and maxims show us that the keys to a harmonious society are kindness, fairness, and education. As we close this chapter, remember that the ancient lessons of Ptah-hotep can still guide us in our daily lives.

The Legend of Moses

Now, let's embark on an epic journey through the sands of time to uncover the incredible story of Moses—the courageous religious leader who changed the course of history!

Our tale begins in the Land of Goshen, a land blessed by the Nile's fertile waters and home to the Israelites, who were the chosen people of the Christian god according to legend. It was here that Moses was born, a child destined for greatness in a time of hardship. Though he was born into a world where slavery was rampant and cruelty reigned supreme, Moses would rise to become a beacon of hope for his people.

A Leader Emerges

As Moses grew, he witnessed firsthand the injustices suffered by his fellow Israelites at the hands of their Egyptian masters. Slavery was a common practice in ancient Egypt. As such, the Israelites were stripped of their humanity by their oppressors. But Moses refused to stand idly by while his people suffered. He knew that he was destined for something greater and had a divine purpose to fulfill.

The Exodus

Driven by a deep sense of justice and guided by the hand of destiny, Moses embarked on a courageous quest to free his people from bondage. With unwavering faith and unyielding determination, he led the Israelites on a daring journey out of Egypt and into the wilderness beyond. Though it was dangerous and difficult, Moses never gave up.

The Lawgiver

As they journeyed through the desert, Moses received divine guidance from the "Almighty" (his Christian god). He climbed Mount Sinai, where he received the Ten Commandments—divine laws that his god had created to serve as the foundation of a just and righteous society. So, Moses became not only a liberator but also a lawgiver, bestowing upon his people the gift of freedom and the wisdom to govern themselves with justice and compassion.

Legacy and Inspiration

Though Moses's time on Earth has long since passed, his legacy endures as a symbol of courage, compassion, and unwavering faith. His story has inspired countless generations to stand up against oppression, fight for justice, and never lose hope in the face of adversity. From the banks of the Nile to the shores of distant lands, the tale of Moses continues to captivate the hearts and minds of people around the world.

The Remarkable Life of Ibn Khaldun

After discussing one of Christianity's most famous icons, we now move on to a lesser-known legend named Ibn Khaldun. Ibn Khaldun was born into a wealthy and influential family. Despite his privileged upbringing, Ibn Khaldun faced many challenges during his youth. Tragedy struck when he lost his parents at a young age, which thrust him into a world of hardship and uncertainty. But even in the face of these difficulties, Ibn Khaldun was still hungry for knowledge.

Ibn Khaldun was blessed with a keen intellect and a passion for learning. He studied under the guidance of respected teachers and scholars, soaking up knowledge like a sponge. But Ibn Khaldun's quest for wisdom extended beyond the confines of the classroom—he was a tireless reader and seeker of truth. Despite his wealth, Ibn Khaldun faced many obstacles on his path to enlightenment. However, his determination could not be stopped.

A Voice of Dissent

As Ibn Khaldun matured, he became increasingly disappointed with the complexities of politics and governance. He witnessed firsthand the corruption and injustice that were like a sickness in his society. So, he decided to speak out against tyranny and oppression. But his outspoken views came at a cost—when he dared to challenge the status quo, he was put in prison. Yet even in the darkest of times, Ibn Khaldun remained true to his beliefs.

Scholar and Philosopher

Upon his release from prison, Ibn Khaldun embarked on a new chapter of his life as a scholar and philosopher. He poured his insights and observations into writing, publishing numerous books that would shape the course of intellectual history. His magnum opus, "The Muqaddimah," is a masterpiece of historical analysis and social theory. It even laid the groundwork for modern sociology and historiography, which are two very important fields of study about humans and history.

Legacy and Impact

Ibn Khaldun's writings transcended the boundaries of time and space, resonating with readers across generations and continents. His profound insights into society, culture, and human behavior continue to inspire scholars and thinkers to this day. Ibn Khaldun's legacy endures as a testament to the power of knowledge and resilience. May his story serve as a beacon of inspiration for all who dare to dream, question, and seek the truth in an uncertain world.

Muhammad Ali: The Father of Modern Egypt

Now let's move on from one of Egypt's greatest thinkers to one of its greatest leaders! , We'll now delve into the remarkable story of Muhammad Ali—the visionary leader known as the "Father of Modern Egypt." Join us as we uncover his journey of reform and transformation as he forever changed the course of Egyptian history!

Muhammad Ali was a trailblazer, reformist, and visionary leader who left an important mark on the sands of time. As he was born in the late 18th century, Muhammad Ali rose to prominence during a period of great change and conflict in Egypt.

A Man of Vision

From an early age, Muhammad Ali possessed a bold and modern vision for Egypt's future. He recognized the need to modernize Egypt's military and institutions, laying the groundwork for a stronger, more prosperous nation.

Modernization and Reform

Muhammad Ali wasted no time in reforming Egypt. He rapidly modernized the military, cultivating a skilled Egyptian elite trained in European academic institutions. Under his leadership, Egypt underwent a period of unprecedented transformation, embracing new technologies, industries, and ideas.

Legacy of Leadership

Muhammad Ali's legacy as the "Father of Modern Egypt" is celebrated by Egyptians far and wide. His tireless efforts to elevate Egypt's status on the world stage earned him the respect and admiration for centuries to come.

And so, dear readers, we bid farewell to Muhammad Ali—the visionary leader whose legacy continues to inspire and uplift the people of Egypt. May his story serve as enduring inspiration and remind us of the power of leadership, vision, and determination.

Chapter Conclusion

From Muhammad Ali's role in profound change to Imhotep's many talents, these stories show us that anyone can achieve greatness. Whether it's through building magnificent structures, embarking on daring adventures, or sharing wise words to guide others, each hero we met had their own unique way of leaving a mark on the world. These men and legends prove that bravery, intelligence, and kindness never go out of style.

Remember, heroes aren't just characters in stories; they're real people who do extraordinary things. Maybe one day, you'll tell your own heroic tale! Keep dreaming big, staying curious, and learning from those who came before us. Who knows? Maybe you're the next great hero in the making!

CONCLUSION

As our journey through the land of ancient Egypt draws to a close, we bid farewell to the legendary figures, majestic monuments, and timeless tales that have captivated our hearts and minds. From the towering pyramids of Giza to the mystical rituals of mummification, we have explored the many wonders of a civilization that has left a lasting mark on history.

As we reflect on the stories we have encountered, we are reminded of the rich tapestry of culture, tradition, and mythology that defined ancient Egypt. We have witnessed the power and majesty of the pharaohs, the wisdom and strength of the queens, and the divine grace of the gods and goddesses who ruled over the heavens and the earth.

Through the tales of heroes and legends, we have learned valuable lessons of courage, resilience, and compassion. From the visionary leaders who transformed their kingdom to the ordinary people who dared to defy the odds, each story has inspired us to dream big, overcome obstacles, and strive for greatness.

So, though our journey may be coming to an end, the spirit of ancient Egypt lives on in our hearts and minds. As we close the pages of this book, we carry with us the memories of the pharaohs, the echoes of the gods, and the timeless wisdom of the ages. Let us cherish these stories and pass them on to future generations, so that the legacy of ancient Egypt may endure for all time.

And so, dear readers, we bid farewell to the cradle of civilization. May the magic of ancient Egypt continue to inspire and enchant us, guiding us on new adventures and discoveries.

Until we meet again, may the sands of time carry your dreams to distant shores, where the legacy of Egypt shines bright as the stars in the night sky.

Bye for now!

THE EXTRA PART

So now that we've journeyed through the magnificent stories of ancient Egypt, met powerful pharaohs, glamorous queens, and learned about mighty gods and legendary heroes,, let's check how much you've remembered. Take this quiz to see how many correct answers you can get. Are you ready to prove that you're a true historian of ancient Egypt?

Why is King Tutankhamun often referred to as "The Boy King"?

A) He became pharaoh at a very old age.
B) He was known for his youthful energy.
C) He became pharaoh when he was very young.
D) He ruled for a very long time.

What is Pharaoh Djoser best known for?

A) Building the first true pyramid.
B) His military conquests.
C) Establishing the first schools in Egypt.
D) Writing important laws.

What title is Ramses II often given due to his achievements?

A) The Great Architect.
B) The Great and Powerful.
C) The Great Explorer.
D) The Great Writer.

What major change did Akhenaten bring during his reign?

A) He introduced the worship of many gods.
B) He banned the worship of all gods but one, Aten.
C) He improved the economy.
D) He wrote a famous book.

What was Snefru known for in ancient Egypt?

A) Building a famous temple.
B) Constructing several pyramids.
C) His long peaceful reign.
D) Discovering papyrus.

How did Queen Hatshepsut make her mark as a ruler of Egypt?

A) She was known for her beautiful singing.
B) She dressed as a man to assert her authority as pharaoh.
C) She wrote a popular book on governance.
D) She discovered gold mines.

What was the primary purpose of mummification?

A) To ensure the deceased looked their best.
B) To protect the dead from wildlife.
C) To preserve the body for the afterlife.
D) To mark the social status of the deceased.

Ra was the god of…?

A) The underworld.
B) The moon.
C) The sun.
D) The ocean.

In The Tale of the Shipwrecked Sailor, what unusual character does the sailor meet?

A) A talking hippopotamus.
B) A giant serpent king.
C) A ghost of a pharaoh.
D) An enchanted cat.

What is Ptah-hotep best remembered for?

A) His military strategies.
B) His architectural designs.
C) His maxims or wise sayings.
D) His treasure discoveries.

ANSWERS

C) He became pharaoh when he was very young.

A) Building the first true pyramid.

B) The Great and Powerful.

B) He banned the worship of all gods but one, Aten.

B) Constructing several pyramids.

B) She dressed as a man to assert her authority as pharaoh.

C) To preserve the body for the afterlife.

C) The sun.

B) A giant serpent king.

C) His maxims or wise sayings.

THE EXTRA, EXTRA PART

These riddles are designed to test your knowledge about the fascinating world of ancient Egypt. Each one relates to the pharaohs, queens, gods, and mythical tales we've discussed. So, put on your thinking caps! Are you prepared to decode these enigmas and discover hidden truths? Grab a pencil, gather your friends, and see who can solve these ancient puzzles first!

Pharaohs and Pyramids:

I was made of stone and stood for eternity, a tomb for Pharaoh but without a key. What am I?

Mystical Queens:

I ruled as a king but was not a man, under my reign Egypt expanded its span. Who am I?

Gods and Goddesses:

I have the head of a falcon, and the sun is my mark, I protect the Pharaohs even in the dark. Who am I?

Legendary Creatures:

Part man and part lion, I guard and protect, solving my riddle you must not neglect. What am I?

The Afterlife:

I am not alive, but I walk and talk, preserved for eternity, in bandages I'm locked. What am I?

Hieroglyphics:

Symbols and pictures that speak without sound, and in tombs and temples, with me, messages are found. What am I?

Ancient Wisdom:

I am old but wise, with advice in a book, to find a life of harmony, in my pages, you should look. Who am I?

Heroic Tales:

I left my home under a cloud of fear, but returned a hero, to the land I hold dear. Who am I?

ANSWERS

Pharaohs and Pyramids:

Answer: A pyramid.

Mystical Queens:

Answer: Queen Hatshepsut.

Gods and Goddesses:

Answer: Horus.

Legendary Creatures:

Answer: The Sphinx.

The Afterlife:

Answer: A mummy.

Hieroglyphics:

Answer: Hieroglyphics.

Ancient Wisdom:

Answer: Ptah-hotep.

Heroic Tales:

Answer: Sinuhe.

GREEK LEGENDS FOR KIDS

GREEK LEGENDS FOR KIDS

a licensed professional before attempting any techniques outlined in this book.

By reading this document, the reader agrees that under no circumstances is the author responsible for any losses, direct or indirect, that are incurred as a result of the use of the information contained within this document, including, but not limited to, errors, omissions, or inaccuracies.

FREE BONUS FROM HBA: EBOOK BUNDLE

Greetings!

First of all, thank you for reading our books. As fellow passionate readers of History and Mythology, we aim to create the very best books for our readers.

Now, we invite you to join our VIP list. As a welcome gift, we offer the History & Mythology Ebook Bundle below for free. Plus, you can be the first to receive new books and exclusives! Remember it's 100% free to join.

Simply scan the QR code to join.

CONTENTS

INTRODUCTION

Welcome, welcome to a magical, mystical world full of gods, goddesses, heroes, monsters and more! Prepare yourselves to enter the world of Greek mythology where we'll embark on a thrilling adventure through the lands of ancient Greece. Allow us to invite you back to those days when the gods ruled the heavens, whilst brave heroes and scary monsters battled as wise goddesses guarded the lands. For hundreds and thousands of years their tales have been retold and told countless times.

Passed through generations like the sands of time, to this day they continue to captivate, make us laugh, smile and inspire us to dream big. Young friends, you're part of the new generation that is being given the noble task of passing on these epic myths. Inside this very book are the most epic stories, heroes, gods, goddesses, monsters and more from Greek mythology.

We're sure you've heard some of these Greek myths once or twice or maybe more! Maybe you've heard of the daring feats of the mighty Hercules? Or how about the scary Gorgon, Medusa with snakes for hair? These are just some of the fascinating Greek myths that have lasted the tests of time. Prepare to meet Zeus, Athena, Hercules and many other fantastic characters.

It's a journey that will take you through mystical lands where you encounter dangerous monsters and learn vital lessons along the way. Imagine cracking a code that opens the doors to a magical dimension of knowledge…. well that's what learning Greek mythology is like! Truly you're about to discover so many new lessons and experiences holding timeless value.

Are you ready to embark on the journey, young adventurers? Well please fasten your seatbelts for this is about to be a joyous ride packed with magic, wonder and legendary tales that have entertained curious children just like you for a very long time. And pay attention, because there is not a second to waste!

Here is a sneak peak of what to expect inside this book.…

In part 1 we'll learn about the gods & goddesses of mount olympus. You'll discover Zeus, king of all gods, Aphrodite goddess of love and many more deities.

In part 2 we'll learn about the gorgons, warriors & monsters. You'll discover the maze of the minotaur, the warrior Amazonian women and many more legends.

In part 3 we'll explore heroic quests & epic journeys. Including Hercules & his twelve labours, the fall of Icarus and many more fantastic tales.

In part 4 we'll discover myths & legends such as Pandora's box - a cautionary tale of curiosity and the Trojan war - an epic battle of heroes, gods & a wooden horse.

In part 5 we'll learn about even more gods & goddesses! Including Hades - lord of the underworld, Eros (cupid) - the mischievous god of love and many more.

In part 6 we'll learn about Greek culture & legacy. You'll discover ancient Greek heroes in the modern world, the Greek olympics - honouring the gods through sports and much more.

After we conclude our book stay tuned for you will also find some excellent activities including, mythological riddles, mythological quiz show and mythical cooking.

Greek mythology has lasted for many years because it's full of treasures of wonderful stories that will truly amaze you. Although these are more than just stories; they also contain valuable lessons about friendship, bravery and doing the right thing. Do you want to learn more and to make new friends? Of course, you do! AND we're sure you want to be brave! Well, you'll learn all of these important lessons, traits and much more from Greek mythology.

Now prepare your imaginations, fasten your seatbelts and join us on a magnificent and wondrous journey into the world of Greek mythology. This will be a journey that you'll never forget!

PART 1
GODS & GODDESSES OF MOUNT OLYMPUS

CHAPTER 1

ZEUS - RULER OF THE MIGHTY OLYMPIANS

Meet the powerful and intelligent Zeus, the supreme ruler of all Gods! Actually, there is only one God king, and since he is the one in charge, he is also the most powerful god in Greek mythology. Welcome on board this journey as we investigate the magnificent and fascinating world of Zeus and his amazing exploits.

The story of Zeus begins many, many years ago in the wonderful region of ancient Greece. Born to Cronus and Rhea he faced danger right from his birth! His father, Cronus was an anxious ruler, who feared that one day his children would grow up to dethrone him. So, in his madness and greed he swallowed every child that his wife Rhea gave birth to!

Rhea knew this, but of course as a mother she deeply loved her children. Thus, she protected young Zeus by skillfully tricking Cronus to swallow a rock instead. With Cronus distracted she took the opportunity to hide Zeus in a quiet cave on the Greek island of Crete. It is here that the great, God king grew up safely on an island overflowing with majestic, wild and wonderful animals...all whilst having amazing adventures! Imagine such a place!

Young Zeus grew to be older, wiser and stronger. In due time, he went to confront his father and release his siblings from Cronus's belly. With the help of several mighty allies, he crushed Cronus and saved his siblings. Relieved the young gods and goddesses were eternally grateful and chose him as their commander. Drum roll cue...and so he became ruler of Mount Olympus!

In this heavenly realm the ancient gods and goddesses resided in majestic palaces and oversaw the Earth below. With Zeus in charge everything ran smoothly and fairly. With his strong and considerate rule, he safeguarded the world. In times of threat, he would hurl his famous thunderbolts into the sky and create thunderstorms.

The family tree of Zeus

Imagine a spiralling, massive family tree, rather like a giant puzzle. Well, this is kind of what the family tree of Zeus looked like! Poseidon the god of sea and Hades the ruler of the Underworld were his brothers. Then there was his wife, Queen Hera. Then there were his sisters Demeter and Hestia. Under them were his children….and this is where things became even more fascinating. Zeus fathered countless children with many goddesses, and even mortal women. We'll hear all about his kids later! From Athena the clever goddess of wisdom to Hermes the swift messenger, and of course Hercules the mighty half god, half human. Can you imagine a more powerful family?

Famous Zeus Myths

Zeus was at the helm of many amazing myths and stories. One of the most fascinating tales was The Titanomachy. Truly this was an epic battle of the gods versus the Titans, in fact it's one of the most famous Greek myths of all time. In this epic story the Titans attacked Zeus and his crew on Mount Olympus. However, they bit off more than they could chew! Zeus and his family fought back with vengeance to retain their place as the bosses of the universe!

Another famous myth involving Zeus was with Prometheus, a cunning Titan who stole fire from the gods and gave it to the humans. Stealing from Zeus made him furious! Zeus caught up with Prometheus and dished him out a harsh punishment, by chaining him to a rock. Here an eagle would feast on his liver every day…yikes!

Besides all this doom and gloom Zeus was also a rather amusing god. Imagine this scene. One day he disguised himself as a glamorous white bull in an attempt to seduce a beautiful princess named Europa! She was captivated by the bull's charm and climbed onto his back. Zeus galloped away and took her to the island of Crete for a magical and romantic time. Queen Hera would later find out and scold Zeus!

Young readers as our journey into the domain of Zeus the king of the gods comes to an end let us remember everything from his unusual birth and early life to his role as leader of Mount Olympus. Remember his interesting family tree, his epic tales and his legend that lives on through his most classic myths. Not only are his stories exciting, they also teach us valuable lessons about courage, leadership and that family is very, very important. Young friends anytime you hear thunder or see a flash of lightning in the sky remember that Zeus is watching over all of us with his thunderbolts!

CHAPTER 2

HERA - THE QUEEN OF MOUNT OLYMPUS

Good day young explorers! Are you ready to meet with a gorgeous and powerful queen? Well join us on an amazing voyage into the world of Hera the Queen of the Gods. Wait a minute though, let's first clear up a rumour. Being a queen wasn't all about wearing a sparkling crown and sitting on a throne. Not at all! Listen, Hera was a symbol of power, grace, and divine wisdom. So, are you ready to learn all about her stories and life lessons along the way?

Hera the daughter of Cronus and Rhea was born with beauty more mesmerising than a thousand sunsets. Zeus the king of all gods fell in love with her instantly. He was so mystified by her beauty that he just had to make her his queen. Their wedding was a spectacular event that was attended by all of the gods and goddesses of Mount Olympus. The day was magnificent, full of laughing, happiness and celebration. On this day Hera not only became the queen of the gods, but she also became the goddess of marriage. From this day onwards it was her duty to safeguard the connection of love between couples.

Along with her husband Zeus she reigned over the skies. Whenever she waved her hands, the winds would blow, and the clouds would gather to create thunderstorms. Although she was more than just a great natural force.

Hera was also a clever and strategic thinker. She took responsibility and presided with intelligence over families and their children. With her blessings families would enjoy loving relationships.

Oh, but everyone is not perfect young readers. Even though Hera was powerful and smart, she also had a weakness. Jealousy plagued her, particularly when it came to Zeus who was infamous for his roving eye. The great god king had an unhealthy habit of falling in love with other women…and this drove Hera crazy!

One infamous story of her envy involves the mighty Hercules. Hercules was the son of Zeus' affair with a mortal woman named Alcmena. Hera learned of this and became so furious that she sent snakes to attack Hercules as a young child. But even as a boy Hercules was strong and fearless. He easily defeated the snakes and proved his destiny for greatness.

Besides her jealousy Hera did have a kind side. She frequently defended those in need and blessed the relationships of loving families. In one famous myth a mad Zeus changed a woman into a cow to shield him from Hera's wrath. With kindness Hera chose to save the woman and made her one of her priestesses.

The Marriage Goddess

Whenever couples encountered difficulties in ancient Greece, they would seek advice from Hera. She guided them through all the trials and tribulations of marriage. She taught the importance of loyalty, trust and compromise in relationships. Teaching that loves and respect are the pillars of lasting relationships.

As we approach the end of our wondrous journey into the realm of Hera, the mighty queen of the Gods, let's take a moment to reflect on the magical path we've travelled. From her origins to her incredible stories and her role as the guardian of marriage and families. Her marriage with Zeus, the king of the gods was nothing short of epic. Together they ruled with a majestic grace that showed us that even the most powerful beings can find strength in the bonds of love and commitment.

Hera's tale is a tapestry of wonders that has left a legendary mark on Greek mythology. When you gaze upon a colourful rainbow painted across the sky, remember that it might just be her way of showering love and wisdom upon our world. As we bid farewell to this enchanting journey, may her stories continue to live in your heart. And may you too find the strength to weather life's challenges and celebrate the joys of love, unity and understanding.

CHAPTER 3

POSEIDON - GOD OF THE MIGHTY SEAS

Ahoy there young sailors! Join us as we set sail across the deep blue, ocean waters where we will discover the magical world of Poseidon. Put on your diving masks and flippers as we dive deep into this sea god's kingdom to explore his incredible powers and the fascinating stories that have made him a legend in Greek mythology. Are you ready? Well then take a deep breath!

Imagine the vast seas with Poseidon standing upon them, tall and majestic. With his trident in hand, he ruled over the waves and all of the mystical animals that lived underneath the water. But did you know that he's more than simply a sea god? He's also a master of earthquakes! Whenever the earth shakes or rumbles underneath us it is a sign to remind us of his epic power…. boom!

Hold on, and that's not all! Did you know that he created horses? It's quite funny how this all happened actually.

Allow us to explain. Poseidon loved to compete. One day the goddess of wisdom Athena challenged him to design a useful present for humanity. Poseidon, not one to turn down a challenge, took his trident and smashed it into the sea. Guess what? Out popped a horse!

Meanwhile Athena planted an olive tree. Poseidon smugly smiled assuming he had won. But he wasn't the judge here…humans were given the task of choosing which was more useful: the olive tree or the horse? After thinking long and hard, they chose the olive tree. But why? Well horses are cool, but the olive tree gave them much more. It provided them with food, oil and wood. However, Poseidon's horses remain a symbol of his might and majesty.

The Mythology of Posiedon

Now we know Poseidon was a mighty God, but he did have one really bad temper! Whenever he was in a bad mood it was better to avoid him because he might unleash massive storms or huge disasters! Sailors or anyone in his way would surely perish. One such story of his infamous temper involves Odysseus. Well, oopsy, because this hero made the mistake of getting Poseidon so angry that he stirred up huge storms around him! Odysseus with daring actions and smart thinking was able to navigate out and return safely to his home.

Poseidon's Marine Creatures

Poseidon ruled over the seas which overflowed with fantastic creatures that would awe any of you young explorers. He was frequently joined by his friends, the dolphins and many other fantastic creatures. Dolphins would dance with him in the waters and send his messages to passing sailors. Besides the beautiful creatures, his kingdom was also home to many dangerous monsters such as the frightening Kraken and the scary Leviathan. These fearsome sea monsters were a testament to Poseidon's epic rule!

As our journey across the seas exploring Poseidon draws to an end let us remember his powers and rule over the oceans and the earthquakes. Never forget his creation of the magnificent horses, his tails of fury and his legacy along the majesty of the seas. The next time you visit the beach and feel the salty breeze on your face, or you see the waves crashing into the sands, remember his power is all around you. Poseidon's tales will continue to captivate young sailors just like you. Allow them to inspire you to discover the wonders of the sea and the mysteries that lay beneath!

CHAPTER 4

DEMETER - GODDESS OF AGRICULTURE

Good day young farmers and nature lovers! Prepare yourselves to enter the fantastic world of Demeter, the goddess of agriculture. Join us as we unravel the mysteries of her enchanted domain. Are you ready to begin an exciting journey through the seasons, farmlands and to solve some puzzling mysteries? Well then let's go!

Born the daughter of the Titans Cronus and Rhea, Demeter was a beautiful goddess with golden hair and a heart as warm as the sun. She was the sister of Zeus and Hera; those other powerful gods and goddesses we talked about earlier. Just like them, great things surrounded her.

Demeter and The Changing Seasons

Have you ever wondered why the weather changes so much? Why is it cold in winter and hot in summer? Allow us to explain, well let's let Demeters tale do the talking!

The story of the seasons begins with Demeters stunningly beautiful daughter, Persephone. One fine day she was wandering through the fields when she came across a charming stranger named Hades.

He was the god of the underworld, and he was captivated by her beauty. Hades really, really, really wanted to take her to the darkest realms of his kingdom. But she wasn't so sure! Would you be? Anyway, despite her protests Hades chose her as his queen.

Demeter was left feeling heartbroken and sad to lose her daughter. Her grief was so intense that the plants wilted and the ground became empty around her. It was as if the world was in sorrow with her. The gods became concerned that there would be no crops or harvest without her touch. So Zeus intervened and requested that Hades return Persephone to her mother. He said ok, but it wasn't so simple. Whilst in the underground Persephone had eaten some pomegranate seeds. This was a sneaky trick played by Hades which meant she had to spend a part of each year with him.

When she was free Persephone returned to her mother's side. During this time Demeters mood improved. Flowers bloomed and began to spring as she showered the earth with her blessings once more. With her daughter by her side, wonderful plants blossomed and prospered. But when the time came for Persephone to return to the underworld Demeter became sad. Her glum mood threw a heavy shadow over the land. The world entered the harsh days of winter. Thanks to Hades' mischief we have the seasons of spring, summer, autumn and winter.

The Eleusinian Mysteries

The Eleusinian Mysteries were special festivals for Demeter and Persephone. These special rituals took place in Eleusis; it is here that Demeter's gifts to humanity were honoured in secret ceremonies. People would travel many far from all around ancient Greece to take part in these sacred rituals. During these rituals they would be taken on a spiritual journey learning all about the secrets of life, death and the natural cycles. Those who took part in the ceremonies were thought to be blessed by Demeter. The rituals were so special that they were attended by powerful monarchs and famous philosophers such as Alexander the Great and Plato.

Demeter's presence was critical for crop prosperity and farmer well-being in ancient Greece. Farmers prayed to Demeter while they ploughed the fields, hoping for her favour and large crops to grow. She was their protector and guide, making certain that the seeds hatched and flourished into healthy plants. Ancient Greek farmers were well aware of this and expressed their appreciation and celebration of Demeter. They asked for her continuous blessings because they feared without her their crops would not grow.

Young nature lovers as we come to the end of our journey through Demeters world, let's remember her endearing relationship with her daughter Persephone. Remember the reason for the shifting seasons and their crucial role in ancient Greek agriculture. The next time you see the fields bursting with golden grains or you feel the earth underneath your feet let it remind of her magnificence. Love and appreciate the beauty of nature just like the ancient Greeks did in celebration of their beloved goddess Demeter!

CHAPTER 5

APOLLO - GOD OF THE SUN & ARTS

Well, hello there and welcome to the fascinating world of Apollo, God of the sun and arts! Here we will reveal his extraordinary birth and early life on the island of Delos. Joins us to explore his fascinating duties both as the god of sun and the arts. On our journey we will make a stop to meet the mystical Oracle at Delphi. Plus, we will travel back to explore the thrilling myths of Apollo and his role in the Trojan War. Are you ready?

Apollo was born to Zeus, king of all gods and the beautiful Leto. However, their relationship was a secret (don't tell anyone) and so when Leto was pregnant with Apollo, she took shelter on the island of Delos. Apollo was born on this lovely island, among golden rays of sunlight. From the beginning he was a cute and lovely child, with his golden hair and charming grin.

Apollo was gifted with powers as diverse and dazzling as the sun itself. Each day he rode his sparkling chariot across the sky providing light and warmth to the whole world. Yet his gifts went far beyond the sun. Did you know he was also a talented musician? Apollo played the lyre with grace and enchanted everyone who heard him. Oh, and he was also the god of poetry, inspiring storytellers, and their works. Wait and one more thing! Did you know he was also the god of healing? Apollo was famous for his ability to cure illness and help those in times of distress. His sacred temples, such as the one at Epidaurus, became places of recovery for the ill and sick.

The Oracle at Delphi

The mysterious Oracle at Delphi was one of the most fascinating figures related to Apollo. Ancient Greeks would visit her seeking advice on everything from personal to business decisions and much more. In a trance-like state, she would give replies that were thought to be messages from Apollo himself. In ancient Greece, her prophecies influenced key events and shaped the path of history. To this day she is celebrated as a higher power for seeking guidance. She was kind of an ancient version of Google or ChatGPT!

Myths Featuring Apollo

The adventures and travels of Apollo are intertwined with some of Greek mythologies' most fascinating stories. Have you ever heard of the Trojan war? Well Apollo was a key figure in this epic battle where the Trojans hid in a large horse to surprise their enemies.

When Agamemnon refused to release a captive priestess, Chryseis, unleashed a fatal plague on the Greek camp. He also directed Paris's arrow to puncture the invincible Achilles' heel, resulting in the hero's demise. Such drama! Apollo's love affairs were also dramatic. He fell madly in love with Daphne but she escaped his advances by turning into a tree!

As we come to the end of our journey exploring Apollo let us remember his fascinating birth and early life on the island of Delos. A god with multiple talents and his skills. Let us also remember that he was a great healer who provided profound answers to those who sought advice from the mysterious Oracle at Delphi.

Forever Apollo's stories will motivate us to embrace our unique skills and to offer healing to the world. His relationship with the Oracle of Delphi inspires us to seek wisdom and guidance from our elders whenever we're struggling in life. Sometimes we won't know all the answers but remember there are people around you who might. Embrace your abilities, seek wisdom AND remember that you have the potential to bring your greatest gifts to the world around you!

CHAPTER 6

ARTEMIS - GODDESS OF THE HUNT & MOON

Good day young hunters and explorers! Welcome to a journey into the enchanting world of Artemis, goddess of the hunt and moon. Here we'll explore her dual nature as both a hunter and protector along with her most famous myths. But that's not all! You're in for a treat because you'll also learn about the sacred animals and symbols associated with her in Greek mythology. Indeed, these are powerful lessons to learn, so stay tuned!

Artemis was a very unique goddess, so unique that she had two parts to her personality. In one part she was a goddess of the hunt, a skilled archer with the perfect aim. She roamed in the wild hunting with a silver bow and arrows to fiercely protect all wild creatures. In particular she had a fondness for deer and bears.

Her other side was as a protector of young children and women. As the goddess of childbirth, she watched over pregnant women to ensure the children's safe delivery. In Greek mythology she is often portrayed as a crescent moon crown to signify her connection with the moon.

Artemis Famous Myths and Battles

There are many, many famous myths and battles showcasing the bravery and power of Artemis. In one famous myth she helped her brother Apollo defeat a huge, super python. This slithery, scary creature had been sent to harm her mother Leto. Thank goodness she was able to defeat it!

In another famous tale a hunter named Actaeon accidentally stumbled upon Artemis taking a bath in a sacred spring. As punishment for sneaking up and looking at her, she transformed him into a deer. He was then hunted down and killed by his own dogs…a lesson not to be sneaky!

The Sacred Animals and Symbols of Artemis

Artemis was associated with several, sacred animals reflecting her roles as the goddess of the hunt and protection. Deer, with their grace and swiftness, were very special to her. Often she was shown with a deer by her side. Whoever was caught harming a deer would be in big trouble.

Other living things sacred to Artemis included bears, wild boars, hares and the cypress tree.

If you're reading or listening to this at night take a look up at the sky and look for the moon. The moon was very important in Greek mythology, and Artemis played a very important role in this connection. People believed it to be a symbol of Artemis's power and beauty. She was often referred to as "Phoebe," meaning "bright" or "radiant,". This was a sign of her connection to the luminous glow of the moon.

Artemis was the twin sister of Apollo and he was the God of the Sun, further making a strong connection between the moon and the sun. The ancient Greeks believed that the sun and the moon were heavenly chariots driven by Apollo and Artemis, lighting up the sky and guiding the world. Imagine that the next time you look up!

As we conclude our thrilling journey into the world of Artemis, the goddess of the hunt and the moon, let us be inspired by her stories. Remember her role in nature and let it remind you to be kind to nature and all of its animals. We must also be kind to all of the other people around us, and especially to protect our loved ones.

So young explorers the next time you take a walk out into nature or when you look up at the moon in the sky, remember the goddess Artemis. Let her spirit inspire you to protect and care for our beautiful world with all of its lovely creatures.

CHAPTER 7

ARES - THE GOD OF WAR

Good day brave young adventurers! Prepare yourselves to enter the world of the mighty god of war, Ares. This powerful god represented the fierce and brave warriors of ancient Greece. Are you ready to be inspired with courage and strength? Well let's enter the world of the great and powerful Ares!

Ares was the son of Zeus, the supreme ruler of the gods, and Hera, the majestic queen of Olympus, was a force to be reckoned with. With his powerful build and fierce presence, he was a true warrior. Clad in gleaming armour and wielding his mighty spear, Ares was a symbol of strength and determination.

For the ancient Greeks, Ares represented everything related to war and conflict. His domain was battle and chaos of which he thrived in.

When warriors clashed in the battlefield they believed that Ares was watching over them. Warriors and soldiers sought courage from him to fight with bravery and determination.

But there's more to Ares than just his warrior spirit! Stories from Greek mythology whisper about his secret affection for Aphrodite, the goddess of love and beauty. Despite her marriage to Hephaestus, the god of craftsmanship, Ares's heart held a hidden flame for Aphrodite, igniting dramatic tales that echoed through the ages.

Ares was the father of many mythological characters, including Phobos and Deimos, the gods of fear, and Eros, the god of love. His offspring inherited his father's powerful attributes of a god. Consequently, they also had a significant influence on ancient Greece.

The Mythology of Ares

Ares can be found in many famous myths and stories from Greek mythology which showcase his strength and wisdom. In one famous myth Ares stood with the Olympian gods against some fearsome giants. Long ago the earth trembled beneath the steps of these fearsome giants who challenged the Olympian gods for the very order of the cosmos.

The mighty Ares stepped onto the battlefield and stood shoulder to shoulder with his Olympian companions, ready to confront the towering foes. As the battle raged on, the giants unleashed their devastating power upon the world. Mountains shook, rivers surged, and the very air crackled with their manic energy. But Ares was not one to be scared easily. With a roar that echoed through the heavens, he charged into battle, wielding his powerful weapons. A huge battle of epic proportions ensued! With bravery and perseverance, the Olympian gods defeated the giants. Finally, the world breathed a sigh of relief! Ares's bravery had helped them to win, his unwavering courage a siren of hope that inspired all who witnessed his heroic stand.

Perhaps another and maybe one of the most famous chapters in Ares's legendary exploits was his involvement in the Trojan War. This colossal conflict raged between the proud city of Troy and the determined forces of the Greeks. As the war's thunderous drums of battle echoed across the land, Ares took to the battlefield once again with a thunderous roar. His very presence ignited the hearts of the Trojan warriors, filling them with unwavering determination and inspiration. With his spear gleaming and armour shining, he led the charge with a ferocity that sent shockwaves through the enemy. Through the twists and turns of destiny, his presence ultimately contributed to the Trojans' success on the battlefield.

As we near the end of our journey exploring the mighty Ares let us remember his lasting impact on ancient Greek mythology. Indeed, he represented the brutal side of the world that is at war. But he also inspired people with bravery and courage in times of conflict. To this day the Greeks honour him with rituals and prayers as they seek his guidance before heading into battles. These are often battling not just of fighting but battles of life and business. Even though at times he was reckless, he was also fierce and wise. He inspired many to stand up for themselves in times of adversity. So brave young warriors the next time you hear the rumble of thunder or when you are faced with challenges or bullies, remember Ares the powerful god of war. Let him inspire within your bravery and to face all of your challenges with determination. Stay strong!

CHAPTER 8

ATHENA - GODDESS OF WISDOM & WAR

Hello, hello young scholars and heroic warriors! It is here in this exciting chapter that we'll discover the fascinating world of Athena, goddess of wisdom and war. Prepare yourself to learn the truth about her unusual birth and stay tuned as we explore her special link with the city of Athens. Can you imagine someone so amazing they named a city after them? Get ready to learn all about this wise and powerful goddess!

Imagine the grand entrance of this goddess. It was unlike any other in the realms of the gods and goddesses. For she did not enter the earth in a normal way…no she sprang out from the head of her father Zeus, the king of the Gods! One cloudy day Zeus was having a horrible headache. Actually, it was so terrible that he asked a strong blacksmith to split open his skull with a magical axe! The blacksmith smashed his axe into Zeus's skull. To everyone's shock out popped Athena fully grown, with a spear and shield in hand.

Athena was no ordinary goddess. From the beginning she was both intelligent and powerful demonstrating that wisdom and strength can unite in one.

The citizens of ancient Athens regarded her as their protector and guardian. With her wisdom and direction, they believed their city would prosper. As we know her love of the city was so great they named it after her! To worship her, the residents built the pantheon, a mighty structure which housed a magnificent temple. Once fully built it included a famous statue of Athena holding a shield along with a small statue of Nike, the goddess of victory in her other hand.

The Athens-Poseidon Rivalry

It's well known that Poseidon the great sea god and Athena once held a friendly (and sometimes not so friendly) competition to see who would become Athens patron god or goddess. Whoever could offer the most helpful gift for the city would emerge the winner. Poseidon smashed his trident into the ground causing a powerful spring of salt water that would benefit the sailors and traders of Athens. But Athena had something better in store for the Athenians. She planted an olive tree which provided them with food, oil and wood for construction. Athena won and became their protector forever. The olive tree became a symbol of peace and wealth for Athens.

The Mythology of Athena

Athena was not just a strong warrior she was also smart and intelligent. Heroes would frequently visit her to seek guidance and courage in times of need. Her knowledge was unparalleled and unrivalled among the gods and goddesses. She became a great ally for people in search of direction and insight. When the mighty hero Odysseus faced difficulties on his return from the Trojan War, Athena was by his side guiding him.

As we come to the end of our thrilling voyage through the world of Athena let us remember her remarkable birth from the head of Zeus. With honour she guided Athens and as a wise counsellor and protected it with fever. Along with her smart intellectual powers she was also a skilled warrior. She stood tall wearing a helmet with a shield and spear ready to defend her great city of Athens. Any opponents who dared to challenge her would surely perish. Wisdom and strength can exist together as Athena exemplified.

Young warriors the next time you face a difficulty remember to seek wisdom and direction from the wise. Imagine Athena and be inspired by her just as the heroes of ancient Greece were. Let wise knowledge continue to guide you as you work to become your best selves. May you also attain greatness and become the heroes of your own epic adventures!

CHAPTER 9

HEPHAESTUS - CRAFTSMAN OF THE GODS

Good day young students. Allow us to introduce you to a god with remarkable skills that could shape the very fabric of reality. Marvellous did you say? Well, this god was certainly marvellous. His name was Hephaestus, a masterful blacksmith and a craftsman of the gods. With imagination and brilliance, he created magnificent weapons, stunning works of arts and even shaped the fabric of life itself!

Hephaestus was a truly unique figure among the Olympian gods. Born to Zeus and Hera, he was not only known for being an excellent craftsman but also for his persistence. However, he faced challenges for he was born with a disability that left him with a limp. Now he might have been disabled but he was not one to let it define him. No instead he embraced his unique talents and focused on his craft.

His creative hands breathed life into the weapons and tools that gods and heroes wielded, shaping the fates of those who inhabited this mystical world. With basic raw material he could create magnificent works of art.

One of his most famous creations was a powerful weapon for the gods. Have you ever seen the lightning bolts of Zeus? Well, those were famously created by him. How about Poseidon's trident, and Artemis' silver bow? Those were also created by him, just to name a few. His skills were in demand, and his creations could be found across the heavens. He even constructed magnificent palaces for the gods, including Mount Olympus itself!

Hephaestus' Role in Mythology

Hephaestus wielded his divine talents to forge not only celestial weapons but also the very essence of Greek mythology itself. One of the most famous episodes involving Hephaestus involves his crafty ingenuity in creating some golden chains. You might think they would be jewellery, right? Well not quite! You see, to keep a god still you are going to need some strong chains. Hephaestus crafted some hefty gold chains to bind Prometheus to a rock as punishment for his stealing fire from the heavens. It was Hephaestus's skillful hand that meticulously crafted this unbreakable chain, forever binding the Titan to his rocky prison.

Another famous mythological story involving Hephaestus is the creation of Pandora, the first human woman. Zeus the king of all gods had ordered Hephaestus to shape Pandora out of clay and give her various qualities and gifts. However, she was also born with the gift of curiosity. In her possession was a forbidden box that she was told not to open. But her curiosity overcame her and she could no longer resist temptation. She opened the box, out of which spilled many troubles into the world.

Hephaestus's tales have etched a profound mark upon the canvas of ancient Greek. They teach us that with unwavering determination, creativity and hard work, even the most formidable challenges can be surmounted. His narrative is a testament to the incredible potential that is within each individual. No matter what may appear impossible, even if they come in the form of significant disabilities.

We each have unique talents and capabilities waiting to be unleashed. Maybe you wish to paint beautiful pictures, construct epic buildings or even simply to overcome challenges you encounter in life. Just as Hephaestus masterfully crafted extraordinary works, you too have the power to create remarkable achievements.

Imagine him, the next time you gaze upon a masterpiece of art or stand in awe before an amazing building. Let his story inspire the power of brilliance within you, whatever you undertake. Whether your canvas is a blank sheet, stones and rubble or the very challenges of life, remember that the power to create something extraordinary is within you.

CHAPTER 10

APHRODITE - GODDESS OF LOVE & BEAUTY

Greetings young romantics and lovers of beauty! Prepare yourselves to be fascinated by Aphrodite the goddess of love and beauty. Here in this chapter, we'll learn all about her creation, magical powers and her impact on love. Imagine a world where every moment is filled with love's gentle touch and every corner shines with beauty. That's the world where Aphrodite reigns, spreading her love far and wide.

Legend has it that Aphrodite's birth was as magical as a shimmering seashell. Once upon a time in the vast expanse of the seas, a stormy clash between the gods created waves. Among these crashing waves, something extraordinary happened. Cronus, one of the mighty Titans, decided to do a bit of spring cleaning in the sky and threw his father Uranus's severed body parts into the sea.

As his watery body met the waves, a mystical froth formed, dancing on the surface like a thousand twinkling stars. From that froth emerged none other than Aphrodite! She stepped onto the shore, her radiance matching the sun's golden glow. With every step she took, flowers bloomed in her wake, painting the land with vibrant colours that had never been seen before. Her beauty was so enchanting that even the birds paused their songs just to gaze at her in awe!

Aphrodite was married to Hephaestus, the skilled blacksmith of the gods, known for crafting majestic weapons and remarkable treasures. But her heart danced to a different tune – it beat in rhythm with Ares, the daring God of War. Their love was like the clash of thunder and the sparkle of stars all at once! While Aphrodite's heart leaned towards Ares, she tried to be a loyal wife to Hephaestus. But in the world of gods, secrets are hard to keep. Gossipy breezes whispered through the heavens, and soon, everyone knew of the love that bloomed between Aphrodite and Ares.

The Power of Aphrodite

Beyond love Aphrodite was also a goddess of desire and fertility. Her powers encompassed all types of passionate feelings including those shared by friends and family. Whenever someone felt feelings of love or affection it was thought that her magical touch was at work.

All forms of beauty were thought to be gifts from Aphrodite herself. From beautiful flowers to radiant sunsets and to wondrous works of art. Furthermore, couples from all corners of the world whispered their hopes and dreams to Aphrodite. When they wanted to start families they sought her blessings. When their hearts felt tangled like a puzzle, they knew she was the one to help unravel the knots. Young lovers would gather flowers and offer them to her, asking for guidance in matters of the heart. They hoped to win the affection of those they admired, and they believed Aphrodite's magic could make even the shyest heart beat a little louder.

As we end this chapter exploring the beautiful realm of Aphrodite the goddess of love, fertility and beauty let us remember her magical creation, her powers of love, family, desire and beauty. The next time you see a flower or your heart flutters with love, remember her power is all around you. May her stories continue to inspire love and joy in your hearts. Love will come and go, and when it goes you will feel grief at its loss, but grief is a price worth paying for love. Appreciate and be grateful for all of the beauty and love all around you whilst it's here. Embrace this beautiful world around you with love.

CHAPTER 11

HERMES - MESSENGER OF THE GODS & TRICKSTER

Salutations young explorers and clever thinkers! Welcome to the world of Hermes, the cunning and mysterious messenger of the gods. Join us as we learn about the myths of Hermes. Our journey will take Hermes to meet with Perseus guiding souls to the underworld to his remarkable patronage over travellers, merchants and daring thieves. Hold on tight it will be a speedy ride!

Hermes was the son of Zeus and the gorgeous Maya. Upon Mount Olympus his smart wit and charm landed him in many adventures. With extraordinary speed and amazing flexibility, he travelled quickly between the realms of gods and mortals. Thus, he was chosen as a heavenly messenger.

In the twinkle of an eye with his winged sandals and helmet he could quickly travel exceedingly long distances. But watch because he was also extremely mischievous! Hermes loved to play tricks on his fellow gods and humans. Everywhere he went havoc and laughter followed him.

Hermes inventions

Do you know what a lyre is? No, it's not what you're thinking! It's actually a musical instrument. Imagine a kind of guitar, well this is what people used to play in the ancient Greek times. It was created by Herme. With his powerful imagination he took a tortoise shell and strung it with cow tendons to create this magical musical instrument. He added this along with his signature wings and sandals which allowed him to fly across the skies like a bird on a mission.

Hermes in Famous Myths

Hermes can be found in many fascinating stories and adventures. Tales that showcase his vast talents and kindness. In one such tale Hermes famously bestowed upon Perseus his wings, sandals and magical helmet of invisibility. With those precious gifts, Perseus was able to defeat the scary monster, Medusa.

In many tales and myths Hermes played an important role in guiding souls towards the underworld. He was an expert in transporting souls to the underworld domain of Hades whilst ensuring their safe passage. Yet his influence went far beyond the worlds of gods and mortals. He was also a patron to many different groups of people. Travellers sought Hermes' protection, trusting him to keep a watchful eye on their voyages and assure safe passage through unknown lands. Merchants and traders sought direction from Hermes, who was as god of trade, bringing wealth and fortune to their enterprises. He was even known to have a soft spot for courageous criminals. He frequently bestowed them with luck and cunning, encouraging them to practise their profession skillfully. But be warned everything you do should be lawful!

Now young geniuses we are almost at the end of our journey into the world of Hermes. In a speedy journey we've explored his cunning and mysterious nature. We've learned about his creation of the lyre and the winged sandals. Plus, we've explored the thrilling myths featuring Hermes and his role in guiding souls, travellers, merchants and even daring thieves. What can we learn from all this? Firstly, Hermes teaches us the power of always learning more, to inspire us to discover joy in everyday life and to enjoy the art of mischief…but in moderation! Allow his story to inspire you to embrace your uniqueness, embark on daring adventures, and approach life with a fun spirit. Now go ahead and let your gifts shine brightly, just like the speedy messenger of the gods!

CHAPTER 12

DIONYSUS - GOD OF WINE & FESTIVITY

Welcome young explorers to the enchanted world of Dionysus, the God of wine and festivity! Join us on an exciting journey to discover his unique birth and upbringing on Mount Olympus. We welcome you to explore his roles as the god of wine, joy, lunacy and the lively! Hold steady because this will be a bumpy ride revealing extravagant festivals, lavish celebrations, intriguing myths and much more.

Dionysus was born in a very, very weird way…. Semele, the human princess, was his mother, and Zeus, king of the Gods, was his father. Once again Zeus cheated and fell completely in love with a new woman. This time it was the mortal Semele. When Zeus' wife, Hera, discovered the truth, she became very jealous and tricked Semele into looking at Zeus in his godly form.

The power of Zeus was so overwhelming that Semele died as he appeared in his celestial brilliance. Zeus was helpless but he managed to save their unborn child by stitching Dionysus into his thigh until he was ready to be born. Once born, he brought Dionysus to Mount Olympus to be nurtured among the immortals.

Dionysus had a personality as colourful and varied as the colours of a rainbow! As the god of wine, he offered gifts of grapes and taught people how to make wine. He urged individuals to accept their inner impulses and to express themselves freely using wine as a symbol of joy and pleasure. Such fun it was to be around him!

Dionysus also had a darker side. Beware young readers that too much wine or alcohol might get you in trouble! He tried hard to hide his insanity and craziness. Nonetheless, he showed that there might be a balance between craziness and calmness…. even amid madness!

Ancient Greek Dionysian Festivals and Celebrations

The celebrations of Dionysus were known as Dionysia in ancient Greece. They were loud and joyous affairs! The City Dionysia in Athens, a major festival organised in his honour, was one of the most magnificent festivals. Residents would build outdoor theatres for theatrical events, including tragedies and comedies. The plays, like Dionysus' dual nature, explored human emotions and how they are often played as an inner battle between order and chaos. We have to learn to practise self-control even when we are tempted by something wrong.

The Myths of Dionysus

Dionysus embarked on many fascinating adventures with both humans and immortals. One such famous myth was his journey into the other underworld to save his mother. He journeyed deep into the dangerous underworld where Hades ruled to save his mother Semele. This demonstrated his strength and willingness to do what was right and to save his family.

Another famous myth involving him is that of King Midas. King Midas had an uncontrollable desire and this created a problem for him. Everything he touched turned to gold! Now that might seem cool, right? But what happens when you just want to eat something or to hold the hands of a loved one? Dionysus later taught him the value of simple pleasures and the importance of self-control.

Did you enjoy this journey into the exploration of Dionysus? Let us remember his dual nature as the god of joy, wine and madness! Remember the festivals that celebrate him in ancient Greece to this day. Remember the thrilling myths of his encounters with both the mortal and the immortals.

As we conclude our journey into the realm of Dionysus let us remember that we should moderate and balance in our lives. Too much excess is often a bad thing. Strive for balance young readers. Learn to appreciate the simple things in life. After all there's more to life than materialistic things or comparing yourself to someone else. Be grateful for the life you have and let the spirit of Dionysus inspire you to celebrate your loved ones. Gratitude and appreciation with moderation will lead to fulfilment.

PART 2
GORGONS, WARRIORS & MONSTER

CHAPTER 13

THE MAZE OF THE MINOTAUR - CONQUERING THE LABYRINTHS MONSTER

Long ago, in the mysterious times of ancient Greece, where myths and legends came to life, there was once a mighty king named Minos. He ruled over a lavish kingdom on the island of Crete. Imagine such a paradise with golden sands, blue oceans and a majestic palace upon rocks. Very nice indeed! But there was a small problem, well actually a big problem! At the centre of his paradise kingdom lay a secret that would send shivers down spines. A fearsome creature known as the Minotaur!

Now the Minotaur was not an ordinary monster. Imagine this…its head was a fierce bull whilst its body was that of a powerful man. So ugly! Unfortunately, this beast was sent as a curse by the gods to punish King Minos for his greediness. Having a monster running loose in your kingdom could be a serious issue, as you can imagine. Everywhere it went, chaos and mayhem followed, terrorizing the residents of Crete.

The Maze of the Minotaur

King Minos built a massive maze beneath his palace to keep the Minotaur hidden. Deep within this labyrinth the Minotaur roamed, hungry for flesh and blood.

Only the bravest (or stupidest) of souls dared to enter into the labyrinth. With its high walls, dark corridors, twists and turns it could easily confuse the smartest of heroes. But in the land of heroes, there lived a young prince named Theseus. It was he who was determined to put an end to the Minotaur's reign of terror. And as you're about to find out, he was no fool!

Theseus bravely volunteered to enter the labyrinth and face the beast. With a sword gifted from his father and a ball of thread gifted from his lover, princess Ariadne, he entered the labyrinth. At the entrance he tied one end of the thread and as he walked in deeper it unravelled behind him. This clever trick would later help him to find his way back out.

After many twists and turns, finally he reached the heart of the labyrinth where the Minotaur awaited. With his sword in hand and courage in his heart, he faced the fearsome beast. A mighty battle began and the labyrinth echoed with the clash of steel. Theseus fought with courage, using his wits and strength to conquer the beast. Finally, his sword found its mark, a weak point on the beast's neck. With one swift strike the Minotaur was defeated!

Theseus followed the thread back out through the labyrinth's twists and turns, emerging victorious. With the monster's defeat, the curse that had haunted King Minos' kingdom was lifted. The people of Crete celebrated his bravery… and for finally being freed from terror!

Theseus became a hero whose name would be forever remembered for generations to come. His story teaches us the importance of courage, determination and of facing our fears. Young adventurers, even in the darkest of mazes of life, there is always a way out. Just like Theseus found his way out, we too can overcome daunting challenges. When we stay focused, persistent and seek solutions towards our goals we too can succeed. Never give up even when it gets difficult!

So young adventurers, the next time you find yourself in a tricky situation just remember Theseus and his clever moves to emerge from the labyrinth victorious. Imagine yourself wearing his bravery like a superhero cape, armed with your own courage and clever thinking. In the labyrinth of life, every twist and turn are a chance for you to show off your own heroic spirit!

CHAPTER 14

THE AMAZONS - WARRIOR WOMEN

In the legends of Greek mythology, there once lived a group of mighty, women warriors known as the Amazons. Now these weren't your everyday heroes. Far from it! In a world where men usually ruled, the Amazons stood out like bright stars in the night sky. These fierce women held powerful positions, making choices that echoed through time. Equality wasn't just a word for them, it was a way of life.

Men and women stood side by side, sharing responsibilities and opportunities as equals. With every arrow they shot and every battle they fought, the Amazons proved that courage had no gender boundaries. They didn't just rewrite myths; they rewrote the rules of their world, showing us that true strength comes from unity and that anyone can be a hero, no matter their gender.

At a place, far at the edge of the world they lived surrounded by wild nature and never ending challenges. From a young age they were trained in the arts of combat, archery and horse riding. With unmatched abilities they rode into battle with supreme confidence instilled from their training.

Their armour shined and defended against sharp attacks. And with powerful weapons in hand they defended and led their lands with determination. Yet they were more than leaders, they were also involved in many legendary tales and as we are about to discover…they feared no one!

Amazon Stories

Stories of the Amazons and their adventures can be found in many legendary Greek myths. One famous myth features Hercules on his quest to complete the twelve labours, a series of incredible challenges. During one of these labours, he crossed paths with the Amazons on a challenge to obtain the belt of their Queen, Hippolyta.

Hercules faced a tough challenge. He knew full well of the Amazon warriors powers and respected them greatly. Only a fool would dare to battle them alone. Hercules was no fool and eventually came to an agreement where both he and the Amazon warriors were happy.

Theseus was another Greek hero who found himself up against the powerful Amazons' when he came across their fierce queen, Antiope. But here's where the story takes an unexpected turn, like a river flowing into foreign lands. Theseus and Antiope fell in love! Despite being from different worlds, their hearts connected and they fell in love. They threw down their wellness and joined forces. Love truly has the power to cross boundaries and cultures.

The tales of the Amazons, those legendary warrior women, continue to teach us powerful lessons that resonate across time and culture. Their stories are not just accounts of bravery and skill, but also hold within them deeper insights that remind us of the enduring strength of the human spirit. They weren't merely a force of fierce warriors but champions of teamwork, where different talents, backgrounds, and skills came together to create an undeniable force.

Young heroes, when you are faced with a challenge that seems impossible, think of the Amazons! In moments of doubt let the tales of these brave women who triumphed against the toughest of challenges inspire you. But remember that their victories weren't achieved alone. Just like they stood side by side and lifted each other, you too can reach higher heights through teamwork.

Regardless of where we are from or who we are, each one of us carries great potential to achieve magnificent feats. The wisdom of the Amazons teaches us to treat each and every person with fairness and value. Now venture forth with the knowledge that through unity, diversity and hard work you too can achieve greatness!

CHAPTER 15

MEDUSA - THE CURSED GORGON & HER PETRIFYING STARE

Greetings young adventures and curious minds! Have you ever heard of Medusa? Well, she was one scary monster, she had a chilling curse and some serious hair issues, snakes! In this chapter we'll learn about her origin, why she looked the way she did and the thrilling encounters she faced with brave heroes like Perseus. Finally, we'll learn about her influence in Greek arts and mythology, let's go!

Medusa was one of three Gorgon sisters who were daughters of the sea gods Phorcys and Ceto. Now the Gorgons were not like any other creatures in Greek mythology because they looked very, very different. Just imagine this…instead of beautiful hair, they had venomous snakes for hair! Oh, and their eyes had a petrifying glare. Legend has it that one look into their eyes could turn anyone who dared to gaze into them into stone!

Medusa, with her fierce gaze and snake hair, was the most dreadful of the Gorgons. But why did she look like this? Well once upon a time she caught the eye of the sea god, Poseidon. It was in the temple of the goddess Athena that Poseidon and Medusa secretly met and fell in love. Athena heard about this and became incredibly angry. How dare they flirt in her temple, a place of purity! With vengeance she punished Medusa by transforming her beautiful hair into a bunch of venomous snakes! And that's not all…she also cursed her with a gaze that would turn any living creature to stone. Now as you can imagine, it's difficult to fall in love if everytime you stare at someone they freeze!

Cast out from society and cursed, Medusa wandered the desolate lands, seeking to hide from the world. Her terrifying reputation spread far and wide, reaching the ears of the heroic Perseus. With the help of Athena and other gods, he set out on a daring quest to slay the fearsome Gorgon and claim her head as a trophy.

Athena helped Perseus to find Medusa's lair where he took a polished shield as a mirror to avoid her dangerous gaze.

With a swift strike of his sword he beheaded the monstrous Gorgon. His triumphant victory was a testament to bravery and resourcefulness. Perseus proved that even the most fearsome foes could be overcome with courage and quick thinking.

The Symbolism of Medusa

In Greek art and mythology, Medusa's image represents the duality of beauty and terror. The Greeks believed in the power of both positive and negative forces within the world. On one side there is beauty but another side also has danger. Life is often this way.

Medusa's petrifying gaze served as a cautionary tale, reminding mortals of the consequences of disrespecting the gods or of lying. Her image was often used as a protective talisman to scare away evil spirits and danger. Her head was often engraved on shields and armour of warriors. When faced with adversity it inspired them with courage and determination whilst setting fear in the eyes of their enemies.

As we conclude our thrilling exploration into the world of Medusa, the Gorgon with a chilling curse. Let us remember her origins, her thrilling encounters with heroes like Perseus, and her lasting symbolism in Greek mythology. Medusa's tale, or story offers us many lessons. First of all let us learn that appearances can be deceiving, and the true character of a person is on their inside. Actions will always speak louder than words. Be truthful and honest in your intentions.

Finally let the mythology of Medusa be a lesson in empathy and courage. Embrace the power of persistence and adapting like Perseus did on his quest. Remember that even in the face of the most difficult challenges, your bravery and intelligence will help you to win. May the story of Medusa inspire you to see the beauty within each soul and to conquer the challenges of your own heroic journey!

CHAPTER 16

ENCHANTING SIRENS & MYSTERIOUS CREATURES

Good day young adventurous! Are you ready to dive deep into the realms of Greek mythology? Fantastic! Get ready to uncover the mysteries of some enchanting creatures that have captivated the hearts and minds of storytellers for generations. Prepare yourself to be mesmerised by the bewitching sirens….and prepare yourself even more for other mysterious beings such as the Centaur and the Sphinx. Now let us dive into the deep waters as we dive deep into timeless lessons and fascinating moments from their captivating stories!

The Enchanting Allure of the Sirens

Far beyond the shimmering waves of the Aegean Sea up on the rocky shores, dwelt the alluring sirens. With the voices of angels and a magical beauty these enchanting creatures possessed irresistible charm. Sailors and adventurers alike were lured by their charms. With hypnotical songs they captivated even the bravest of hearts, luring ships and sailors close to their perilous shores. But one hero, named Odysseus avoided the perils.

In an epic journey home, the wise hero came across the Sirens. They called out to him with hypnotic songs. Danger came closer and he had to act quickly. To protect his crew from their mesmerising songs he filled their ears with beeswax and had himself tied to the ship's mast.

Odysseus very well understood their power and allure. His quick thinking and courage allowed him to safely pass their shores.

The sirens and their songs serve as a cautionary tale which teach us to be aware of the dangers of giving in to temptation. When we give into short fix, pleasure often it comes at the expense of wisdom and reason. Stay strong young explorers when you're tempted and practice self-control. Think long term. When you practise self-control and planning ahead it always pays off. In turn you will become stronger each time.

Other Mythical Creatures: The Centaurs & The Sphinx

Far beyond the shores of the sirens, lived many more extraordinary mythical creatures from Greek mythology. Brace yourself young friend for you are about to encounter the wild Centaurs and the powerful Sphinx!

The Centaurs

Half human and half horse, the Centaurs were a lively and unruly bunch, living in the untamed wild. They were famous for their wild behaviour and could often be found at the centre of chaos. One famous Centaur was the wise centaur Chiron, who was a mentor to many heroes, including Achilles and Jason.

The Sphinx

With the head of a woman, the body of a lion, and the wings of a bird, the Sphinx was a mysterious and puzzling creature. She guarded the entrance to the city of Thebes and those seeking entry first had to pass her riddles. Only one famous adventurer named Oedipus is known to have solved her riddle. As for the rest? Well one can only imagine, or lest forget!

Young explorers as we come to the end of this chapter let us explore the lessons from these mythical creatures. The Centaurs teach us about the struggle between our civilised and our wild instincts. Whilst the Sphinx challenges us to confront our knowledge and to be introspective.

Through these stories we have learned about the importance of courage, wisdom and of being self-aware. Such mythical creatures represent our own struggles and potential for greatness. Allow them to inspire you to face challenges with courage and to seek wisdom in times of doubt. As you venture out on your own heroic quests may their wisdom be your guide. May these stories inspire you with curiosity and adventure within your hearts. Until we set sail on our next voyage may these stories continue to captivate and inspire you on your own journey through life.

PART 3

HEROIS QUESTS & EPIC JOURNEYS

CHAPTER 19

HERCULES & THE 12 LABOURS

Once upon a time in ancient Greece, there was a mighty hero named Hercules (also known as Heracles). But he was no ordinary hero; he was the strongest and mightiest of them all! Born the son of Zeus the king of all gods and Alcmena, a mortal woman. From birth he possessed incredible strength and courage. He could bend a steel bar and wrestle a lion, at the same time! But just like all heroes he faced tough challenges. His journey of greatness began with a series of incredible tasks known as the twelve labours. Are you ready to join us on a thrilling adventure to learn about his legendary feats?

The Twelve Labors Begin

The beginning of Hercules' stories starts when he tragically lost control of his actions due to a curse. In order to seek redemption, King Eurystheus tasked him with completing twelve seemingly impossible tasks. But Hercules was good friends with the impossible! So, let's join him for the twelve labours, a test of strength, wit and courage.

Labour 1: Hercules and the Mighty Nemean Lion

Hercules first task was to defeat a lion, but this was no ordinary lion. The Nemean Lion was so ferocious and powerful that it struck fear into the hearts of all who heard its name. Its coat of golden fur was so thick and strong that neither arrows or swords could pierce it. Everywhere it roamed, mayhem and terror followed.

Hercules set out on a journey through deep forests and across rivers as he followed the lion's tracks to its lair in a deep and dark cave. As he entered the cave the growls and roars of the lion echoed off the walls. But Hercules stood tall and confident, ready for whatever came his way.

The lion leapt out of the shadows and dazzled Hercules with his fierce eyes and sharp teeth. But our brave hero was ready;

he dodged the Lions' razor sharp claws and dangerous attacks. With his strength and speed he was always one step ahead.

After many hours, Hercules finally wrestled the lion onto its back. The lion roared and wriggled but Hercules held on with all of his might. He drew his sword and found a weak spot on the lion's neck. Then with one strike he slayed the fearsome beast!

With the lion slain, Hercules tore off its tough skin and used it as a coat for both victory and protection. King Eurystheus was shocked to see Hercules return with the lion's skin draped over his shoulder. Many men had been killed by the Nemean Lion, but Hercules was no ordinary man. He was a true hero who with determination and strength conquered the impossible! And it wasn't just muscles, he also used his brain to conquer the mightiest of obstacles.

Labour 2: Hercules Battles the Terrifying Lernaean Hydra

After successfully defeating the Nemean Lion, Hercules was ready for his next challenge. Only this time he would face a creature that was even more fearsome and dangerous! His target? A monstrous serpent that struck fear into the hearts of all who heard its name. Its name? The Lernaean Hydra and it lived in the murky swamps near the town of Lerna.

Now this was no ordinary snake. First of all it was big, really big. And if that's not scary enough it had nine heads which grew back every time someone tried to chop it off! Slaying such a hideous monster seemed impossible to most. But

Hercules wasn't most and he was determined to prove himself once again.

With his trusty sword in hand he entered the swamps where the Hydra lurked. The air was thick with a foul smell surrounding him and the ground squished underneath his feet. Suddenly the Hydra sprang out from the water hissing and snarling. A dangerous battle began! Hercules swung his sword at the heads of the Hydra. But as soon as he cut off one head two more would sprout back in its place! It seemed like an impossible fight.

Hercules undeterred, was smart as well as strong. Something else would need to be done and so he called upon his clever nephew, Iolaus, for help. Together, they came up with a plan. When Hercules chopped off one head of the Hydra, Iolaus would burn the neck to prevent new heads from growing. Slowly and surely they chopped and burned away at the Hydra. Finally, Hercules chopped off the last head of the Hydra and returned to King Eurystheus with its remains. Once again, the King was amazed and impressed by Hercules. With teamwork, creativity and persistence Hercules had once again overcome a huge obstacle. You see strength doesn't only come from muscles but also from our adaptability to think quickly and find new ways to our goals.

Labour 3: Hercules and the Swift Ceryneian Hind

After slaying the monstrous Hydra, Hercules was given his next challenge, to capture a magnificent deer known as the Ceryneian Hind. With its golden antlers and incredible speed, this was no ordinary deer. So of course, catching it would require someone far from orignary!

The Ceryneian Hind lived in the lush forests of a distant land. With its swift legs it could outrun even the fastest of hunters. With its golden antlers it shone brightly like the sun. King Eurystheus, who had assigned Hercules this labour, believed that capturing such a rare and swift creature would be nearly impossible.

Hercules knew better and was confident in himself as always. Deep into the wilderness he ventured, marvelling at the beauty of nature as he travelled. After many days of searching he finally spotted the Ceryneian Hind grazing near a crystal-clear stream. The Hind noticed Hercules and darted away with lightning speed, disappearing into the dense woods. Capturing such a swift creature would not be easy.

Hercules chased after the Hind, racing over steep hills and under deep valleys. With a relentless pursuit he caught up with Hinds speed. As the chase continued Hercules skillfully manoeuvred the Hind into a corner. The Hind was nervous but with kind words and soothing gestures Hercules gently approached. Miraculously, it seemed to understand that he came without harm and stood still as Hercules secured a golden rope around its neck. With grace Hercules led it back to King Eurystheus who was amazed at his ability to capture such an elusive creature without causing it harm. Respectfully he realised that Hercules was not only strong, but was also kind and clever.

Labour 4: Hercules and the Wild Erymanthian Boar

After capturing the Ceryneian Hind Hercules was faced with yet another challenge. Another capture! This time it was the challenge of capturing the Erymanthian Boar, a wild and mighty beast that caused chaos wherever it roamed.

Hercules ventured deep into the lush forests on the slopes of Mount Erymanthus where the bore resided. After many days of searching Hercules finally saw the wild boar tearing through the forest with sharp tusks and powerful hooves. Scrambling up a snowy slope he chased the beast where slippery grounds made it difficult for the boar to maintain its balance. As the beast slipped down the ice, Hercules skillfully trapped it in a net.

The wild boar thrashed around in the net but Hercules held on with all of his might. With the boar thrashing in his hand he journeyed back through fierce storms and across treacherous cliffs. Finally, he arrived back to present the Erymanthian Boar to a shocked King Eurystheus. The king congratulated Hercules for his strength to capture this fearsome beast and his resourcefulness to return with it. In a dangerous and impossible situation he had once again emerged triumphant

Labour 5: Hercules and the Augean Stables

After capturing the Erymanthian Boar, Hercules faced a new task assigned by King Eurystheus. After all the capturing it was time for something else, to clean the Augean Stables in a single day. However, these were not ordinary stables.

Home to a vast number of cattle and they had not been cleaned for many years, creating a colossal mess!

Our hero Hercules was not lazy and did not procrastinate. He approached the Augean Stables with a determined spirit, even though he could smell the stench from miles away. The size of the stables was overwhelming, but Hercules was not one to back down from any challenge. With his powerful muscles and sharp mind, he devised a clever strategy to clean the stables in a record time. With bare hands he dug deep tunnels to redirect nearby rivers to flow through the stables and wash away the filth. The waters crashed in and washed away years of filth. Once again, the air was filled with freshness, ahh.

King Eurystheus was astounded when he learned of how quickly Hercules had completed the seemingly impossible task. Finally, the Augean Stables were clean and free from the mess that had plagued them for so long. Hercules used his intelligence and creativity to find an innovative solution to the task at hand. With hard work we can achieve a goal. But sometimes we have to think creatively to adapt. Instead of avoiding enormous tasks, roll up your sleeves and get to work!

Labour 6: Hercules and the Stymphalian Birds

For his sixth labour Hercules was faced with a winged menace, the Stymphalian Birds. These were gigantic birds with sharp beaks and feathers that were tough as metal. Those unfortunate souls nearby lived in fear as the nasty birds caused havoc and terror.

Hercules set out to end their reign of terror. As he arrived at the marshes where they lived he noticed that they were swift and elusive. So instead of rushing in, he thought carefully about a plan to defeat the birds on their own terrain. You see, oftentimes instead of rushing in with overconfidence we need to take a step back and think of a more creative solution.

Hercules took a pair of bronze clappers gifted from the goddess Athena to scare the birds out of their hiding spots. With a loud noise from the clappers, he scared the birds into flight. As the birds soared into the sky, Hercules aimed his arrows. With a sharp aim he shot down the menacing birds one by one. Finally, peace was returned back to the land.

Labour 7: Hercules and the Cretan Bull

For his seventh labour, Hercules faced a fearsome beast known as the Cretan Bull. This was an enormous bull with powerful muscles and sharp horns that could pierce through anything. Destruction and devastation lay in its tracks. Farmers, where the bull roamed were fed up and so they called upon Hercules to save them.

Hercules set out for Crete where he found the bull wreaking havoc, but he was not one to be intimidated. As the bull charged at him he grabbed onto its powerful horns and with his incredible strength wrestled it to the ground. With his bare hands he submitted the mighty beast. After capturing the bull, he was faced with the challenge of getting it back to King Eurystheus. With big muscles like a powerlifter, the mighty Hercules simply lifted the bull onto his shoulders and carried it all the way back to the king!

With determination and resourcefulness Hercules was again successful. Even though he was strong, he was also compassionate. He didn't use his advantages to bully or to harm others. Instead, he used it to protect and to help those in need. Remember that our talents and abilities should be used to make the world a better place.

Labour 8: Hercules and the Mares of Diomedes.

Onto the next adventure! For his eighth labour Hercules faced wild and dangerous creatures, the Mares of Diomedes. These were a group of fierce and hungry horses that loved to feast on humans! A cruel King named Diomedes was their owner and he was happy to let them feed on captured travellers. Meanwhile villagers living nearby were terrified of the monstrous creatures and begged Hercules for help.

Our hero Hercules set out on a journey to capture the horses and bring them to King Eurystheus. Protected by his lion's skin and with his trusty club in hand he arrived at the stables where the horses lived. As he approached he saw their red eyes gleaming with hunger. Hercules took a step back and waited until night time. The horses would be sleeping then. Under the cover of darkness he sneaked into the stables. Using his big muscular strength he submitted and tied up the horses.

But it didn't end here....King Diomedes learned that someone was daring enough to steal his prized horses. Furiously he gathered an army and attacked Hercules. A dangerous battle ensued. But Hercules was no pushover! With his mighty club in hand and quick thinking he defeated the king's soldiers. He led the tamed horses back to King Eurystheus, who congratulated his bravery and determination. Once again he proved his ability to conquer even the most ferocious beasts. And just like Hercules, you too have the power to stand up against challenges and make a positive difference.

Labour 9: Hercules and the Belt of Hippolyta

Hercules continued his daring adventures with each labour testing his courage and strength. The ninth labour was no exception, for on this adventure his task was to obtain the magical belt of Hippolyta!

Hippolyta was the queen of the Amazons, a tribe of warrior women. She possessed a beautiful and powerful belt. Legend has it that this belt would give strength and protection to its wearer. King Eurystheus sent Hercules on a mission to capture this remarkable belt.

Hercules arrived and asked Hippolyta to give him the belt peacefully. Why not she thought? After all, she was impressed by Hercules's bravery and agreed to give him the belt as a gift. However, the jealous goddess Hera, who always caused trouble for Hercules, decided to meddle in their encounter. She stirred up and spread rumours that Hercules was planning to capture Hippolyta, then steal the belt. Confused and misled, her warriors clashed with Hercules in battle. Hercules tried to explain but in the end he had to forcefully capture the belt. With the belt in his hand he left the land of the Amazons saddened by what had occurred.

Sometimes young adventures our messages and intentions can be misunderstood. We must listen, clarify and trust each other. Just like Hercules, try to always find peaceful solutions to our problems. Keep a clear head and never allow rumours to cloud your judgement.

Labour 10: Hercules and the Cattle of Geryon

On his tenth labour Hercules would have his courage and determination tested once again. This time he was tasked with capturing the magnificent Cattle of Geryon. Now Geryon was a farmer but he was not an ordinary farmer…he was a giant with three heads and six arms!

Geryon owned cattle that were dazzling with red hides and were famous for their strength and speed. King Eurystheus, commanded Hercules to bring back these extraordinary cattle. Hercules travelled across deserts, mountains, and vast lands on his journey to the far western reaches of the world where the cattle grazed. As he arrived at the dwelling of Geryon he was faced with a fierce two-headed guard dog named Orthrus. With his powerful club, Hercules smashed Orthrus and moved forward to face the next part of his quest.

Finally, our brave hero encountered the giant Geryon, but he was not happy to see intruders on his land. Hercules wrestled with Geryon's multiple arms. Once again, his strength was the strongest. He emerged victorious and went on to capture the cattle of Geryon. Hercules created a massive bronze vessel to carry the cattle across the seas back to King Eurystheus.

However, the journey back was not a smooth one for along the way Hercules was met with the god Helios. Frustrated by the blazing heat Hercules shot an arrow at the sun. Helios was impressed and gifted him with a magical golden cup allowing him to travel over the sea with ease. Eventually Hercules reached King Eurystheus and presented him the Cattle of Geryon. With determination, creativity, and a willingness to face challenges head-on, Hercules completed his tenth labour.

Labour 11: Hercules and the Apples of the Hesperides

For his eleventh labour Hercules faced an incredible challenge. His mission? To retrieve some golden apples which were guarded by the Hesperides, three skilled and powerful women who lived in a magical garden at the edge of the world.

The golden apples were said to be a gift of immortality to anyone who ate them. Of course, everyone wanted a bite! Including King Eurystheus who sent Hercules to bring back these special apples as part of his ongoing trials. And so he set out on his journey to the Garden of the Hesperides.

Once he reached the garden, Hercules was faced with a fierce dragon named Ladon. Its many heads and sharp teeth made it a dangerous opponent. But Hercules was not scared and with bravery he slayed the fierce dragon. However, he was soon faced with a new challenge. For now, he was met with the Hesperides, who were the daughters of the titan Atlas. With their magical skills they created powerful illusions and tricks to confuse and distract Hercules.

Hercules offered their father, Atlas, a deal. He would temporarily hold up the sky (which was Atlas's punishment) in exchange for Atlas retrieving the golden apples for him. Atlas agreed, and as Hercules held up the sky, he went to the tree and retrieved the apples. However, Atlas tried to trick Hercules to continue to hold up the sky, but Hercules was no fool. Hold this a minute, he said to Atlas as he escaped with the golden apples.

Hercules triumphantly returned to King Eurystheus with the golden apples in hand. The golden apples became a symbol of Hercules's ability to find innovative solutions and use strength to achieve goals. As you face your own adventures, Hercules's journey to retrieve the golden apples inspires you to think outside the box, believe in your abilities, and never give up.

Labour 12: Hercules and the Capture of Cerberus

Are you ready to embark on one last thrilling adventure? Join Hercules on his twelfth and final labour where he was faced with capturing the Cerberus. Again a capture mission! This time to catch a horrible dog with three heads, sharp teeth and a tail made of serpents!

Cerberus lurked in the Underworld which was a tricky place to find. Hercules asked for help and was guided by the goddess Athena. Once he reached the gates of the Underworld he was met with Cerberus. The dog barked and growled at him with eyes that glowed with fire. Hercules wrestled with Cerberus, its three heads snarled and snapped, but he held on tightly. Slowly, the horrible dog faded as he was brought under Hercules's control.

With the dog in hand, Hercules journeyed back to the world above and presented it to King Eurystheus. The king was both amazed (and frightened) to see the dog with its three heads. Once again Hercules had proven himself as the greatest hero of all time!

Hercules' Twelve Labors proved his amazing abilities, strength and determination. Time and time again he proved that with a strong heart and fast thinking, even the most difficult challenges could be overcome. For when faced with seemingly impossible challenges, he never gave up. Instead, he looked at it from a different angle or thought creatively of solutions to emerge victorious. Not only with his strong muscles but also using his brain and brilliance. Hercules' reminds us that hard work, persistence and creativity will help you to conquer many obstacles in your life. With the right mindset and the belief in yourself, you too can emerge victorious in your own challenges!

CHAPTER 20

THE FALL OF ICARUS - A LESSON IN CONSEQUENCES

Once upon a time in the world of ancient Greek mythology there lived a daring and adventurous young boy named Icarus. Together with his father Daedalus, he lived on the island of Crete. Daedalus was a brilliant inventor, world famous for his amazing creations and brilliant inventions. But guess what? He was hiding a huge secret! What do you suppose it might be? Keep reading to learn more about this amazing invention that was so thrilling it was like putting a rainbow in a jar.

One rainy day, Daedalus and Icarus found themselves trapped on an island by a wicked king who refused them to leave. The king knew very well that Daedalus skills were just too valuable to lose. Daedalus on the other hand could not wait to escape back home with his son. And so, he went to work on a fabulous invention, creating a pair of wings to escape. Crafted with the threads of courage and dreams of home, these wings were given to young Icarus.

Daedalus gifted Icarus the glorious new wings. He showed his son how to wear them and how to soar gracefully in the skies. However, they came with a serious disclaimer. Now listen closely because such a warning should not be taken lightly! Daedalus cautioned his son to be careful, don't fly too low or the sea would clog his wings. Additionally, he warned him not to fly too high because the sun's heat would melt them.

Icarus jumped into the air and with the magnificent wings he took flight, his heart racing with excitement. As he soared into the skies, he felt amazing and couldn't contain his joy. Higher and higher he flew, feeling like he was invincible. But as he flew higher, he became careless and ignored his father's advice. Soon he came very close to the warm sun. Feeling its enticing warmth, he thought if he could just touch the sun, it might make him even more powerful. So, ignoring the voice of reason in his head, he flew closer to the hot sun.

Suddenly disaster struck! The wax that held his wings together started to melt as he got closer to the sun. Icarus felt his wings collapsing, and he fell swiftly towards the sea below. Desperately he flapped his wings as the winds whipped around him, but it was too late. He crashed into the sea, falling at a place that was named the Icarian Sea in his memory.

Lessons from a cautionary tale

Now what can we learn from this cautionary tale of Icarus? First of all, we must always be cautious with pride and arrogance. You see Icarus was carried away by his overconfidence and excitement. This created an attitude of arrogance which eventually got the better of him and turned things sour. In his ignorance he didn't listen to his father's warnings. He thought he could rise above the laws of nature. Such foolish actions eventually led to his downfall.

Young explorers, whenever you see the birds flying across the sky or you feel the warmth of the sun, remember the story of Icarus. Be careful to stay humble even when the dazzling lights of praise flash upon you. Understand that often when our dreams come to life, it can be all too easy to fall from grace. Just like Icarus dreamed to fly yet quickly crashed into the sea. Stay humble with an open mind and listen to those wise people who care about you. Dream big, but stay humble and who knows, you might discover your own wings of wisdom!

CHAPTER 21

ODYSSEUS' EPIC ODYSSEY - THE CLEVER TRAVELS OF A HERO

Once upon a time in the ancient world of Greek mythology there lived a hero named Odysseus. But he was unlike many of the other heroes you've heard about so far. So far, we've heard tales of the strong and mighty. But Odysseus was famous for his intelligence, quick thinking, and creative solutions even in the trickiest of challenges. Let's visit him to see how sometimes a strong brain is more useful than titan size muscles!

Born in the city of Ithaca, Odysseus fought bravely in the Trojan War. After ten long years this epic battle finally came to an end. The Greeks emerged victorious and Odysseus set sail for his homeland ready to reunite with his family. However, his journey back would not be a smooth one.

For he sailed across a massive and chaotic sea where he was met with many, many challenges. In Greek mythology his journey became known as "The Odyssey". It is a legendary tale of bravery, perseverance and creativity. Now, let's dive into the adventure!

The Odyssey

Picture Odysseus, a captain with a heart full of courage as he sets sail back to his beloved Ithaca. But before he even set sail, the waves themselves held a grudge! Poseidon, the mighty sea god, was furious at Odysseus for blinding his son, Polyphemus, during the Trojan War. So, he stirred up storms that wreaked havoc on their ship, pushing them toward the clutches of the one-eyed giant, Polyphemus, also known as a Cyclops.

Fear not, for wit and bravery were abundant in Odysseus' and his loyal crewmates! In the belly of the beast, they hatched a clever scheme. They presented themselves as "Nobody" to the Cyclops. And when Polyphemus cried for help, "Nobody" was to blame! The cunning plan worked, and with eyelids heavy from laughter, they managed to escape the giant's grasp.

But the adventures didn't stop there! Every island in their pathway seemed to hold a new challenge and presented a new twist to their story. As they passed one island the sailors met the Lotus Eaters. They tricked the sailors with fruits that made them forget their homes, like a temporary spell of forgetfulness. If that wasn't enough on another island they met the Sirens. Their mesmerising melodies lured sailors toward danger, crashing close to the rocks. However, with sharp wits they steered away from danger.

Further on they sailed, only to be met with Circe, a sorceress with many sneaky tricks rolled up her sleeves. She tried to turn Odysseus' crew into animals! But once again with his sharp mind, he outsmarted her spells, steering his ship away from her tricks. Next Calypso, a captivating beauty, offered him the allure of eternal life. Only this came at the price of forever leaving his homeland behind. Not such a great deal!

Even in the tight grip of a sea monster called Scylla and a swirling whirlpool, Odysseus kept his crew's courage afloat. He used his wit to navigate through narrow straits, just like threading a needle through a stormy sea. With each challenge, he stood as a beacon of bravery and cleverness. He played the hero's part, unravelling problems with his quick thinking and persistence. Throughout his adventure, Odysseus used creative solutions, bravery and determination to rescue his crew.

Finally, Odysseus returned to Ithaca. But even there, his journey was far from over. For it was here that he had to prove his identity to his own wife, Penelope and scare off the men who tried to marry her. He called for help from his son Telemachus and the goddess Athena. Together with their help, Odysseus once again emerged victorious.

So, young adventurers, what can we learn from this? Understand that the key to success is not just being stronger but being smarter. Beyond having muscles like a titan, it's also about flexing your brainpower! Odysseus faced monsters, tricky challenges, and even heartache. But with intelligence, resourcefulness and persistence he always succeeded.

As you sail through your own adventures, remember his lessons. For you also don't need a sharp sword or big muscles to conquer challenges. A sharp mind with a brave heart is often more useful. Just like Odysseus, navigate the seas of life with cleverness and courage. In doing so you'll find that even the toughest challenges can be conquered with a clever mind and a sprinkle of bravery.

CHAPTER 22

ECHO & NARCISSUS - A LOVE STORY OF ECHOING HEARTS

Once upon a time in the magical world of Greek mythology, there was a young beautiful woman named Echo. She was famous for her beautiful singing voice which could mimic any sound that she heard. Echo loved to wander through the deep forests singing and imitating the calls of the birds and animals.

One day she came across the king of all gods Zeus. He was a flirtatious God but he was married to Hera. Anyway, he was the mighty king of all gods, so what! And so he flirted with Echo. Hera learned of their betrayal and as punishment she cursed Echo by taking away her ability to speak her own words. From then on, she could only repeat the last words that were spoken to her.

Echo still wandered through the woods day after day. One day she came across a handsome youth named Narcissus. He was famous far and wide for his handsome looks, but he had a flaw. Narcissus was so obsessed with himself, he cared for no one or nothing else but himself. Thus, he reflected the affections of all who loved him.

Narcissus was famous for breaking hearts with indifference. Many of the most beautiful women fell in love hopelessly with him. One of those was Echo. She longed to express her feelings to Narcissus. But she was only able to repeat words. Day after day she followed him through the woods hoping he would notice her.

One day, as Narcissus was separated from his companions, he called out, "Who's here?" Echo, as she always did, repeated his words, "Who's here?" Confused, Narcissus looked around and saw no one. He called out again, "Come!" And once again, Echo echoed his words, "Come!" But still, he saw no one.

Now he was even more confused and also a little annoyed, he called out, "Let's meet!" Echo echoed his words, "Let's meet!" Unable to understand that the voice was his own repeating, Narcissus grew frustrated and yelled, "Leave me alone!" And yet again, Echo echoed his words, "Leave me alone!"

Feeling frustrated and embarrassed, Narcissus ignored the voice and continued his journey. However, he didn't realise that the voice belonged to the young girl who had fallen in love with him. Echo's heart ached as she watched him walk away, knowing that he would never truly see her or hear her feelings.

Narcissus' self-centred attitude eventually led to his own downfall. As he looked at his own reflection in a pool of water he fell in love with what he saw. Unable to tear himself away, he wasted away as he longed for his own reflection until he transformed into a beautiful flower – the narcissus flower.

The story of Echo and Narcissus represents love and self obsession. The voice of Echo lives on as a natural phenomenon of an echo or a reminder of a love that was never truly heard. Whilst the narcissus flower blooms as a reminder of the dangers of excessive self love and vanity.

Let their tragic love story remind us of how important empathy, understanding and valuing the feelings of others really are. For love is not a selfish act, it is a shared feeling. And remember that true beauty is not just in someone's physical looks but it also in their hearts and actions.

CHAPTER 23

THE DARK RIVERS OF THE UNDERWOLRD

Did you know that a second world once existed deep beneath the surface? Would you be interested in learning the mysteries of it? In ancient Greek mythology, the underworld was the name for this mysterious place. After leaving the world of the living, the spirits of the dead had to travel here. However, to reach there, one first had to navigate the vast Underworld rivers guided by a chilling character named Charon.

The underworld was surrounded by dark rivers flowing through caverns and tunnels. But these rivers were not like the ones we see on Earth; they were magical and held great powers. One of the most important rivers was the River Styx. According to legend it was the boundary between the word of the living and the dead. One had to cross this river on their journey to the afterlife. But they needed to please someone first.

Charon, The Ferryman of the Underworld

Meet Charon, a fascinating and mysterious character. It was he who played a very important role in journeying souls to the underworld.

Imagine an old hooded man with a long grey beard. Each and every day the old man would ferry the souls of the deceased across the River Styx to the underworld.

His boat was a magical ship that could transport souls from this world to the afterlife. But he wouldn't just take anyone across that river. Deceased souls had to pay him with a special coin which would be traditionally placed under their tongues before they were buried. This coin, known as an obol, was accepted as payment to guarantee a secure journey to the Underworld.

And for those who couldn't afford the payment. Well, their fate was to wander the shores of the River Styx for one hundred years unable to cross nor find any rest. This is why it was so important for the ancient Greeks to always place coins on the eyes and mouths of their deceased. Because they wanted to ensure that their trip to the end of the world was secure. Be sure to save some money too!

Dear young friends remember, the River Styx isn't just a mythological river! It is also a reminder of the challenges and choices we will all face. Just like Charon guided souls, you too will also have to guide your life through many challenges. But if you focus on being prepared and consider the consequences of your choices then you will make better decisions.

In this tale, those who didn't pay Charon were stuck on the shore of the River Styx, unable to cross. It's a reminder that when we're not prepared, we might miss out on opportunities or face setbacks. So, young adventurers, take this lesson to heart. Make responsible choices and be prepared for whatever life brings your way. So as you journey through your own rivers of life keep these lessons in mind. Prepare, make smart choices and steer your boat with confidence!

CHAPTER 24

JASON & HIS QUEST FOR THE GOLDEN FLEECE

Good day young adventurers and brave explorers! Welcome to an epic journey where we will join the mighty Jason and his brave crew, the Argonauts on their quest for the mysterious Golden Fleece. Are you ready for a journey across the seas with this team of smart and strong adventurers? Stay tuned to learn all about the great challenges and adventures they faced on their thrilling search for the Golden Fleece. Truly, this is one of the most famous adventures in Greek mythology!

We begin the story with Jason, a brave hero who set out to claim his rightful place as the king of Iolcus. He stood at a crossroads of life with a huge decision before him. In order to claim his throne, he would first need to fetch the Golden Fleece.

Whoever claimed the mysterious and powerful fleece would be worthy of a crown. However, the quest for the elusive fleece would test his strength, intelligence and heart.

Jason and the Argonauts

Jason gathered together a fearless band of heroes known as the Argonauts. Together they boarded a magnificent boat built by skillful craftsmen and followed the guidance of the goddess Athena herself. Far off to the distant land of Colchis they set sail on their great adventure. It is here that the elusive Golden Fleece was guarded by both mortal and supernatural challenges.

But wait! Because before we get there we must sail across dangerous waters. On these very waters the courageous team battled ferocious monsters and faced the wrath of the gods. In one challenge they came close to clashing against the rocks as huge boulders smashed down the cliffs! But with the guidance of the goddess Athena, Jason and his crew safely manoeuvred through the perils.

When they reached the land of Colchis, Jason faced his most challenging task, he had to convince King Aeetes to give him the Golden Fleece. Jason stood before the mighty king. With determination shining in his eyes, he pleaded with the king to grant him the Golden Fleece. But the old king was not about to hand over his most treasured possession so easily. For his heart was as tough as armour, and he refused to part with his cherished prize!

It seemed like all hope was lost, that is until a glimmering figure stepped onto the stage of destiny. Who might this figure be, you ask? None other than Medea, the daughter of King Aeetes. She was no ordinary princess. More than that she was also a sorceress with a heart full of kindness and…. a spark of love for our hero, Jason. Ah, young love! Her heart was swayed by the bravery of our daring hero and she decided to help him.

With a touch of magic, Medea put the fearsome dragon that guarded the Golden Fleece into a sleep so deep that even his snoring would rival a symphony! With the dragon snuggled up in dreamland, Jason seized the moment. With silent steps and a heart pounding, he tiptoed past the sleeping dragon and claimed the Golden Fleece for his own.

The Power of Teamwork

The story of Jason and the Argonauts teaches us that courage and teamwork are powerful forces in life. Imagine you're playing a game with your friends, and everyone brings their own special skills to the table. One friend's super good at solving puzzles, another's amazing at telling funny jokes, and yet another is the fastest runner you've ever seen. When all these talents come together, it's like a magical recipe for success, just like it was for Jason and his Argonaut friends.

So, young readers, remember this epic story. It's not just about a fancy fleece, really it's about the incredible power of true friendship. Just like how Jason and the Argonauts had each other's backs, you too can achieve amazing things when you have friends who believe in you. Team up with friends who cheer for you, support you and help you reach for the stars. Who knows, you might discover your very own Golden Fleece!

CHAPTER 25

ORPHEUS THE MUSICIAN - A TRAGIC JOURNEY INTO THE UNDERWORLD

Hello there young learners. Would you like to hear about a famous musician? In this chapter we're about to learn about Orpheus, an extraordinary musician with an enchanted instrument. Here we'll embark on a captivating journey to discover his exceptional talents and the magic of his instrument. Our journey will also explore the tragic and touching tale of Orpheus and his lover Eurydice as they fell into the depths of the underworld. Finally, our journey will conclude the legacy of his melodies in Ancient Greek culture.

Orpheus was born a talented musician. From a young age he showed amazing musical talents that enchanted anyone who ever listened.

With a lyre in hand (a kind of stringed instrument) he could create magical melodies that stirred the hearts of gods and mortals alike. With a gentle strum he could bring tears of joy and with powerful chords he could ignite the deepest of emotions. Legend has it that even wild beasts and trees would sway to the rhythm of his music!

Orpheus & Eurydice, A Tale of Tragic Romance

Once upon a time Orpheus fell in love with Eurydice, a beautiful young woman. She was mesmerised by the melodies Orpheus played on his lyre. But tragically, she was bitten by a venomous snake and was taken far too soon from the world of the living. Orpheus could not bear to live without his beloved. And so he set out on a daring journey to the realm of the dead, the Underworld and bring her back to the world of the living.

With his enchanting music he charmed the moody, underworld god Hades and his queen, Perspone. Mesmerised and moved by his songs they allowed him to take Eurydice back to the world above. Only on one condition… he must not look back until they had reached the world of the living. In one moment of doubt he turned around to ensure Eurydice was still with him. This mistake cost him dearly and he lost her forever. Eurydice vanished back into the shadows of the Underworld, leaving Orpheus heartbroken and alone.

The Legacy of Orpheus

Orpheus's music had a magical impact on anyone who listened. They felt emotions and were transcended beyond the boundaries of time and space. He was also a gifted poet and storyteller, using his lyrical verses to share emotional and captivating tales. His creative gifts had the power to heal hearts, inspire courage and express deep emotions of the human soul. His melodies continue to resonate throughout ancient Greek culture and beyond. To this day his legacy lives on in the hearts of those who appreciate the power of music and storytelling. Meanwhile his story has become a symbol of undying love and the consequences of recklessness.

As we near the end of our journey into the life of Orpheus, the extraordinary musician and his heart wrenching journey into the underworld. Let us remember his extraordinary talents and praise the melodies he played. There are lessons from the touching tale of Orpheus and Eurydice. It reminds us to cherish every moment with our loved ones and to never take love for granted. Time can slip away just like notes from a lyre. Like Orpheus's timeless melodies, may your own creativity and love resonate in the hearts of others.

CHAPTER 26
THE MUSES - GIFTS OF CREATIVITY & INSPIRATION

Long ago in the magical realm of ancient Greece, lived nine extraordinary beings. Together they were known as the Muses. Art, science and creativity were just a few of the wonderful things inspired by them. Each Muse had their own special talents and together they covered a wide range of fascinating subjects. Could you imagine having nine extra, magical friends to spark your imagination, teach you, or to inspire your creativity. Wouldn't that be wonderful? Well, that's what The Muses are here for. Now without further ado, let's share their gifts with you!

Calliope, The Muse of Poetry

Meet Calliope, the wisest and eldest Muse. Imagine her as the storyteller of ancient Greece, inspiring poets to write epic tales. You know, the kind that makes your imagination take flight like Pegasus! She's the reason words dance on the pages, creating magic that tickles your soul.

Clio, The Muse of History

Step into the realm of Clio, the Muse of history. She's a gateway to the past, helping historians scribble down important moments so they're never forgotten. Imagine her with a magical pen, making sure that the stories of brave heroes and legends are passed on.

Erato, The Muse of Love Poetry

Erato is the Muse of love poetry and she's like a mini Cupid spreading love through words. She whispers sweet verses into the ears of poets, making their hearts sing with love. When you read beautiful, romantic poems, you can be sure that she had something to do with them.

Euterpe, The Muse of Music

Euterpe is all about music. She's the maestro of melodies, guiding musicians to create songs that make toes tap and hearts hum. When you listen to a catchy tune that makes you want to dance, think of her leading the symphony of sounds.

Melpomene, The Muse of Tragedy

If you're in the mood for some drama, Melpomene is your Muse. She's the guide behind stories that tug at your heartstrings and make you feel all sorts of emotions. She helps playwrights write about sadness and challenges, reminding us that even in tough times, stories can help us to understand the world.

Polyhymnia, The Muse of Sacred Poetry

Polyhymnia is the poet-priestess of the Muses. She inspires poets to write meaningful words that honour the gods and send blessings to people. Imagine her words as small prayers floating on the winds, carrying good wishes to those in need.

Terpsichore, The Muse of Dance

Meet Terpsichore, the dancing Muse. She's the one who makes dancers twirl, leap and spin like leaves caught in a playful breeze. When you watch a graceful ballet or energetic hip-hop, it's like her magic is bringing the stories to life through dance.

Thalia, The Muse of Comedy

Got a case of the giggles? Thalia's to blame! She's the funny one of the Muses, inspiring writers to write funny stories that make us laugh. Imagine her as a jokester, sprinkling chuckles and joy wherever she goes.

Urania, The Muse of Astronomy

Take a look out at the starry night. Well, say hello to Urania, the Muse of astronomy! She's a cosmic explorer, inspiring astronomers to study the mysteries of the vast universe. When you gaze up at the night sky, remember that her presence is there.

Think about what it would be like to have these Muses as your friends. Wouldn't that be wonderful? When you wanted to write poems, Calliope would whisper tales in your ear. When you wanted to be a musician, Euterpe could guide your fingers on the strings or voice to sing. Or maybe you wanted to study history, well Clio could share stories from the past with you. Together the Muses should inspire us all to explore our talents and then to share our ideas with the world. Go ahead, just like the ancient Greeks you too can be inspired by their magical powers!

CHAPTER 27

PERSEUS - THE SLAYER OF MEDUSA

Greetings, young heroes and adventurers! Prepare yourselves for we are about to dive into the epic tale of Perseus, a brave character who slayed the fearsome monster Medusa. Join us on this epic journey where we learn all about this hero, his quest and his legacy in Greek mythology. With brave courage and cunning wit, Perseus etched his name into the legends of history, inspiring countless generations to come.

Perseus was born to the mighty Zeus, King of the Gods, and the mortal princess Danaë. Blessed he was, however from the start his life was filled with danger! King Acrisius, his grandfather, was afraid of a prophecy saying that he would fall at the hands of Perseus. And so, to avoid this fate, he locked Danaë and Perseus in a chest which he threw into the sea. The chest crashed into the sea and washed ashore on the island of Seriphos where a kind fisherman rescued them. On the island Perseus grew up to be a strong and fearless young man. Yet he was unaware of his divine heritage.

Perseus' life was going well until one day it took a bad turn when the wicked King Polydectes plotted against him. Polydectes devised a sneaky plan. He set Perseus a seemingly impossible task, demanding that he bring him the head of the dreaded Gorgon, Medusa as a gift. Medusa was one of the three Gorgon sisters, with snakes for hair and a gaze that could turn anyone into stone. Many had dared to challenge her. And many had fallen or frozen in her stare. Armed with a magical sword from the gods and a polished shield, Perseus set out on his dangerous quest.

Hermes the messenger god and Athena the goddess of wisdom helped Perseus find the lair of Medusa. To avoid her deathly gaze he used his polished shield to look at Medusa's reflection instead of directly at her. Carefully he aimed his sword. With a swift strike, he cut off her head. But the quest was not over yet!

On his way back home, Perseus came across the beautiful princess Andromeda who was about to be sacrificed to a monster. Perseus couldn't bear to see an innocent girl suffer. With bravery he rescued her just in time using Medusa's petrifying head to freeze the monster. Andromeda's parents

King Cepheus and Queen Cassiopeia were forever grateful. They welcomed Perseus into their family, he married Andromeda and they lived happily ever after.

Perseus's adventures and heroic feats contributed to him as a beloved figure in Greek mythology. He became a symbol of courage, cleverness, and determination. And he proved that even mortals could achieve greatness! His legacy continued through the generations, with many famous heroes and demigods tracing their ancestry back to him, including the great Heracles (Hercules). Forever more he became an inspiration for countless heroes and adventurers.

As we conclude our epic journey into the world of Perseus, the heroic slayer of Medusa, let us remember his courageous quests and his enduring legacy in Greek mythology. His stories teach us that bravery and determination can conquer even the most difficult of challenges. Along with the help of our friends and family we can overcome difficult challenges that might lay ahead.

So, young heroes, as you face your own adventures in life, remember Perseus. Let his bravery inspire you to be strong, smart and a great friend. May his legacy continue to inspire generations of brave souls like you. For even ordinary individuals like us can achieve amazing things!

CHAPTER 28

PRINCE THESEUS & HIS HEROIC ADVENTURES

Well hello there, young adventurers! Get ready to buckle up for a journey into the legendary tales of Theseus, the heroic Cretan Prince. Join us as we dive headfirst into his epic travels to claim his city of Athens. Are you ready to learn about his amazing adventures and his legacy as a leader of Athens? Well hurry up, the journey begins now!

Our story begins with the birth of Theseus, a prince like no other. His mother, Princess Aethra and his father, King Aegeus, had a unique plan. Under a massive rock, they laid a sword and sandals like a hidden treasure. Once Theseus could lift that rock to take those treasures, it would be his cue to travel to Athens and claim his royal destiny.

When the time was ready, Theseus headed out for the adventure of a lifetime. But hold on tight, because his journey was definitely not an easy one! Almost right away, he crossed paths with a gang of menacing thieves.

Theseus wasn't one to back down in the face of these troublemakers' attempts to stop him. The brave prince faced them head-on. And what do you know? He triumphed! Theseus demonstrated that true bravery and quick thinking can overcome even the most brutal of bullies.

But that was just a small taste of his epic journeys! So young adventurers let us continue to unravel the tales of Theseus. Buckle up your seatbelts as our journey will be filled with twists, turns and triumph. Prepare to be inspired, to laugh, to gasp and to embark on an adventure you'll never forget!

Theseus's Famous Adventures

One of Theseus's most famous adventures was his encounter with the dreaded Minotaur. This fearsome creature with the head of a bull and the body of a man, was confined in a labyrinth below the island of Crete where King

Minos ruled. Every year the mean king demanded that Athens send human sacrifices to the Minotaur. Theseus was determined to put an end to this cruel tradition. When he arrived, Princess Ariadne, the daughter of King Minos, fell in love with him and helped him to slay the Minotaur. But we won't give you all the gory details here, for full details check out - CHAPTER 13: THE MAZE OF THE MINOTAUR!

Anyway, if you're still reading, this is what happened next! After successfully defeating the Minotaur, Theseus set sail for Athens with Princess Ariadne at his side. All that sailing was tiring and so they stopped for a snooze on the island of Naxos. Unfortunately, whilst Theseus was sleeping, the trickster god Dionysus lured Ariadne into his divine realm. Heartbroken, Theseus was left alone to continue his journey. Along the way encountered many more challenges, including battles with the fierce Amazons.

When he reached the city of Athens, Theseus became a wise and courageous leader. The story of his triumph over the Minotaur brought hope and inspiration to the people. He rose to fame as a beloved hero who stood for justice and power. Under his rule he united many regions and turned Athens into a great city.

As we near the end of our journey into the thrilling world of Theseus, the heroic Cretan Prince. Let us remember his courageous journey to Athens, his victory over the Minotaur and his inspiring leadership of Athens. Let us also remember his tragic love story with Ariadne. His stories teach us the importance of bravery, leadership and determination in the face of adversity. Even in the darkest of times, with the help of clever solutions and loyal friends, we can overcome the most challenging obstacles. Or when faced with mean bullies we can stand up for ourselves, be brave. So young adventurers let the story of Theseus inspire you to be courageous leaders and brave heroes in your own lives.

PART 4
MYTHS & LEGENDS

CHAPTER 29

PANDORA'S BOX - A CAUTIONARY TALE OF CURIOSITY

Greetings young seekers of knowledge and wisdom! In this chapter we're going to explore the curious tale of Pandora, the first woman created by the gods. Are you ready to learn about her infamous curiosity that led to the myth of "Pandora's box"? Great, because many valuable lessons can be found in this myth so, please pay close attention!

Pandora was a very special creation for she was sculpted by the gods themselves. They took great care and craftsmanship with each deity providing their own gifts to her. Pandora was a true wonder, meant to be the most perfect creature to ever walk the earth. Hephaestus the blacksmith, gave her the gifts of beauty, intelligence and charm. Lastly, he also gave her one more very special gift. Stay tuned as we will soon discover the impact of one gift of particular interest, her insatiable curiosity.

Pandora's Box

Along with her many splendid gifts, the gods gave Pandora a mysterious box that was sealed tightly. But she was strictly instructed never to open it. Despite serious warnings from the gods, her curiosity grew and grew.

The mystery inside the box was just too much to resist opening it. With her heart racing she slowly opened the lid, not knowing what to expect. As she opened the box to her shock and surprise, a whole swarm of troubles escaped out into the world! Pain, sickness, envy and all sorts of bad things spread out like a virus among humans causing sadness.

Pandora felt helpless, but, just when things seemed at their darkest she heard a faint whisper coming from inside the box. It was the last remaining spirit, hiding in there all along. Can you guess what it was? It was the spirit of hope! Even though Pandora had let lose lots of trouble into the world, she had also been given something precious, the gift of hope. Hope was still there like a glowing torch lighting up the night to guide people through even the darkest of times.

With the spirit of hope by her side, Pandora felt a surge of determination. She understood that while troubles and challenges were now a part of the world, hope was the key to overcoming them. The spirit of hope offered her a silent promise, that no matter how bad things got, there would always be a glimmer of light to guide others through the darkest of times.

Lessons from Pandora

The myth of Pandora's Box teaches us valuable lessons that are as old as time itself. You see, being curious is a natural part of being human…something that kids, like you, know very well! But just like crossing a busy street, we must be careful and follow the advice of those with more wisdom. Think of it like having a map when you're exploring a new place. We should always consider the consequences of our actions, just like a captain steering a ship through stormy seas. Stay curious because having an open mind is like a key that can open many doorways to endless discoveries. But remember, just like you'd wear a helmet while biking, always be careful and stay aware.

But wait, there's more to learn! Pandora also reminds us that life isn't always smooth sailing. Nope, sometimes we face challenges and difficulties that can feel like a bumpy roller coaster ride. But guess what? The power of hope can guide us even in the most difficult of times. Remember that even in the darkest of times, hope will always be there to guide you. Imagine hope as you're superhero friend who always has your back, that's the power of hope!

CHAPTER 30

THE TROJAN WAR - AN EPIC BATTLE OF HEREOS, GODS & WOODEN HORSE

Greetings, young warriors and history lovers! Prepare yourselves for tales from the epic Trojan War. In this chapter, we'll embark on an exciting journey to learn about the causes and key players of the Trojan War. But that's not all! We'll also discover the fascinating role of the gods and goddesses in the war. Then later we'll learn about the tragic aftermath of the war and its legacy in Greek mythology.

Now let's start at the beginning to discover what the Trojan War was all about. This legendary conflict took place between the ancient city of Troy and the mighty Greeks. The war was caused by a love affair between Prince Paris of Troy, and the beautiful Helen, wife of King Menelaus of Sparta. When Paris kidnapped Helen, Menelaus and his brother Agamemnon sent their armies to save her. The result was an epic war that captured the imagination of generations to come.

Many key characters and legends were involved in the Trojan War including brave heroes like Achilles, Hector, Odysseus, and Ajax leading the Greek forces. Valiant warriors such as Aeneas and Priam defended Troy.

Meanwhile the gods and goddesses of Olympus also played key roles in the war. Battles were swayed by them as they took sides in the conflict, supporting either the Greeks or the Trojans.

Athena, the wise goddess, sided with the Greeks. She offered her guidance, strategy and protection to their heroes. Hera, the queen of the gods, also supported the Greeks, as did Poseidon, god of the sea, and Hermes, the messenger god. On the other side, Aphrodite, the goddess of love, favoured the Trojans. In fact, it was her involvement in the judgement of Paris, which started the whole affair. Apollo and Ares were among the gods and goddesses who supported the Trojans.

The Wooden Horse

After ten years of intense war the Greeks devised a sneaky plan to finally get inside the highly guarded walls of Troy. Long battles had led to a stalemate and so they built a massive wooden horse. Inside it they hid their finest warriors to be sneaked in. Meanwhile the rest of the Greek army tricked the Trojans by pretending to retreat, leaving the wooden horse as a supposed peace offering.

The Trojans were tricked into a false sense of safety. Victory was in their hands they thought and moved the wooden horse into their city as a trophy. But little did they know that inside of it, Greek warriors were hidden! Inside the warriors waited for nightfall and under the cover of darkness they emerged from the wooden horse. They opened the city gates, allowing the rest of the Greek army to enter the city and in the chaos that followed Troy was defeated. A trail of sorrow and tragedy followed in the aftermath. Hector, the great Trojan hero, was killed by Achilles. Then more drama followed as Achilles was then slain by Paris to avenge the death of his brother. Finally, the noble king of Troy was killed and the city was left in ruins.

The Trojan War became a legend in Greek mythology. Over many years, its stories have been retold and passed down through history. May you receive this timeless tale to fuel your own love for history and mythology! Valuable lessons of honour, courage and wisdom can be found in it. So, young warriors and history lovers, let the legend of the Trojan War inspire you to face challenges! For with honour, courage and wisdom you may overcome challenges. Let it guide you on your own epic adventures and quests for knowledge!

PART 5
EVEN MORE GODS & GODDESSES!

CHAPTER 31

THE TITANS & THEIR EPIC CLASH

Welcome brave young adventurers! Are you enjoying the journey so far? Well, it's great to have you here and in this magnificent chapter you're about to discover the Titans! Once upon a time these ancient and powerful gods ruled the cosmos in Greek mythology. In this chapter, we'll uncover their origins, significance in Greek Mythology and witness their epic clash, known as the Titanomachy!

Long, very long ago in fact before the reign of the Olympian gods, the Titans were born. Children of the heavens and earth, together they ruled over a vast and infinite universe.

With immense power they embodied the elements of the earth, sky and sea. Each Titan possessed unique abilities that influenced the balance of the universe.

Clash of the Titans!

Picture this: an incredible showdown between the mighty Titans and their descendants, the Olympic Gods. Brace yourselves, for this legendary clash is known as the Titanomachy! It all began when Uranus, the first ruler of the Titans, was overthrown by his very own son, Cronus. Talk about a family feud! But Cronus, afraid of meeting the same fate as his father, had a rather strange solution…he would eat his own children as soon as they were born, yikes!

Cronus' wife Rhea couldn't bear to see her precious children gobbled up. So, she hatched a clever plan. When she gave birth to Zeus, she disguised him as a stone. Zeus grew up in secret, gaining strength and power. And guess what? He eventually became the ruler of all gods, the big boss up in Olympus!

But the story doesn't end there. Once Zeus was strong enough, he confronted his dad, Cronus, and released his siblings from their belly-imprisonment. It was like a family reunion of mythic proportions! And thus began the ultimate battle between the young and powerful Olympian gods and the Titans.

Can you imagine the cosmic clash that followed? Thunderbolts clashed, earth shook, and the sky rumbled as gods and Titans clashed for control of the universe. After a truly epic showdown the Olympian gods emerged victorious! They sent the Titans packing, banishing them deep into the shadows of Tartarus within the Underworld.

The Titans Legacy

As you gaze upon the stars and ponder the mysteries of the universe, remember the Titans and their legacy. Even in the world of gods and titans, the struggle for power and control is real. But with courage, determination, and maybe a bit of clever trickery, the underdogs – or in this case, the young Olympians – can rise to greatness. This myth reminds us that strength and unity can conquer even the mightiest challenges, making it a timeless tale of victory against all odds!

In the dance of the stars, galaxies and the mysteries of the universe together many questions are waiting to be explored. As you embark on your own journey of learning, approach it with an open mind and an eager heart. Just as the Titans dared to challenge the boundaries of the heavens, you too must challenge the limitations of your own understanding. Embrace change as the Titans did when they faced a new generation of gods, adapting in the face of adversity.

The universe, much like the Titans' struggle, is always moving and changing. With each passing discovery you are stepping into the realm of the unknown. Step forth with courage and determination young learners. For we must be willing to adapt to change, keep learning and stay hungry in our pursuit of knowledge.

CHAPTER 32

HADES - LORD OF THE UNDERWORLD

Greetings young explorers and brave adventurers! Are you ready to venture deep into the underworld? Prepare yourselves for some scary and enchanting tales within the realms of Hades, the powerful lord, God of the underworld. Don't worry we'll hold your hand as we uncover the scary but fascinating Hades! Welcome to his domain, the underworld, the afterlife and the Eleusinian Mysteries.

Hades was the brother of Zeus and Poseidon. As the mighty lord, God of the underworld he was responsible for judging souls that entered into his realm. He reigned over the underworld, a place that was hidden, deep beneath the earth. It was here in this kingdom that the spirits of the deceased travelled to after they had left the mortal world. Imagine such a mysterious and eerie place where the afterlife lived on! But it wasn't all doom and gloom...as we'll soon discover.

Actually, there was more to it than meets the eye. While "Tartarus" was a place of punishment for the wicked, the "Fields of Asphodel" were a neutral and peaceful place for ordinary souls. And of course, there were the "Isles of the Blessed" which were a paradise for heroes and virtuous souls.

Within the underworld was The River Styx, another fascinating place. It was a boundary between the mortal world and the underworld. Those souls who came to the underworld first had to cross the Styx in the boat of Charon who would only accept payment in one way. One had to place a coin under the tongue of the dead!

The Elysian Mysteries

In the heart of the Underworld was a place of eternal beauty known as Elysium. Heroes and anyone who had lived honourable lives were granted a special afterlife here. The

Elysian Mysteries were not just about the physical wonders of Elysium but also about its magical secrets and rituals. Mysteries that unlocked the hidden treasures of the Underworld, allowing only those who were worthy to experience its true magic.

But how did one join the Elysian Mysteries? Well, it wasn't as simple as raising your hand and saying, "I want to join!" No, the process was a bit more mystical. It involved special rituals, ceremonies, and tests to prove one's worthiness.

The Elysian Mysteries were a celebration of life and its potential for greatness. They encouraged people to strive for goodness, to be kind to others, and to embrace their inner hero. And just as heroes were welcomed into Elysium, those who celebrated the mysteries were also welcomed into the special community.

The Story of Hades and Persephone

The tale of Hades and Persephone is one of the most magical love stories in Greek mythology. One day, as Hades was roaming the fields of the human world when he came across the radiant Persephone. She was the daughter of Demeter, the Goddess of Agriculture. Her beauty mesmerised and captivated Hades. He was so obsessed and just had to make her his Queen of the underworld.

Hades hatched his cunning plan and on one, fateful day as Persephone was picking flowers he appeared before her in a chariot drawn by majestic, black horses. He swept her away to his kingdom, but this caused great distress to her mother Demeter. Persephone also felt lonely and homesick in the underworld. She yearned to return to the world of living.

Hades insisted on making her his queen and tricked her into eating some pomegranate seeds. Such a trick unknowingly sealed her fate to spend part of every year in the end of the world. From then on Persephone would have to spend six months of every year with Hades in the underworld. Without her radiant beauty the earth became cold and experienced harsh winters during. When she returned to her mother Demeter, the world would bloom with joy and beauty.

Now as we conclude our own journey…but not one into the underworld but rather one onwards in our own lives let us remember the cautious tales of Hades. Seek the truth, young friend. Understand that many times we will explore further the stories or rumours to find out what the truth is. Because sometimes what is talked about as being bad may have something good going on behind the scenes. Just like the underworld and its hidden paradises. Remember there are dark and light sides to everything. When we seek the truth that we are moving more towards the light. Remember that all of your actions have consequences, and if you practise honesty then you will live a virtuous life.

CHAPTER 33

THE FATES - WEAVERS OF DESTINY

Once upon a time, long, long ago in the magical world of ancient Greece there lived three special sisters with powers to shape the future. Togethery they were known as the fates and together they guided the lives of everyone in the world. Each had their own unique role in the process of creating destiny. The future of mortals, gods and even you would be influenced by them! Are you ready to look into the future? Brave you are indeed! Now let's learn more about these mysterious women.

Clotho: The Spinner of Life

Clotho was the youngest of the three sisters and hers was a very important job. She was known as the spinner of life. Imagine her sitting by a giant spinning wheel where she would spin the threads of people's lives. With every twist and turn of her wheel, she threaded out a new life journey. Thankfully she was kind and generous, making sure that everyone had a fair chance.

Lachesis: The Measurer of Fate

Lachesis was the middle sister. She was the measurer of fate and her role required great care. With her magical measuring stick, she measured the threads spun by Clotho.

With the thread in her hands, she calculated how long each person's journey would be. It might be a quick trip or it might be a lengthy one. Who knows? Lachesis did. She knew exactly how long each person needed to experience the world.

Atropos: The Cutter of Threads

Atropos was the eldest sister and her task was the most mysterious. Once Lachesis measured the thread, Atropos would decide when it was time for it to end. With her sharp scissors, she would carefully cut the thread to signal the end of a person's life. Now this might sound sad, but Atropos knew that every ending was also the beginning of something new. It all depended on how one viewed it.

Together the three fates worked, weaving the tapestry of life for everyone in the world. Imagine them as masterful artists creating fantastic patterns. Patterns that told the lives of heroes, kings, queens, gods and even ordinary people like us. No two threads were the same and every person's thread was unique. The fates made sure life was full of surprises, challenges and opportunities along the way.

Young scholars as you journey through life remember the fates and their magical work. Let them remind you that life is a beautiful tapestry woven with love, laughter, challenges and adventures. Make the most of every moment and cherish the time that you have on this earth. Stay present and grateful. Just like the fates we have the power to shape our own destinies by the choices that we make. Regardless of where we are from or the cards we were dealt, it is in our hands. Venture forth with a smile and let your unique thread of life lead you on a wonderful journey!

CHAPTER 34

PROMETHEUS - THE GIFT GIVER

Good day young adventurers! Are you ready to begin a thrilling new quest? Join us as we journey into the extraordinary tales of Prometheus. This heroic Titan gifted humanity with a wonderful treasure, fire! Here in this chapter, we'll first discover the creation of humans and how Prometheus was involved in the process. Finally, we'll learn about how he stole fire from the gods to help humanity and the cruel punishment he received. Let's go!

In the olden days, the gods of Mount Olympus ruled from above the heavens whilst the mighty Titans ruled the earth. After taking in the wonders of the world, the Olympians decided to create something new. Something was missing in the world below, what was it they wondered? Humans! Prometheus, a Titan, was given the responsibility of creating humans by Zeus the ruler of the gods.

Prometheus was famous for his intelligence, making him the perfect guardian of humanity. He took great care in creating humans, giving them various gifts and abilities. He taught them how to build homes, farm the lands, and how to work with tools and weapons. Finally, he gave them the gifts of power, intelligence, curiosity and taught them all about the world around them.

Prometheus Steals Fire from the Gods

In the realms of Mount Olympus fire was a sacred treasure that was possessed only by the gods. It brought light and warmth, but more importantly it symbolised knowledge and civilization. These were the very elements that could help humanity to reach new heights. Prometheus saw the potential of fire to help his human creations. However, he would first have to steal it from the gods. As you can imagine this would be a daring and dangerous task.

Now, let's set the scene. Picture Mount Olympus, the grand home of the mighty gods. One fateful night, as the gods peacefully slept, Prometheus tiptoed into their divine home. His heart pounded like drum beats when he saw the fire of the gods. With courage he silently approached, his palms sweaty with anticipation. Gently, as though cradling a star in his hands, he captured a single glowing ember from the flames. Oh, the excitement! It sent shivers down his spine.

And so, with the radiant gift of fire tucked safely into his possession, Prometheus began his descent from the heavenly realm. The air around him crackled with energy and the stars above twinkled. As he journeyed back to the world of mortals, held within his hands was a treasure that would forever change humanity. The gift lighted up their lives, providing warmth against the cold and providing light in the darkness.

But wait! Zeus, the all-seeing ruler of the gods, soon found out about Prometheus's tricky act. And he was furious! Angrily he chained him to a mountainside where an eagle would feast on his liver everyday. What a horrible fate! But this punishment did not break his spirit. Even though he was in a lot of pain, he would not plead with Zeus. In the end, he knew that any suffering was worth giving the humans the gift of fire.

Prometheus became more than a hero. For the humans he was their light on a pathway through dark times. Through the ages his very name was whispered like a secret promise of empowerment. Indeed, his heroic efforts came at a great personal cost, that locked him in chains. But despite his suffering, his spirit remained unconquerable, thus demonstrating the power of the human spirit.

As you read the tales of Prometheus, let his dedication remind you that even in the face of challenges, you have the power to spark change. Just as Prometheus lit the fire for humans, your own efforts can ignite a flame of positive change for others. And as you venture through life let your light shine brightly like a raging fire!

Think of your dearest friends, those kindred spirits who light up your world with their presence. With his arrows of affection, he weaves strong bonds of friendship.

CHAPTER 35

EROS (CUPID) - THE MISCHIEVOUS GOD OF LOVE

Ah, love is in the air, young hearts! In this dear chapter we're about to learn about Eros, the mischievous and delightful god of love. Prepare to be carried away on the wings of this god in adventure where we'll learn all about him and the magical effect of his love arrows. Now let us dive into the depths of Greek mythology to explore love and passion in the enchanting world of Eros. Are you ready to embark?

High up on Mount Olympus where the gods and goddesses lived, Eros reigned as the god of love. Ever heard the name Cupid? Well, that was also his name and he was the son of Aphrodite, goddess of love, beauty and desire. We're sure you've seen him before. He's the winged, playful god with a magical bow and arrows in his hands. But these are no ordinary arrows…they're love arrows! With one strike they had the power to make mortals or even gods fall in love with whomever the arrow might strike.

In Greek mythology, Eros was not only a symbol of romantic love. He was much more. Imagine the gentle affection shared between parents and children. Eros's touch can be felt in the laughter exchanged between siblings, the soothing embrace of a mother's arms and the protective watch of a father's gaze.

Think of your dearest friends, those kindred spirits who light up your world with their presence. With his arrows of affection, he weaves strong bonds of friendship.

Eros' Mischievous Adventures

With his bow and love arrows in hand, Eros went on many great adventures, stirring up emotions of the gods and mortals alike. He loved to matchmake and find couples to fall in love with each other. Whenever he fired his arrows, couples would fall head over heels for each other. Often it led to happy, romantic and heartfelt connections. Even the mighty gods and goddesses could not resist Eros' love arrows! Amazingly some of the gods and goddesses even fell in love with humans. Of course, this led to some dramatic love stories!

In Greek mythology Eros represents the force of love that binds humans together which inspires affection, compassion and devotion. With his love arrows he sparks the flames of passion leading to both joyous, and sometimes dramatic affairs.

Tales of Eros remind us of love's powerful force that can bring joy, healing and unity. Love goes beyond couples. There is also love between friends, family and the world around us. Indeed, it has the potential of heartache but grief is a price worthy of paying for love. For love is an important part of being human. Maybe the most important part.

As we conclude this loving chapter let us remember the magic of Eros and his tales of love and adventure. Let it all remind you of the importance of love in our lives. Love your friends and family with warmth. Share your love with the world. For love is a wondrous force and we should cherish those precious moments together with our loved ones. Be kind to the world around you and love all of its creatures. May the spirit of Eros' love always dance within your hearts!

PART 6
GREEK CULTURE & LEGACY

CHAPTER 36
ANCIENT GREEK HEREOS
IN THE MODERN WORLD

Greetings young scholars of Greek mythology. Welcome to the beginning of a new journey into exploring how ancient Greek myths and heroes have continued to influence us today. From books to movies and to artwork we're about to delve into some of the famous retellings and adaptations of Greek myths in popular culture. Many years later in this present day you'll discover why they still captivate audiences. In addition, we'll also discover examples of Greek mythology in our everyday language. Are you ready to discover the timeless wonders of Greek mythology? Well then let's begin.

Ahh Greek Mythology, its allure is mesmerising and it continues to be found in modern culture. Writers, filmmakers and artists from around the world continue to draw inspiration from the epic tales of ancient Greece. In books many famous authors have created compelling stories that were inspired by Greek myths whose heroes set out on epic quests to overcome challenges and dilemmas. Themes of bravery, sacrifice, and the struggle between good and evil are still popular to this day because they carry universal messages. Naturally this makes them relatable to readers of diverse backgrounds.

The magic of Greek mythology has also found its way into the cinema. Directors and screenwriters continue to be inspired by classic myths in blockbuster movies. We've seen on screen the myths of Perseus, Hercules and Medusa. All of these and many more have been reimagined and recreated in a number of different variations on the silver screen. Filling a spectrum of emotions and thrilling tales.

In the world of fine art ancient Greek influences can still be found to this day. From the majestic statues of Greek gods and goddesses found in public places to the paintings of mythological scenes. The vibrant legacy of ancient Greece continues to inspire artists to create masterpieces around the world.

Famous Retellings and Adaptations of Greek Myths

Rick Riordan's "Percy Jackson & the Olympians" series, brings Greek gods and heroes into the modern world. Readers can escape into the thrilling adventures and humorous escapades.

The film "Troy" explores the legendary Trojan War, showcasing the valour of Achilles and the struggles of Hector. New audiences can enjoy the epic saga once again.

"Wonder Woman," the beloved superheroine, draws inspiration from the Amazonian warrior princess. Again, the epics of Greek mythology are found in modern storytelling.

Greek Mythology in Modern Language

Greek mythology has even found its way into our everyday modern language.

Phrases like "Achilles' heel" to refer to a weak point.

Whilst "Pandora's box" relates to something that might create unwanted consequences.

Then there is the saying of a "Herculean task". One would imagine a tremendous challenge in this case!

Even some of the stars in the night sky are named after characters from Greek myths. The constellation Orion is named after the great hunter Orion. Whilst the Pleiades, constellation is named after the seven daughters of the Titan Atlas.

We can all find some similarities in Greek mythology because ultimately, they connect with the experience of being human. These ancient tales resonate with our emotions, dreams and struggles. They capture our dilemmas and troubles which are timeless and universal. Struggles of heroes reflect courage and echo through the ages. Whilst moral dilemmas of the gods send important messages across generations.

Truly these stories are timeless and will live on forever in our world. Forever they will connect us to the amazing experience of being human which spans cultures, centuries and transcends language. Timeless tales touch the heart and ignite our imagination. Indeed, we can all relate them to our own struggles, triumphs and dreams.

Since the beginning of time humanity has pursued greatness. We have sought love and friendship. At the same time, we fight an eternal struggle between light and darkness. May the legacy of Greek Mythology inspire you on your own journeys and heroic quests! For many, many years (since before you were born) these myths have captivated the minds of the world. And for many more years they will!

CHAPTER 37

THE GREEK OLYMPICS - HONOURING THE GODS THROUGH SPORTS

Get ready to step into the thrilling world of the ancient Greek olympics! An event of the strongest, fastest and fittest. Here athletes gathered to showcase their skills in honour of the mighty gods and goddesses of Mount Olympus. Within this chapter we'll journey back in time to uncover the origins of the Greek olympics which have lasted until this day. As we uncover this grand sporting event let us also explore its connection to Greek religion and mythology. Get ready, it's time to stretch your muscles and tie up your shoelaces!

We begin our journey back to 776 BC in the city state of Olympia. It was at this moment that the ancient Greek Olympics began in honour of Zeus the king of gods. Greeks from various cities united in this event of competition and camaraderie. Held every four years, these games soon became a celebrated tradition.

The Olympics were of great importance both culturally and religiously for the Greeks. Athletes had the opportunity to show off their physical skills. But more than that it represented the harmony between the human world and the heavens above. Winners in the games were celebrated as heroic athletes and the favourites of the gods. Their victories were believed to be the results of God's blessings.

Olympic Sports

The Greek Olympics included many different sports and competitions. Each with their own demanding skills and abilities. Among some of the most popular events were:

Running races

The stadium where the Greek Olympics were held featured a track for short sprints and long running races. Speed and endurance would be demonstrated by the finest runners of those times.

Wrestling

Two athletes would face each other in this intense sport. Whoved submitted their opponent to the ground would emerge victorious.

Discus Throw

Strong athletes would throw a heavy discus (kind of like a heavy frisbee) as far as possible. Whoever could throw the discus furthest would emerge victorious.

Javelin Throw

Mighty athletes would throw a javelin (kind of like a spear) as far as possible. Whoever landed the furthest was the winner.

Chariot Racing

This thrilling sport involved skilled horse riders guiding a chariot connected to the horse in an epic race to the finish line.

Pankration

This was a fierce combination of boxing and wrestling (kind of like mixed martial arts) where athletes had to use all of their skills and powers to emerge victorious.

How the Olympics Connected to Greek Religion and Culture

For the ancient Greeks the Olympics were more than just a sporting event. It was also a sacred occasion celebrating religious beliefs to further connect them to the gods. Before every Olympic event, athletes and spectators would join in elaborate ceremonies where they would make offerings to the gods seeking their favour.

What's amazing is that many Greek city states were sometimes involved in battle but during the Olympic Games they would pause the war in a truce! This was known as the "Olympic Peace,". During this time all wars were suspended. All athletes and fans could now travel safely to and from Olympia without fear of harm. The Olympic Peace was a symbol of unity and demonstrated the shared values of Greek culture. Truly sports and competition has the power to heal.

To this day the Olympics live on as a worldwide event. They are testament to the unity between people and the respect between cultures. Regardless of our differences we can set them aside to celebrate healthy competition and to inspire each other.

Well young athletes as we come to the end of this brilliant chapter let us celebrate the Greek Olympics. Such a magnificent event that honours the gods through sports uniting together people from all corners of ancient Greece. As you run, jump and play, may you remember the spirit of the Greek Olympics. Embrace the spirit of sportsmanship, respect and honour. Let it fuel your own journey to greatness. Until our next adventure may the gods and goddesses blessings be with you on your journey to becoming true champions!

CHAPTER 38

GREEK HEREOS IN EVERYDAY LIFE

Listen closely to young readers because we're about to uncover some hidden lessons from ancient Greek Heroes that will help us in our daily lives. Pay close attention as we dive deep into the virtues and characters of these legendary figures. With the lessons learned it will help to shine a light on our own pathways. Maybe you can also become heroes in the world!

The great heroes of ancient Greece were more than just mighty warriors; they were also wise and virtuous characters. And their stories teach us valuable life lessons that we can apply in our own lives. Let's learn!

Courage

From the fearless Perseus who faced the scary monster Medusa to the brave Hercules who conquered the Twelve Labors. Greek heroes inspired bravery in the face of tough times. Courage doesn't mean that you won't feel afraid. But it is your ability to rise above fear even when you feel it.

Compassion

Heroes like Theseus and Jason showed compassion and empathy towards others. Together with their friends and fellow warriors they achieved great things. Learn from their kindness and compassion. Whatever you want from the world you should learn to give it first, because in giving we can find true strength.

Wisdom

Athena the great goddess of wisdom guided many heroes with her intelligent advice. Wise decisions come from learning and experience. We should seek wisdom from our elders and continue to learn. Thus, we should also learn from our own experiences. Such wisdom will help us to make better decisions in our life.

Perseverance

Do you remember Odysseus' epic journey home? And do you remember Persephone's determination to rescue her kidnapped daughter? These stories and many more from Greek mythology showcase the power of perseverance. Young friends, never give up on your dreams! All too often we stop short when we are very close to achieving our goals. Master perseverance to unlock the doors of your success.

Modern Heroes

Heroes don't just exist in Greek mythology; they also exist in the world around us. Everyday there are heroes who risk their lives for others. Firefighters, police officers, volunteers and first responders are just a few of the many heroes in our modern world. Selfishly they dedicate their time and effort to support those in need. Be inspired by them and consider the ways that you too can help in this modern world.

Remember young readers that being a hero is not only about grand gestures or epic events. Sometimes small acts of kindness and compassion can make a huge difference in the lives of others. For you too young readers have the power to be a hero in your own community and make a positive impact on the world around you. Simple acts of kindness such as helping a friend in need or showing empathy to someone going through a tough time can make a huge difference.

Don't let bullies or injustice continue. Stand up against evil. Get involved in your community, serve others, volunteer and make a positive contribution. You can also be a role model by embodying the virtues of Greek Heroes to inspire others by being your very best self.

As we conclude our journey in this empowering chapter let us again remember that heroism is not just for the extraordinary. Each and every one of us has the power to be a hero in small or big ways. Embrace the virtues of the Greek Myths and let them serve you as guiding stars towards a life of courage and compassion. Never underestimate the power of your actions, young readers, even the smallest acts of kindness can create ripples of positive change. Embrace the hero within yourself. Now more than ever the world needs heroes like you and together we can create a better future.

CONCLUSION

Congratulations young explorers you have reached the grand finale of a thrilling journey through the world of Greek gods, goddesses, heroes and monsters! As we conclude this epic adventure let us remember the legacy of Greek mythology and refresh the valuable lessons from these timeless myths.

Just like the great majestic phoenix rises from the ashes, Greek mythology has continued to stand the test of time. For countless generations its magical tales have continued to captivate imaginations and spark inspiration in hearts. Stories of brave heroes, powerful gods and mythical creatures have lasted for centuries. From the courage and determination of heroes like Hercules and Perseus. To the wisdom and strategic thinking of Athena. Each myth, God, goddess, hero

Virtues of courage, friendship and empathy can be found countless times in Greek mythology. Through triumph and tragedy these larger than life stories and characters have taught us the importance of friendship, honour and perseverance.

Lessons found inside also taught us the consequences of wrongdoing, jealousy and greed. Cautionary tales like these will help us to guide us to better life choices.

Over the centuries authors, play rights and poets have drawn inspiration from the epic tales of the ancient Greek. Mythological elements have been weaved into their masterpieces to enchant and captivate readers. Whilst filmmakers and animators have brought gods, heroes, monsters and mythology to life on the movie screen. Artists too have been inspired; sculpting magnificent statues and crafting inspiring paintings to celebrate the immortal beauty of Greek mythology.

Now today, the magical world of Greek mythology awaits you forevermore! You have a duty to pass these tales down to the next generation. Share them as you embark on your own quest of discovery and continue to learn from these ancient myths. For within them remain infinite opportunities for learning, growth and enlightenment. We encourage you to keep learning and to re-read or re-listen this book because each time new insights will appear related to your current situation.

May your imagination soar high like Icarus and your determination be as strong as Odysseus on his journey home. Let your spirit fly on the wings of Perseus, dive into the deep ocean with Poseidon and solve riddles with the wise Sphinx! Stand brave and strong like Hercules, wise like Athena and kind like Persphone.

As we say goodbye to the world of Greek mythology, we hope you leave your hearts filled with wonder and a mind eager for more adventures. Of course, we will be back soon! Remember young learners that the legacy of Greek mythology can live on through you and every generation that follows. Take on the lessons and values from these ancient tales and share them with the world. You can make a positive change.

And as we close this journey, we leave you with one final thought:

You are the authors of your own destiny, the creators of your own myths and the heroes of your own stories.

Let the spirit of Greek mythology inspire you to dream big, dare greatly and to make a positive impact on the world. Until the next time we meet (coming soon), goodbye young adventurers! May the legacy of Greek mythology forever inspire wonder, strength and wisdom within you!

ACTIVITIES

ACTIVITY INFORMATION

Congratulations, young mythologists! As you conclude your journey through the captivating world of Greek gods, goddesses, and heroes, we have some exciting activities for you. These will help you to explore further and immerse yourself in the enchanting realm of Greek mythology. Not only will these activities entertain you but they will also deepen your understanding and connection with the mythical tales.

So, let's dive right in!

ACTIVITY 1

MYTHOLOGICAL RIDDLES

Welcome to the world of Ancient Greek Riddles!

Are you ready to challenge your knowledge and thinking skills? Prepare yourselves for we are about to present you with some complicated riddles. Now pay close attention to the descriptions and hints which are coming up.

Listen or read closely to the following riddles about some mythological characters. Don't rush, carefully think about the clues and hints found within the riddles. Take a guess at answering the riddles. Ask your friends and family for help. Then once you've made your guess go ahead to the reveal part to discover if you were correct.

Riddle 1

I am mighty and wise, a queen of all gods,

My husband is Zeus, the ruler of skies,

Far and wide my jealous nature cries,

But beware of my wrathe for it's not easy to hide.

Who am I?

Riddle 2

I rule the seas with my trident in hand,

Stormy waves are under my command,

Dolphins and horses they understand,

The depths of the oceans follow my demand.

Who am I?

Riddle 3

I was born from the head of Zeus, wise and fair,

Athens is the city for which I care,

My shield and helmet are symbols so grand,

In peace and war I lend my helping hand.

Who am I?

Riddle 4

Under the darkness i dwell and rule the dead,

The underworld is my home and it is widespread,

My queen Persephone is by my side,

The underworld's secrets here we hide.

Who am I?

Riddle 5

With my wings I fly quicker than a bee,

My messages of gods are the key,

With grace I guide souls, my role profound,

In the underworld my cleverness is renowned.

Who am I?

Riddle 6

With bow and arrows I'm a mischievous lad,

But in matters of love my aim is not bad,

When hearts flutter and emotions ignite,

With a strike of my arrow love burns bright.

Who am I?

Riddle 7

A monster feared with one gaze you will be stone,

With snakes for her she stands alone,

This gorgon is so grim to put you at unease,

One sight of her will make you freeze.

Who am I?

Riddle 8

A strong hero, his legend spreads wide,
Twelve labours he completed with pride,
With the strength of gods in his heart,
And with bare hands he tore beasts apart.
Who am I?

Riddle 9

I am poet who plays a music divine,
With my melodies stands still time,
I went to the underworld to win back love,
And played beautiful songs, gentle as a dove.
Who am I?

Riddle 10

Inside a box lay many mysteries untold,
Be warned if you open it trouble might unfold,
One fair maiden opened it at a cost,
Despair unfolded but hope was not lost.
Who am I?

Dear readers behold the ten riddles! Do you know the answers? Seek wisdom from your friends and family. Now write down your answers and check at the end. If you were successful then celebrate, otherwise study more young friends!

ACTIVITY 2

THE MYTHOLOGY QUIZ SHOW

Greetings and welcome to the mythology quiz show! Your expert mythology skills are about to be tested. Are you ready for the challenge? Listen or read carefully because you are about to be presented with a quiz about many things which you have learned in this book.

You can join with family, friends or alone. But one rule must be followed…don't skip ahead to the answers! For each question you will be given multiple options. Wise young scholars think carefully before choosing your answer. If you're not sure, use your best instincts or ask for advice. Write down all of your answers and when you're finished check the correct answers at the end of this book. Good luck!

Question 1

Who was the king that ruled the gods and goddesses of Mount Olympus?

a) Hera
b) Poseidon
c) Zeus
d) Apollo

Question 2

Which goddess was famous for wisdom and strategy in war?

a) Aphrodite
b) Athena
c) Artemis
d) Hestia

Question 3

Which God ruled the sea, holding a powerful trident?

a) Hades
b) Apollo
c) Poseidon
d) Hermes

Question 4

What was the name of the hero that completed twelve labours?

a) Perseus
b) Theseus
c) Heracles (Hercules)
d) Odysseus

Question 5

What was the name of the goddess of love, beauty and desire?

a) Hera
b) Artemis
c) Demeter
d) Aphrodite

Question 6

What was the name of the god of the messenger of the gods?

a) Hermes
b) Dionysus
c) Ares
d) Hephaestus

Question 7

Who was the goddess connected with the changing seasons?

a) Hera
b) Demeter
c) Athena
d) Hestia

Question 8

Who was the wife of Hades, God of the underworld?

a) Persephone
b) Artemis
c) Athena
d) Aphrodite

Question 9

Which mythical beasts had the head of a human and the body of a lion?

a) Centaur
b) Minotaur
c) Sphinx
d) Chimera

Question 10

Which hero went to the underworld to rescue his lover?

a) Orpheus
b) Jason
c) Theseus
d) Odysseus

Now young mythologists, prepare your answers. It's time to find out how much you truly know! Choose your best answers and check them at the end of this book. Keep a track of your results and continue to learn more about Greek mythology.

ACTIVITY 3

MYTHICAL COOKING

Well, hello there! Are you feeling hungry? All of this learning has for sure will have burned some calories and fueled appetites. Get ready for a feast! We are about to discover some fun and delicious recipes inspired by Greek mythology.

Listen or read carefully these recipes. Make sure you have an adult to help you gather everything you need. Follow the steps to create these mythical dishes. Then when they're ready, enjoy eating them with your friends and families. Now young chefs let's get to the cooking!

Recipe 1: Ambrosia Fruit Salad

Here we go! We are about to discover a divine dish for the gods themselves, Ambrosia Fruit Salad! Ask an adult and let's gather all of the ingredients to create this mythical treat.

Ingredients

- 1 cup of chopped pineapple
- 1 cup of orange cut up
- 1 cup of shredded coconut
- 1 cup of marshmallows
- 1 cup of seedless grapes
- 1 cup of Greek yoghurt

- 1 tablespoon of honey (optional, for a touch of sweetness)
- A handful of cherries (optional)

Instructions

Combine the chopped pineapple, orange cut up, shredded coconut, marshmallows, and seedless grapes. In another bowl mix the Greek yogurt with the optional honey for a creamy and sweet dressing. Pour the creamy dressing over the fruits and gently mix them until all the ingredients are covered.

Put the bowl in the fridge with some plastic wrap to cover it. Leave it there to meld for about thirty minutes. Next you can add some cherries for an extra touch of mythical charm.

Now it's time to enjoy this ambrosial delight! Savour the heavenly taste worthy of the gods and goddesses with your family and friends.

Recipe 2: Hercules' Hero Sandwiches

Hercules was a strong and powerful hero. So of course, he always needed big and hearty meals to fuel his muscles and adventures! The Hercules' Hero Sandwiches is such a hearty meal worthy of this hero.

Now with adult supervision, gather your ingredients and kitchen tools. Let's make these legendary sandwiches.

Ingredients

- 4 slices of buttered bread
- 8 slices of ham or turkey
- 8 slices of cooked bacon
- 4 slices of cheese
- Lettuce leaves
- Sliced tomatoes
- Sliced red onions
- Pickles (optional)
- Mayonnaise or mustard, for spreading

Instructions

Lay out the slices of bread on a clean surface. Spread butter on them. Next spread mayonnaise and mustard on one side of each piece of bread. Layer the ham or turkey, cooked bacon, and cheese on one piece bread. On the next piece of bread add the lettuce leaves, sliced tomatoes, red onions, and pickles. Press the bread slices lightly together and secure them with toothpicks if needed.

Now it's time for you to serve Hercules' Hero Sandwiches with a side of ambrosia fruit salad for a truly mythical feast! Enjoy your epic sandwiches and feel the strength and courage of Hercules as you take each heroic bite!

Young mythologists, savour the flavours of these mythical dishes and share them with your loved ones. May these recipes inspire you to create your own recipes and continue your journey into the enchanting world of Greek mythology!

ACTIVITY ANSWERS

<u>Warning, warning! Don't come here before you have completed the activities!!</u>

Activity One Answers:

Riddle 1: Hera
Riddle 2: Poseidon
Riddle 3: Athena
Riddle 4: Hades
Riddle 5: Hermes
Riddle 6: Eros (Cupid)
Riddle 7: Medusa
Riddle 8: Hercules
Riddle 9: Orpheus
Riddle 10: Pandora

Activity Two Answers:

Question 1

Who was the king that ruled the gods and goddesses of Mount Olympus?

c) Zeus

Question 2

Which goddess was famous for wisdom and strategy in war?

b) Athena

Question 3

Which God ruled the sea, holding a powerful trident?

c) Poseidon

Question 4

What was the name of the hero that completed twelve labours?

c) Heracles (Hercules)

Question 5

What was the name of the goddess of love, beauty and desire?

d) Aphrodite

Question 6

What was the name of the god of the messenger of the gods?

a) Hermes

Question 7

Who was the goddess connected with the changing seasons?

b) Demeter

Question 8

Who was the wife of Hades, God of the underworld?

a) Persephone

Question 9

Which mythical beasts had the head of a human and the body of a lion?

c) Sphinx

Question 10

Which hero went to the underworld to rescue his lover?

a) Orpheus

REFERENCES

PRIMARY REFERENCES

- This book is intended for informational and entertainment purposes only. Readers should not rely solely on its content for making important decisions or drawing conclusions. If you have concerns about the accuracy of any information presented in this book, please seek additional sources and expert advice.

- OpenAI. (2023). ChatGPT 3.5
  https://chat.openai.com

- This book was written with the assistance of ChatGPT, a language model developed by OpenAI, which provided creative input based on the information and instructions provided. While ChatGPT was used to aid in the writing process, the publishers of this book have made every effort to ensure the accuracy of the information presented. Extensive fact-checking and research were conducted to verify the information contained within this book.

- Mid Journey. (2023). https://www.midjourney.com/
- All interior images were created with the use of artificial intelligence, namely Mid Journey.

OTHER BOOKS BY HISTORY BROUGHT ALIVE

Available now in Ebook, Paperback, Hardcover, and Audiobook in all regions.

For Kids:

Other books:

GREEK LEGENDS FOR KIDS

We sincerely hope you enjoyed our new book *"Greek Legends for Kids"*. We would greatly appreciate your feedback with an honest review at the place of purchase.

First and foremost, we are always looking to grow and improve as a team. It is reassuring to hear what works, as well as receive constructive feedback on what should improve. Second, starting out as an unknown author is exceedingly difficult, and Amazon reviews go a long way toward making the journey out of anonymity possible. Please take a few minutes to write an honest review.

Best regards,
History Brought Alive
http://historybroughtalive.com/

www.ingramcontent.com/pod-product-compliance
Lightning Source LLC
Chambersburg PA
CBHW071917150726
47999CB00001B/10